D0153591

Franco

PROFILES IN **POWER**

General Editor: Keith Robbins

Franco

Sheelagh Ellwood

An imprint of **Pearson Education**

Harlow, England · London · New York · Reading, Massachusetts · San Francisco
Toronto · Don Mills, Ontario · Sydney · Tokyo · Singapore · Hong Kong · Seoul
Taipei · Cape Town · Madrid · Mexico City · Amsterdam · Munich · Paris · Milan

Pearson Education Limited
Edinburgh Gate
Harlow
Essex CM20 2JE
England

and Associated Companies around the world

Visit us on the World Wide Web at:
www.pearsoned.co.uk

First published 1994

© Sheelagh Ellwood 1994

The right of Sheelagh Ellwood to be identified as author of
this Work has been asserted by her in accordance with
the Copyright, Designs and Patents Act 1988.

All rights reserved; no part of this publication may be reproduced, stored
in a retrieval system, or transmitted in any form or by any means,
electronic, mechanical, photocopying, recording, or otherwise without
either the prior written permission of the Publishers or a licence
permitting restricted copying in the United Kingdom issued by the
Copyright Licensing Agency Ltd, 90 Tottenham Court Road, London
W1T 4LP.

ISBN: 978-0-582-43753-1

British Library Cataloguing-in-Publication Data
A catalogue record for this book can be obtained from the British Library

Library of Congress Cataloging-in-Publication Data
A catalog record for this book can be obtained from the Library of
Congress

10 9 8 7 6 5
08 07

Produced by Pearson Education Asia Pte Ltd.,
Printed in Malaysia. VVP

CONTENTS

PREFACE

In the course of the twentieth century, Spain has experienced a bewildering succession of political systems and structures: regency; an uneasy period of monarchy; the proclamation, development, crisis and overthrow of a democratic republic; a Civil War; two dictatorships; and, finally, the return of both monarchy and democracy. Paradoxically, the most striking feature of the period is not so much the rapid shifts of the political kaleidoscope, as the fact that four decades of it were occupied by the single regime of General Francisco Franco Bahamonde.

It was unusual in Spain for a Head of State to remain in power for so long. How was it, then, that Franco was able to achieve and enjoy for nearly forty years a position of complete domination over his fellow citizens, without inheriting, or, indeed, creating, a totally monolithic state? This book attempts to provide some of the answers to that question. It is not an exhaustive biography, nor a comprehensive history of twentieth-century Spain, but an examination of the social, economic, political and historical circumstances which permitted Franco's rise to power, and of the personal characteristics which enabled him to take advantage of those circumstances.

It is not easy to say what Franco was 'really like'. The closest he came to an account of his own life was a series of sketchy manuscript 'Notes', written in 1962 as a draft for an autobiography and covering the period 1925–39. While they provide some interesting insights into Franco's view of the monarchy of Alphonso XIII (1902–31) and the Second Republic (1931–36), they are disappointingly brief and fragmentary with respect to the period of the Spanish Civil War (1936–39), and peter out without devoting a single line to the regime headed by him from 1939 onwards. And although Franco was frequently filmed and photographed seated behind a desk covered in documents on which he appeared to be working, there is no public archive replete with the personal papers of the *Generalísimo*; nor does there appear to be an extensive private collection. There exists a profusion of secondary material which enables us accurately to piece together the historical details of Franco's career and of the times in which he lived. We also have the testimony of many who met him, some who worked for him and a few who knew him. And there is the graphic record of thousands of photographs and metres of film. Yet, as his latest and most incisive biographer to date notes, he remains the most enigmatic of this century's dictators.[1] Of one thing we can be certain, however, and that is that Francisco Franco was a man determined to leave his mark on his country. How he did that, and to what extent his mark was indelible, is the subject of the following pages.

The interpretation of contemporary Spain contained in this volume of 'Profiles in Power' is the result of a personal interest in Spanish history and politics which dates back to 1970. I was in Madrid as a post-graduate student when the then President of the Spanish government, Admiral Luis Carrero Blanco, was assassinated by Basque terrorists, in December 1973. I was there again, beginning my doctoral research into the fascist party, Falange Española ('Spanish Phalanx'), when General Franco died, in November 1975. And I was still there in 1981, when a small group of military men attempted to reimpose on newly democratic Spain the kind of authoritarian regime it had known under Franco. That I was able to spend so much time in Spain and, consequently, acquire not only material for my research but also first-hand knowledge of Spanish political history, is due in no small measure to the financial support I received from a number of institutions, in the form of successive scholarships and fellowships: the Spanish Ministry of Foreign Affairs, the Vicente Cañada Blanch Foundation and the British Department of Education and

Science. Without this assistance, my career as an historical researcher would have proved very short-lived.

Over the years, many people have given me the benefit of their knowledge and experience of contemporary Spain: friends, acquaintances and colleagues in Spain and the United Kingdom; the hundred or so men and women with whom I recorded personal interviews between 1976 and 1986; and other historians, such as Sebastian Balfour, Martin Blinkhorn, Julián Casanova, Julio Gil, Helen Graham, Ana Guerrero, Paul Heywood, Enrique Moradiellos, Florentino Portero, Ismael Saz, David Solar, Herbert Southworth and Angel Viñas. My deepest and longest-standing debt of gratitude in this respect is owed to Paul Preston, who, for twenty years, has been unstintingly generous in giving me access to his time, his knowledge and his library. With regard to the present volume, I am particularly grateful to him on two counts. In the first place, for the time and attention he devoted to reading and commenting on earlier drafts. Secondly, for allowing me to read the manuscript of his monumental biography of Franco, a work of remarkable scholarship and research. Without doubt, my own work has been enriched by his.

In writing *Franco*, I have also been fortunate enough to enjoy the help, advice and support of a number of other people. Pride of place must go to the *Profiles in Power* team at Longman Higher Education, including the series editor, Professor Keith Robbins, of St David's University College, Lampeter, Wales. I am grateful to them all for the time and effort they have devoted to the book and, especially, for their seemingly endless patience in the face of repeated delays on my part. Family, friends and colleagues at the Foreign and Commonwealth Office, London, have sustained me on many occasions with words of interest and encouragement; as did Golo, without them. Finally, I am grateful to the Head of Southern European Department at the FCO, David Madden, who kindly read and made many helpful comments on the manuscript in the final stages of its preparation.

It goes without saying that I hold none of these people responsible in any way for the shortcomings which, despite their best efforts, undoubtedly remain in the book. It only remains for me to add that the opinions expressed in this volume are my own and do not necessarily reflect the views of the Foreign and Commonwealth Office.

. . .

NOTES

1. P. Preston, 'Franco Revisited. An Unlikely Dictator' in *LSE Magazine*, London, autumn/winter 1992.

GLOSSARY

africanista	Colloquial term for an officer serving, or who had served, in the Spanish Army of Africa.
BN	Bloque Nacional (National Bloc); monarchist political organization created in 1934, with members of both Alphonsine and Tradionalist sympathies.
Caudillo	A military leader. Spanish equivalent of *Duce* or *Führer*.
CEDA	Confederación Española de Derechas Autónomas (Spanish Confederation of Autonomous Rightist Parties); coalition of conservative political groups formed in February 1933.
Comunión Tradicionalista	(Traditionalist Communion); reactionary monarchist followers of the nineteenth-century absolutist Pretender to the Spanish throne, Don Carlos, and his descendants.
Cortes	Spanish Parliament.
CNT	Confederación Nacional del Trabajo (National Confederation of Labour); anarcho-syndicalist trade union organization, created in 1910.
CTV	Corpo di Truppe Volontarie (Volunteer Troop Corps); Italian forces sent to Spain by the Fascist government to fight for the Nationalists in the Civil War.

ERC	Esquerra Republicana de Catalunya (Republican Left of Catalonia); coalition of moderate left-wing Catalan nationalist parties, created in 1931.
ETA	*Euskadi Ta Askatasuna* (Basque Homeland and Liberty); clandestine, extremist, Basque separatist organization, formed in 1960.
FE	Falange Española (Spanish Phalanx); Spanish fascist party, founded in 1933.
FE de las JONS	Falange Española de las Juntas de Ofensiva Nacional-Sindicalista (Spanish Phalanx of Committees for National Syndicalist Attack); created in 1934 by the fusion of FE and JONS.
FET y de las JONS	Falange Española Tradicionalista y de las Juntas de Ofensiva Nacional-Sindicalista (Spanish Traditionalist Phalanx of Committees for National Syndicalist Attack); Franco's 'single party', created in 1937 by the fusion of FE de las JONS and CT.
FNTT	Federación Nacional de Trabajadores de la Tierra (National Federation of Land Workers); agricultural workers' section of the socialist union, UGT.
gallego	Native of Galicia, north-west Spain.
JONS	Juntas de Ofensiva Nacional-Sindicalista (Committees for National Syndicalist Attack); fascist organization created in 1931.
JSU	Juventudes Socialistas Unificadas (United Socialist Youth Movement); socialist youth organization created in 1936 by the unification of the communist and socialist youth movements.
madrileños	Inhabitants of Madrid.
Nationalists	Supporters of the anti-Republican cause in the Civil War.
Opus Dei	Secretive Catholic association of laymen and priests founded in Spain in 1928 by Mons. José María Escriba.

PCE	Partido Comunista de España (Communist Party of Spain); largest Spanish communist party, founded in 1921.
PNE	Partido Nacionalista Español (Spanish Nationalist Party); extreme right-wing party, created in 1930 and dissolved in late 1933.
POUM	Partido Obrero de Unificacion Marxista (Workers' Party of Marxist Unification), anti-Stalinist, bolshevist communist party, created in 1935.
PSOE	Partido Socialista Obrero Español (Spanish Socialist Workers' Party); principal Spanish socialist party, created in 1879.
Regulares	Moroccan mercenaries serving in the Spanish Army of Africa.
Requeté	Militias of the Comunión Tradicionalista.
RE	Renovación Española (Spanish Renewal); conservative Alphonsine monarchist political organization.
Republicans	Supporters of the Second Spanish Republic, declared in April 1931.
SEU	Sindicato Español Universitario (Spanish University Union); Falangist student organization created in 1933, converted into the official, obligatory students' union of the Franco régime in 1937.
UGT	Unión General de Trabajadores (General Union of Workers); federation of trade unions linked to the PSOE.
UME	Unión Militar Española (Spanish Military Union); clandestine, anti-Republican military organization, created in 1933.
UNGA	United Nations General Assembly.

'Look on my works, ye Mighty, and despair!'
(from P. B. Shelley, 'Ozymandias')

Chapter 1

FROM GALICIA TO CASTILE AND BACK (1892–1912)

On 4 December 1892, in El Ferrol, a small town on the north-west tip of the Spanish coast, the wife of a naval officer gave birth to a son, the second of their children. The mother, Pilar Bahamonde y Pardo de Andrade, was from a middle-class family which traced its descent from the minor nobility of fifteenth-century rural Galicia. The child's father, Nicolás Franco Salgado-Araujo, belonged to a well-known local family and was employed, as five generations of his forebears had been, in the administration of the Spanish Navy. The child, shortly christened Francisco Paulino Hermenegildo Teódulo, had been born on the feast-day of Saint Barbara, patroness of artillerymen. This turned out to be portentous indeed, for, in the course of his long life, Francisco Franco Bahamonde was to have a great deal to do with guns and shooting.

Francisco Franco's childhood was neither more nor less eventful than most. In later life, he recalled that it was 'short and simple, and scarcely contain(ed) any noteworthy events'. He did not lack companions for, in addition to his elder brother, Nicolás and his younger sister and brother, Pilar and Ramón (born, respectively, in 1894 and 1896), he had numerous cousins on both his mother's and his father's side, all of whom lived, as he did, close to the naval base in the port of El Ferrol. His mother, for whom he always showed admiration, was a devoutly Catholic and self-effacing woman, whose caring nature contrasted sharply with that of her husband, whose unfeeling behaviour eventually opened a permanent rift between him and his children. Until the age of twelve, Franco was

1

educated at a private school, run by a Catholic priest, and appears to have been a conscientious, though not outstanding, student. His father was dismissive of his successes, but his mother 'inculcated in her sons the desire to get on, by the only means possible for those of their social class: study. For to have a career meant achieving social progress.'[1] It was, thus, in the bosom of his family that Franco acquired what was to be one of his defining characteristics: ambition. Had doña Pilar lived beyond 1934 she would not have been disappointed by her second-born.

Franco's immediate surroundings were those of a large, modestly well-off, conservative, middle-class family, but the broader context of his early years was one of isolation and deprivation. The region in which he was brought up, Galicia, is cut off from the rest of Spain on two sides by the sea and on a third borders with Portugal. Moreover, in the 1890s the peripheral regions of the country were linked to each other and to the metropolis by only a rudimentary system of roads and railways. In addition to being geographically isolated, Galicia also suffered acute economic penury. Most of the working population was employed in the fishing industry or agriculture, but both provided only a meagre existence. The highly fragmented system of land tenure made it impossible for agriculture to support a rapidly expanding population, driving thousands of people to overseas emigration or migration to the coastal towns and the larger cities elsewhere in the country. Socially, too, like most of rural Spain, turn-of-the-century Galicia was poor and backward, imbued with the anti-egalitarian values of a society whose different sectors had no contact with each other except in terms defined by the rigidly hierarchical structure of the traditional social order. In Franco's particular case, this had two extra dimensions, for he belonged to a service family and civilians and forces personnel each lived in separate worlds, as did seafaring and administrative members of the Navy.[2]

Isolated though life was for this dry-land sailor's son in a small, provincial town, his native Galicia was not entirely divorced from what was going on in the outside world. On the contrary, towns like El Ferrol on the Atlantic seaboard were particularly important and more than usually busy then, for Spain was at war with her South and Central

American colonies, whose struggle for independence had occupied much of the nineteenth century. El Ferrol was one of the Spanish Navy's three home bases and many of the thousands of sailors who served in the colonial wars came from Galicia. One of Franco's closest school (and life-long) friends, Camilo Alonso Vega, lost his father in a naval battle in Cuba in 1898. As children, Franco and his companions may have seen the jerky pictures of an early cinematographic newsreel showing a Spanish battleship, the *Carlos V*, in the Caribbean and the landing of United States troops in the Cuban ports of Daiquiri and Siboney, in June 1898.[3] A month later, the Spanish Atlantic fleet was routed and the Spanish land forces in Cuba were forced to surrender. This resounding defeat enabled Cuba to achieve independence and the United States to assume sovereignty over Puerto Rico and the Philippine Islands, thereby bringing to a close four centuries of Spanish imperial power. At the age of six, Franco could not have understood the full impact of what was immediately referred to as the 1898 'Disaster', but his country's subsequent transition from a long period as a great colonial metropolis to its new role as a lesser power in twentieth-century Europe was a difficult, often violent, process which decisively affected not only the mood of the times in which he grew up but also his own attitudes towards politics and the armed forces. In later life, 1898 meant to him (as to many of his generation) a betrayal of the armed forces by civilian politicians which demanded retribution and redress.

Spain had been at war on a number of occasions since the end of the eighteenth century: against Britain from 1793 to 1805, against a French army of occupation from 1808 to 1814, and against its American colonies from 1810 to 1824 and 1895 to 1898. In terms of domestic politics, too, conflict and instability were the keynotes of the nineteenth century, as the supporters of a traditional, conservative regime in which the monarch both reigned and governed at the top of a hierarchically organized social and political system, sought to exclude from power the partisans of liberal monarchy, in which political power would be based on the popular will expressed in free elections. There were also occasions on which civil war broke out between the partisans of absolutist conservatism and those of more moderate conservative and liberal forms of government. Thus, even when there was a lull in the external fighting, there was war at home. In addition, there was a rising tide of socio-economic unrest, as the mass of the population, who had no say in governmental politics, attempted to make their voice heard against a system which excluded, oppressed and exploited them. The most extreme manifestations of this groundswell of popular discontent were the bombings and assassinations perpetrated by the more radical sector of the anarchist movement. More frequent and more widespread in their effect and level of involvement were the peasant uprisings against the unfair distribution of land, or the strikes staged by industrial workers against low wage levels, poor conditions and inflation. Conservative and liberal governments invariably responded with repression, often carried out by the Army. In so doing, they merely exacerbated the situation, by alienating the working masses further.

In the absence of democratic elections, political change was effected either by the intervention of the monarch or by an appeal to the military. Even when the monarchy was briefly replaced by a Republic (1873–74), the conflict continued between conservative and liberal concepts of how it ought to be organized. The terms of the restoration of the monarchy in 1875, in the person of the Bourbon heir, Alphonso XII, and of the constitution promulgated in 1876 ensured that the liberals were no longer systematically excluded from power. However, it was not until 1885 that a certain political stability was achieved, when the leaders of the Liberal and Conservative parties agreed to take turns in power. But new tensions quickly arose, for military interventionism had simply been replaced by electoral manipulation as the generator of political change. By the turn of the century, the political and administrative effectiveness of the two-party system was in decline, and responsibility for government fell increasingly upon a monarchy which lacked both the expertise and the political and popular support necessary to achieve and sustain political stability.

Above all, nineteenth-century Spain lacked a strong economic base on which to construct a stable political system. Heavy reliance on agriculture (and on a narrow range of crops) made the Spanish economy highly susceptible to factors beyond its control, such as climatic variations, natural disasters or changes in demand. Moreover, in addition to the technical problems posed by an enormous diversity of soil-types, geographic and hydrographic characteristics, and land-holding systems, the whole sector suffered from under-capitalization, under-exploitation and gross inefficiencies in the distribution and use of fertile land. Productivity was generally low and unit costs high, with the exception of labour, of which there was an excessive and, consequently, very cheap supply. The second half of the century saw the beginnings of industrial production in two areas of Spain: Catalonia, where textile manufacture slowly became the main non-agricultural component of the regional economy, and the Basque Country, where rich deposits of iron ore gave rise to ore exporting, steel manufacture, shipbuilding and engineering. By the end of the nineteenth century, however, the gradual loss of Latin American markets made Spanish industry increasingly reliant on domestic consumers whose demand and purchasing power were extremely limited. Neither agriculture nor industry generated surplus capital which might be reinvested, and a state impoverished by a century of war was incapable of providing any assistance other than protectionist policies, which temporarily paliated but did not remedy the underlying structural weaknesses.

The symptoms of decline and crisis manifest throughout the nineteenth century stimulated the idea among politicians, intellectuals and the military that some kind of radical intervention was required to stop the rot and initiate a period of national revival, or 'regeneration'. The loss of the last remnants of the empire in 1898 increased the already exaggerated nationalistic and patriotic component of 'regenerationism', particularly in military circles, where the conviction was growing that it was the ineptitude of politicians and government officials (especially those in the Treasury) that was the cause of Spain's troubles. This was a view to which Francisco Franco was later to subscribe. Looking back at the early part of the twentieth century, Franco wrote in 1962:

The obsession with public finance prevented Spain from realizing that she was being left behind in everything. The loss of our overseas territories, as a result of an unjust war, submerged us in the negative mood of national politics vis à vis our national territorial ambitions . . . . I believed in Spain and in her future possibilities. What was inadmissible was the political status quo, the structures of a system which presided over the complete collapse of our Empire.[4]

The implications of the ferment provoked by the change in his country's fortunes were brought home to Franco in 1907, when he was fifteen years old. Family tradition and personal vocation indicated that he would join the Navy and he therefore received his secondary education at the Naval School in El Ferrol, in preparation for entry to the Naval Academy.[5] However, a century of war and the collapse of the empire had virtually bankrupted the Spanish state and, as part of its efforts to cut military spending, in 1907 the government suspended until further notice the admission of cadets to the Naval Academy. This meant not only the frustration of Franco's ambition to join the Navy, but also that of his family to see one of its sons cross the invisible but crucial boundary between seafaring and non-seafaring sailors. The shattering of both dreams came as a severe disappointment and added a personal grievance to Franco's latent class and generational animosity towards the political Establishment. In response to the government's decision, Franco took what his cousin and life-long companion, Francisco Franco Salgado-Araujo, considered the only option left to 'the young men of El Ferrol who aspired to joining the Navy': the Army.[6] In so doing, Franco began the ascent which was to lead, twenty-nine years later, to the position of Commander-in-Chief of the Armed Forces, Head of Government and Head of State. It is interesting that, despite doña Pilar Bahamonde's belief in study as a means to social advancement, a university career was not even entertained as a possibility for her son, because the conservative classes saw the universities as centres of subversion. Franco retained that opinion all his life.

On 29 August 1907, Franco enrolled as a cadet in the Infantry Academy in Toledo, far south of his native Galicia, in the middle of the high *meseta* which forms the central massif of the Iberian Peninsula. In the absence of his own testimony, it is difficult to know what sentiments that move provoked in the adolescent Franco, but the magnitude of the change cannot but have affected him profoundly. In the first place, having been born and brought up close to the sea, ships and Atlantic rain, he was now in the middle of an arid, land-locked plateau, scorched in summer and frozen in winter. Secondly, the disparate figures of his mother and father were no longer present in his everyday life.[7] Thirdly, from the relative liberty and diversity of civilian existence, he was transferred to a closed, all-male social unit which erased individual identities in the interests of discipline, substituted rules and regulations for freedom of choice, and attempted to make contact with the outside world unnecessary by providing internally for all its members' needs.

Writing of Franco's time in Toledo, one of his first biographers describes him as 'always ready to fulfill the duties, however disagreeable, imposed by the discipline of the Academy'.[8] The Army was not the origin of that attitude, however, but the catalyst of beliefs received in the bosom of a family whose Catholicism, conservatism and authoritarianism made such concepts as hierarchy, discipline and obedience supreme values. His readiness to obey orders was not merely a formal attribute of his professional role, but a fundamental part of his character. It reflected a preference for hierarchical, rather than egalitarian, relationships, and was intimately bound up with the values which, for him, legitimated the exercise of authority. He was ready to accept orders provided they were given by people he considered empowered to do so by their formal position and their affinity with his own code of behaviour. The second was the key consideration. People and, above all, their opinions, were seen through a Manichaean prism which led him to reject, fear and try to eliminate those views which differed from his own. As his participation in the military rising of 18 July 1936 was to show, however, his obedience was far from guaranteed when he did not subscribe to the ideas of those in power, even when they were his superiors.

If Franco's strict upbringing had conditioned him to the submissive role required of Army recruits, it seems also to have predisposed him towards embracing the camaraderie of military life. As an institution, the Army did not reproach him with his physical shortcomings – his weedy build and a slight speech impediment – nor did it frown, as other professional circles might have done, on his provincial accent. Dressed in the same way as the other cadets, he 'belonged' in the Academy and felt reassured by the outward respectability with which uniforms are intended to invest their wearers. Nevertheless, the military uniform masked only partially Franco's underlying insecurity. He was constantly reminded of his small stature by the nickname he was given by his companions – the diminutive of his own surname, 'Franquito' – while his penchant for 'swotting' made him the butt of barrack-room practical jokes, to which he responded with unsmiling abnegation. Unlike the other cadets, he did not take part 'in the lively sexual forays customary among soldiers' – a reluctance not due to anti-machismo on Franco's part, but to his 'inferiority complex'.[9]

Despite his reputedly studious nature, Franco's academic performance was unremarkable. Of the 312 cadets who completed their training at the same time, he came well down the list, in 251st position. He graduated from Toledo on 13 July 1910, with the rank of Second Lieutenant, and was posted to his native El Ferrol, with the 8th 'Zamora' Regiment. He had tried to enlist for service in Spanish Morocco, but was unable to do so on account of his junior rank. The return to Galicia, although lacking the promise of rapid promotion, was an opportunity to go home wearing the uniform which was the visible sign of his membership of a respected élite; a chance to show his family and friends that he had made it (rather like the *gallego* emigrés to Cuba and Argentina, who returned only when and if they had made money overseas). His immediate satisfaction was short-lived, however, for although he now had a distinct role in life, there was nothing prestigious or glamorous about being a low-ranking Army officer in a small, provincial garrison town. Moreover, the salary of a Second Lieutenant was low and, with Spain at peace, promotion would come only slowly, by virtue of years of service.

It would seem logical that such considerations should go

through the mind of a young, professional soldier. Franco left no personal testimony of his feelings at that time, but the fact remains that as soon as an opportunity arose to leave El Ferrol, he jumped at it. In August 1911, and after an uneasy two-year lull, the hostility which had existed for centuries between Spain and Morocco flared again into war. Franco volunteered to join the troops leaving Spain for North Africa and, in February 1912, arrived in Melilla, one of Spain's military bases on the Mediterranean coast of Morocco. Not only had he disembarked in a new continent, he was also on the threshold of what turned out to be an experience which played a vital role in shaping the rest of his life: active service in Africa.

.   .   .

NOTES

1.   L. Suárez Fernández, *Francisco Franco y Su Tiempo* (hereafter, *FFST*), (8 vols) Madrid: Ediciones Azor 1984, vol. I, p. 62.
2.   Cf. G.P. del Acqua, *Los grandes protagonistas de la II Guerra Mundial: Franco*, Barcelona: Ediciones Orbis 1985, p. 7.
3.   RadioTelevisión Española (RTVE), *Ejército ayer y hoy*, broadcast 28 May 1982.
4.   Suárez Fernández, *FFST*, vol. I, pp.123–4.
5.   J. Arrarás, *Franco*, San Sebastian: Librería Internacional 1937, p. 16.
6.   F. Franco Salgado-Araujo, *Mi vida junto a Franco* (hereafter, *Mi vida*), Barcelona: Editorial Planeta 1977, p. 16.
7.   That same year, Franco's parents effectively separated when don Nicolás Franco was posted to Madrid and set up house with another woman. Francisco never forgave his father for the pain this caused his mother.
8.   Arrarás, *Franco*, p. 16
9.   Del Acqua, *Los grandes protagonistas*, p. 8.

Chapter 2

AFRICA, MADRID, ZARAGOZA (1912–31)

Without any doubt, the eleven years that Francisco Franco spent in Spanish Morocco, between 1912 and 1926, were crucial to the formation of his professional, personal and political character. It was there that he initiated a meteoric ascent of the promotional ladder; there that he became part of a tightly-knit group of officers – the *africanistas* – the bond of whose *esprit de corps* was, precisely, their Moroccan experience; and there that he came not only to sympathize with, but also to share, the hostility felt by military officers towards politicians. It was in North Africa, too, that the legend began to be woven that Franco was endowed with special qualities of heroism and leadership; and there that he learned the tactics of slow, relentless occupation of enemy territory which he would employ to devastating effect years later, in the Spanish Civil War.

Spain's presence in North Africa dates back to the fifteenth century. In 1497 the small town of Melilla, on the north-east coast of Morocco, was conquered by the Spanish Duke of Medina-Sidonia and later (in 1556) ceded to the Spanish Crown. With the addition (in 1640) of the Portuguese colonial town of Ceuta, situated almost directly opposite the Rock of Gibraltar, Spain possessed two enclaves in Morocco, on the coastal plain of a mountainous, isolated area known as the Rif. For the next 200 years, the protection of these two outposts of Spanish military power from the incursions of the tribes which inhabited the Rif was a continuous task for the troops garrisoned there, but marked the limit of Spain's aspirations in North Africa.

The relative tranquillity of this situation changed in the nineteenth century, adding yet another element of conflict to that turbulent period. The idea of the conquest of Morocco began to take shape as a means of rallying national sentiment and placating the military. Accordingly, in 1860, a campaign was launched to take the town of Tetuán, south of Ceuta. In spite of the 7,000 deaths in what was a badly planned and badly equipped expedition, the success of the operation 'raised Spain from her prostration', in the words of the contemporary Spanish Prime Minister, Leopoldo O'Donnell.[1]

The Tetuán campaign was 'a war of honour, not based on economic interest',[2] and, as such, had the general backing of the Spanish public. The same was not true, however, when 'economic interest' *was* the motive force. In July 1909, the military commander of Melilla asked for reinforcements to defend an Hispano-German iron mining concern, the Compañía Española de Minas del Rif, set up near Melilla in 1908. The political and labour organizations of the Left had become strongly opposed to Spain's military involvement in Morocco, partly because they were against the expenditure of public money on the protection of private interests, and partly because it was the sons of the working and lower middle classes who, as conscripts, sustained most of the casualties in such ventures. Protest demonstrations and press campaigns had already been organized in 1908. When the Conservative Prime Minister, Antonio Maura, authorized the mobilization of the reservists in July 1909, there was outcry on the Left. In Barcelona, where the troops were to embark for Africa, socialists, anarchists, the populist revolutionaries of the Radical Republican Party and the partisans of an independent labour movement, Solidaridad Obrera (Workers Solidarity) called a general strike, which quickly turned into a violent confrontation with the forces of law and order. Barricades were built in the streets and, as so often happened at times of civil strife, churches and convents were raided and burnt as a sign of rebellion against a Church considered to be the ally of the property-owning élite. The situation was aggravated by fresh news from Morocco, which told of the massacre of thousands of Spanish troops in the Wolf's Gully (el Barranco del Lobo), close to Melilla.

The government response was to declare a state of war in Barcelona and send in the army to restore order. The week of violence in Barcelona, subsequently known as the 'Tragic Week', resulted in hundreds of dead and wounded, and nearly 2,000 arrests.[3] Outraged by the revolt, the main Catalan Conservative Party, the Lliga Regionalista (Regionalist League), demanded retribution. Although it was far from clear who was responsible for the strike, five Catalans of known anarchist sympathies were accused of being the organizers and sentenced to death, despite the flimsiness of the case against them. The protests staged by left-wing organizations throughout Europe against the trial and the sentences merely hardened the Spanish government's resolve and persuaded the conservative classes that there was an international, Leftist conspiracy to subvert the existing order in Spain. At the military academy in Toledo, Franco had no firsthand knowledge of the events of the 'Tragic Week', but evidently shared that belief. His opinion that 'the demonstrations organized in many European cities were simply a show of international Masonic solidarity'[4] was an early sign of an obsession with Freemasonry that was to colour his political judgement to the end of his life.

The events of the 'Tragic Week' strained the political atmosphere further, weakening the credibility of the existing two-party system and strengthening the appeal of those parties excluded from and opposed to it. It was no coincidence that the Spanish Socialist Workers' Party (PSOE) obtained its first parliamentary representative in 1909, nor that the anarchist movement became more organized, creating the Confederación Nacional del Trabajo (National Confederation of Labour, CNT) in 1910. More than that, the July crisis and its aftermath focused and increased a view which had been gaining support since the turn of the century, namely that it was not only the two-party system which needed to be done away with, but the monarchy which simultaneously upheld and was upheld by it. Both the Conservative and Liberal parties were disintegrating into squabbling factions and were clearly incapable either of containing the rising tide of opposition and unrest, or of resolving the underlying social, economic and political problems. Yet the monarch, King Alphonso XIII (who had ascended the throne in 1902) continued to look to them for the formation of his cabinets. In the wake of the Tragic Week, the Conservative Prime Minister, Maura, was replaced by a Liberal, Segismundo Moret, until José Canalejas became leader of the Liberal Party and Prime Minister in 1910. When Canalejas was assassinated in November 1912, the premiership was taken over by a Conservative, Eduardo Dato.

It was, thus, against a background of considerable tension and confusion in mainland Spain that Second Lieutenant Francisco Franco Bahamonde disembarked in Melilla in February 1912. He was, of course, fully aware of the significance of the Moroccan war. He had been educated in a tradition handed down from the fifteenth century, which held that Spain's southern frontier was formed by the Atlas mountains, on the North African coast. Moreover, the war had for years been the subject of heated discussion, in Spanish political and trade union circles, in cafés, and in private houses up and down the country. The press talked of little else. As we noted earlier, Franco had tried to get to Morocco on graduation from the Toledo Military Academy in June 1910, and his arrival there two years later was the result of a conscious desire to be where the action was, for, as Raymond Carr observes, Morocco was 'where the monotonous life of the garrison was left behind for "shooting and promotion" '.[5] Franco was not to be disappointed on either count.

At that time, the Spanish Army had some 80,000 men stationed in Morocco (the northern portion of which officially became a Spanish protectorate in 1912). Of these, 15,000 were members of a force known as the Cuerpo de Indígenas Regulares (Regular Native Corps), composed of Moroccan soldiers serving under Spanish officers as part of the regular Spanish Army. As a rule, the Regulares were employed in the front line, as shock troops. On arrival in Melilla, Franco was assigned the command of a unit of Regulares, and on 19 March 1912 he had his first taste of battle, in the vanguard of an attack commanded by Colonel Dámaso Berenguer, then Spanish High Commissioner in Morocco. Soon afterwards, on 13 June, he rose to the rank of first lieutenant. This was the only time in his career that he was promoted by seniority. All his other many promotions were awarded on grounds of merit.

For the next four years, Franco acquitted himself well in numerous actions at the head of his Regulares. In September 1913 his successful leadership of a risky operation against an enemy position won him the Military Cross and ensured that 'from then on, he would no longer be an unknown officer'.[6] By 1915 he had been promoted to the rank of captain. His courage had rapidly gained the respect and admiration not only of the troops he commanded, but also of General Berenguer and other leading officers in Morocco, such as the Commander of Melilla, Major José Sanjurjo, and the Cavalry Commander of Alcazarquivir, in the south-west corner of the territory, Major Gonzalo Queipo de Llano. After the isolation of his childhood, the frustration of an aborted naval career and the lacklustre years as a cadet, Franco now found that he was good at his chosen profession and that he was not only accepted but also admired by his colleagues. Contemporary film footage of the war in Morocco includes scenes of Franco chatting with Sanjurjo and other officers in one of the Spanish camps.[7] The images of a relaxed and smiling Franco are a far cry from the stiff, severe-looking cadet who posed for his passing-out photograph in 1910.

Franco and his fellow *africanistas* saw the conquest of Morocco as a historic mission with which they had been entrusted in order to restore Spain's identity as a great power, to give people a sense of national purpose, and to repair the damage done to the prestige and honour of the armed forces by the Cuban defeat. They were united by this sense of collective enterprise and by their rejection of the political in-fighting of the governing parties and the politicians' incapacity to stamp out, or even contain, the protests and pressure for change from the forces of the Left. The *africanistas* believed that they alone were making sacrifices in order to defend Spain's rightful place in the world. Their conception of this as an enormous burden of responsibility, which honour and duty nevertheless obliged them to accept, along with the very fact of being together in a situation of isolation, hardship and danger, created among them an *esprit de corps*, which was as real as it was indissoluble. It was a bond which was to subsist in Francisco Franco Bahamonde long after he had left the Army of Africa.

Franco's time in Africa was also important for another reason, for it was there that the legend began to be woven that he was immune to enemy slings and arrows. On one occasion, so the story goes, an enemy sniper shot out of Franco's hand the top of a thermos flask into which he was pouring coffee. Franco turned in the direction of the enemy position and shouted, 'Let's see if you can aim better!'[8] Such incidents could not fail to capture the loyalty and admiration of the young captain's men. He was not, however, totally bullet-proof. On 24 June 1916 Franco was shot in the abdomen in the course of an assault on Moroccan guerrilla positions at the village of El Biutz, in the hills near Ceuta. It was a serious wound, and he was not expected to live. The reference to him in the official report of the day's action read like an obituary, praising his 'incomparable bravery, gift for command and the energy he displayed in combat'.[9] In fact, not only did he recover, but that was the only time he was wounded in ten years of fighting – a remarkable feat for a soldier in the front line and 'in a war which cost the lives of 915 officers and 16,000 soldiers between 1916 and 1926'.[10] His survival increased the devotion that his Regulares already felt towards him for his fighting spirit. They said he had *baraka*, a mixture of luck and divine protection afforded to a chosen few. Thus was sown the seed for the belief – to which Franco subscribed and which was subsequently exploited to the full by his propagandists – that his life received guidance of a superhuman nature.

For his part in the El Biutz action, Franco was recommended for promotion to major and for the highest military award for bravery, the Saint Ferdinand Cross with Laurels. The promotion was turned down by the War Ministry, on the grounds that he was too young. In a gesture which revealed Franco's high opinion of himself, he appealed against the decision to the king, who reversed it. Franco thus attained the rank of major on 28 February 1917,[11] but the dispute must have added to the *africanista* conviction that their sacrifices were not fully appreciated by government officials in Madrid. It almost certainly also aggravated an existing division between *africanista* and peninsular soldiers. The former were firm believers in promotion by merit; the latter, by seniority. In January 1917, in Barcelona, a group of soldiers set up a semi-clandestine committee (*junta*) to defend the peninsular position. It was dissolved in May and its members arrested, but the prohibition was lifted a month later and more *juntas* came into being, particularly among cavalry and artillery units, giving rise to a movement which called itself Juntas de la Unión y Defensa (Committees for Union and Defence). They were even given semi-official status as advisory bodies to the Ministry of War. The *africanistas* were outraged at this and more than ever convinced that political interests were undermining the rebuilding of a strong, professional army. Not surprisingly, Franco was among those opposed to the *Juntas*, not least, perhaps, because his own career would have been very different had the promotion-by-seniority-only criterion prevailed. As it was, he had attained in only six years a position which, in peacetime or in the Peninsula, would have required ten to fifteen years to achieve. Despite better passing-out results, many of those who had been at Toledo with him still had not risen above the rank of lieutenant. So ended Franco's first tour of duty in North Africa, for there was no vacancy for a major in Morocco at that time and he had to return to mainland Spain. There he was to encounter once more the realities of Spanish domestic and European politics from which he had been isolated since 1912. In the interim, war had broken out in Europe.

Spain maintained a position of neutrality during the conflict which tore the rest of Europe apart between 1914 and 1918. While she did not participate in the fighting, however, she was very much engaged in providing the belligerents with minerals, foodstuffs and textiles. The mine owners, industrial entrepreneurs and proprietors of agricultural land, together with the bankers and other intermediaries who handled the transactions, reaped substantial profits from this trade, as did the profiteers and black marketeers who inevitably appear at times when the normal rhythm of supply and demand is disrupted by conflict. Others, by contrast, received no rake-offs. The miners, factory workers and landless labourers, vital to the labour-intensive economy that Spain then was, continued to work long hours for wages which were not only low in absolute terms, but increasingly devalued from 1914 onwards, as inflation forced prices up. Spain was predominantly an agrarian society, and trade unionism, essentially an urban and industrial movement, was still in its infancy, having been banned until 1881. Moreover, the efforts of the two principal trade unions, the anarchist CNT and the socialist Unión General de Trabajadores (General Union of Workers, UGT) to improve the lot of the working classes were hindered by their inability to subordinate their ideological differences to the pursuit of common socio-economic aims. Finally, the parliamentary representation of the working classes – one socialist – was absurdly disproportionate to their numerical size and economic importance. As long as government and parliament were in the hands of Liberals and Conservatives who represented the interests of the owners and employers, it would not be possible by parliamentary means significantly to change the distribution of national wealth in favour of the poorer classes.

Nevertheless, the incipient Spanish labour movement was far from acquiescent in this situation. Although the UGT was reformist rather than revolutionary in character, the events of the Tragic Week, in 1909, and fears that the anarchists would dominate the whole of the labour movement had made the socialists participate in the anti-government campaign which followed. They also took part in the strikes and other protests which punctuated the next five years. Spain's ruling classes became increasingly concerned that the socio-political ferment which underlay the European war would spread south of the Pyrenees. Their fears increased in the spring of 1917, when not only did the UGT and CNT reach an agreement on joint action, but dissent began to be expressed by a number of non-unionized socio-economic groups, such as peasants and civil servants. The climax came in August 1917, when the UGT launched a rail strike which, with CNT support, became a general strike. One of the main centres of the strike was Asturias, Spain's principal coal-producing region in the north of the country. It was particularly important to the Spanish economy at a time when the war made it impossible to import better, cheaper, foreign coal. Anxious to end the strike, for economic as well as internal political reasons, the government resorted to force, as it had done in 1909, and called in the troops.

In March 1917 Major Francisco Franco had been posted to the capital of Asturias, Oviedo, where he was to be in command of a battalion of the Prince's Regiment. Conflicting accounts make it difficult to assess with certainty how active was his part in the repressive operations carried out in the province in August. There is no doubt, however, that he was at the head of one of the columns sent out to patrol the hinterland of Oviedo, with orders from the military governor of Asturias, General Burguete, to 'flush out the workers like vermin'.[12] Franco himself maintained that he and his column did nothing, because 'nothing was happening there'. This, of course, begs the question of what he would have done if something *had* happened. His reputation for decisive action, his belief in discipline, and his growing conviction that military intervention was necessary to put a stop to political mismanagement and the threat of revolution make it unlikely that he would have done other than obey Burguete's orders to the letter.

Franco appears to have attached little lasting significance to this episode of his stay in Asturias, despite the fact that this was the 'first revolutionary experience he was to live through'.[13] His notes for a projected (but never realized) autobiography, written in 1962, place only one meaning on this period of his life: 'Asturias = engagement'.[14] After five years of fierce fighting against Moroccan tribesmen in the Rif mountains, hunting down a few hundred miners in the hills of Asturias probably seemed rather tame by comparison; or, at least, no more than the 'normal' way to deal with a rebellion. Be that as it may, his engagement evidently took pride of place in his recollection. His fiancée, María del Carmen Polo y Martínez Valdés, was the daughter of a well-to-do Asturian family. As befitted a girl of her social class, she was a strict Catholic and, indeed, Franco met her on a church outing. Middle-class, religious and conservative in outlook, Carmen Polo's social and cultural profile was very similar to that of Franco's mother.

She did not, however, turn out to be the unobtrusive figure in the background that doña Pilar Bahamonde always was.

The three years that Franco spent in Asturias were sufficient for his relationship with Carmen Polo to become a formal engagement, but not for this to culminate in marriage. The reason was the continuing war in Morocco. In the autumn of 1918, while on a training course in Madrid, Franco met Major José Millán-Astray Terreros. Born in 1879, Millán-Astray was, like Franco, a *gallego*, an *africanista* and an Infantryman. With these three key features in common, Franco and Millán-Astray struck up a friendship which was to last until the latter's death in 1954. By then, Millán-Astray was convinced that 'Franco [was] God's emissary'.[15] In 1918, however, the veteran only saw in the younger man a highly competent soldier with experience in Africa, who shared his own view that the Moroccan war could not be fought efficiently with conscripts, but could only be won with fully professional forces – a view to which the government did not subscribe, mainly on economic grounds. Millán-Astray was eventually authorized by King Alphonso XIII to set up a special, multinational volunteer force, modelled on the French Foreign Legion. In 1920 he offered Franco a post as his second-in-command in Ceuta, where the force was to be based. Franco accepted. Postponing his imminent marriage to Carmen Polo, he returned to Morocco in October 1920, to take up his duties as the commanding officer of the first unit of the Tercio de Voluntarios, or, as Millán-Astray insisted it be called, the Legión Extranjera – the Foreign Legion.

The reputation for bravery which Franco had gained in the first five years of his Moroccan career was confirmed and enhanced in the six which followed his incorporation into the Foreign Legion. Its members soon established a name for themselves as the Spanish Army's hardest men and toughest fighters. His ability to command their respect and obedience and his participation in some of the most difficult operations of the war gave him unrivalled prestige within the Armed Forces and in the eyes of public opinion. In 1922 Millán-Astray wrote of him: 'Franco possesses all the qualities that every good soldier must have, which are: courage, intelligence, military spirit, enthusiasm, love of the profession, the spirit of sacrifice and a virtuous life.'[16] There are no indications that Franco was ever concerned that his progress might be too rapid or that such widespread public admiration caused him discomfort or stimulated self-criticism. On the contrary, he himself believed that these years signified the 'securing of [his] personality'.[17] It is hardly surprising, then, that he should feel piqued that he was not chosen to replace Millán-Astray as chief of the Legion, when Millán was removed from the post in November 1922. This undoubtedly had a bearing on Franco's request to be posted to the mainland. He was sent to Oviedo again in March 1923, but his stay was brief. On 28 May there occurred the first of what might be termed 'providential deaths' in Franco's career: that of Lieutenant-Colonel Rafael Valenzuela, the man who had taken over from Millán-Astray in 1922. Franco was appointed to succeed him, although this meant that his marriage to Carmen Polo had to be postponed again. Her family evidently used to say of him that he was like a gun-dog: as soon as he heard a shot, he was off.[18]

Franco's meteoric career was undoubtedly assisted by the fact that the existence of a war offered the possibility of promotion on merit. He was fortunate, too, that his part in it was to provide the brawn, rather than the brains: he could and did deploy effectively the sheer brute force and resilience of the Legionnaires, but he was not a brilliant strategist. Happily for him, that was the role assigned to others, notably General Goded. Paradoxically, Franco was also helped by the fact that a disastrous defeat at Annoual, in the north of the Protectorate, in July 1921, had strengthened the determination of the Army to vindicate its honour by bringing the whole area under control, thus 'justifying' the prolongation of the war.

However, the Annual massacre and the subsequent campaign to restore Spanish military honour and political control added to the ferment of opposition and unrest in the Peninsula. The Conservative members of parliament agreed to an inquiry into the disaster, to determine military responsibilities, but refused to examine the question of possible political responsibilities. Rumours began to circulate that the king himself was directly implicated. In 1921, the Prime Minister, Eduardo Dato, was assassinated, while the spiral of violence which had begun in Catalonia after the 1917 strike became ever more bloody and insoluble. The reformist Liberal government appointed in 1923 simply could not cope. In September 1923, with the support of the Catalan upper classes, the Captain-General of Barcelona, Don Miguel Primo de Rivera y Orbaneja, declared a *pronunciamiento*. King Alphonso XIII, recognizing that Primo de Rivera was the *deus ex machina* who could save the throne, called him to Madrid and asked him to form a government. Franco did not express support for Primo's coup – because he believed it to have been staged by members of the Juntas de Defensa – but neither did he oppose it. This calculated ambiguity was to become a familiar trait of Franco's response to major political developments.

Primo de Rivera immediately appointed a cabinet (or 'Directorate', as it was called) composed entirely of military men, suspended parliamentary rule (which, *inter alia*, meant that the Annoual inquiry could not continue), and banned political parties and labour organizations. He did not envisage this as a permanent system, but as a temporary period of strong (i.e., authoritarian) government, during which, in the absence of debilitating party-political conflicts, it would be possible to restore economic prosperity, social harmony and national greatness. In line with his 'regenerationist' view of what was needed, Primo de Rivera's policies concentrated on improving Spain's infra-structural condition (particularly its energy and transport sectors) and productive capacity, and introduced a number of measures aimed at improving the educational system and the lot of women. In the final analysis, however, Primo de Rivera was essentially a conservative and politically incapable of carrying out the socio-economic reforms without which the country would inevitably sink further into crisis.

One of the areas in which Primo de Rivera recognized a particularly urgent need for change was the Armed Forces. In particular, he believed that the war in Morocco must be brought rapidly to a close. This was, perhaps, surprising, given that the General was himself an *africanista*. But, if he was conscious that such a policy would (and did) earn him the hostility of a large sector of the Army, he was equally aware that the military, economic and political costs of the war were arguments which outweighed those in favour of continuing it. Franco was among the *africanistas* who were opposed to what they saw as an attack on their own *raison d'être* and a betrayal of the efforts and sacrifices made by the Army in Morocco since the turn of the century. For them, withdrawal from Africa was tantamount to a repetition of what had happened in South and Central America in the previous century: Spain's position as a great world power was being eaten away because the country's leaders were bowing to political pressure. They felt all the more aggrieved because the king, as supreme commander of the armed forces, and Primo de Rivera, as a military man, claimed to have the protection of the Army's best interests at heart.

Primo de Rivera was well aware of Franco's opposition to withdrawal from Africa. Franco explained his position personally to Primo in July 1924 and wrote extensively on the subject in a military journal he helped to found that same year. Nevertheless, his behaviour was totally disciplined. He was even decorated for his part in the withdrawal from the city of Xauen and promoted to the rank of colonel in February 1925. Perhaps because Primo was himself an *africanista*, or because he saw advantage in trying to avoid the total alienation of an important sector of the Army, the general partially changed his mind in 1925. He agreed to an all-out attack via the bay of Alhucemas, south of Ceuta. It was to be carried out, in collaboration with French forces, on 7 September 1925. In the event, the operation was almost a disaster. Franco's role was to go ashore first with his Legionnaires, to establish a bridgehead. This he did, but only after countermanding an order to retreat. He had taken a tremendous risk but, fortunately for him, the enemy forces were ultimately routed. It was thus possible to present the withdrawal from Morocco as a victorious army returning home with its mission fulfilled, playing down the economic and political pressures which were its true motives. Franco was promoted yet again, to brigadier-general. At the age of thirty-three, he was the youngest general in Europe.

The seniority of his new rank again obliged him to return to mainland Spain. A decisive stage in his career was formally over, but the links he had created with his fellow *africanistas*, the military lessons he had learned in combat against the Moroccan guerrilla forces, the reputation he had earned himself as a soldier, and the opinions he had formed on such matters as the role of the Army in political affairs or the reasons for Spain's decline as a world power, were to be carried over into all the successive stages. Franco himself affirmed, years later, 'My years in Africa live on in me with indescribable strength.'

Franco undoubtedly displayed remarkable qualities as a soldier in Africa, despite his mediocre showing at the Toledo Academy and the fact that 'he was by no means up to date with the modern style of warfare', used in Morocco after 1926.[19] It is also true, however, that the Moroccan war was a small conflict in geopolitical terms and one in which a semi-professional Spanish Army was fighting technically inferior guerrilla forces. Successful operations and individual acts of bravery consequently seemed more spectacular than they might have done in a larger, more evenly balanced, conflict. This is not to say that the Moroccan war was a walk-over for the Spanish Army, nor that the conditions in which it was fought were easy. On the contrary, the barren, mountainous terrain, the arid climate, the grossly deficient sanitary and living conditions of the troops, and shortages of arms and munitions, together with the tenacity and ferocity of the enemy, made it a protracted and difficult struggle. What it *is* to say is that it provided Franco with an opportunity for accelerated self-advancement which he would certainly not have had had he stayed with the 8th Zamora Regiment in El Ferrol.

That Franco's performance in the Moroccan war should provide the basis for his future professional and political prestige is partly explained by the fact that Spain in the first half of the twentieth century was a society whose ruling classes believed that the strength of the nation lay essentially in its military strength and for whom military prowess was equated with patriotic zeal. The rest of the explanation lies in the specific political and social significance of this particular war, as a highly controversial last-ditch attempt to salvage national honour and placate the military. Had there been less at stake in the Moroccan conflict, Francisco Franco's role in it would, equally, have been given less attention. It was as much the importance of the war as Franco's personal contribution to it that enabled him to emerge as a heroic figure, and to use it as a springboard to higher personal, professional and, ultimately, political goals.

On his return to the Peninsula, Franco was given command of the two regiments which were based in Madrid. Life in the capital was, of course, very different to what Franco had been used to for the preceding fourteen years, or, indeed, at any previous time in his life. He does not seeem to have been attracted by the social whirl that now surrounded him: 'Franco did not possess inherited wealth and this, together with a certain timorousness, disinclined him to lead a brilliant social life. Nor did he like that kind of thing.'[20] Given Franco's reputation for audacity in combat, his medals for bravery and his promotions for outstanding behaviour on active service, it hardly seems appropriate to describe him as 'timorous'. The economic constraints imposed by the return to the Peninsula, together with the relative seclusion in which military families lived are more likely explanations for his social isolation than any natural diffidence. His economic situation was probably not very buoyant, for he no longer received the additional payments made to those who served in the Legion and/or Africa. Low pay was, in fact, one of the principal grievances of Army officers, and increased their sense of being badly treated by a state and a society which did not appreciate their sacrifices in the name of the Fatherland. In Franco's case, the birth of his daughter, Carmencita, in 1926, placed an additional burden on his domestic economy.

Nevertheless, Franco's transfer to Madrid put him not only at the centre of the country's most important military region, but also at the hub of its political life. He was therefore able to witness at close range a period of profound, often violent, upheaval in Spain, as the Primo de Rivera dictatorship tried to conserve its own and the monarchy's position against a growing swell of discontent. As a result of his attempts to satisfy irreconcilable demands for both change and stability, Primo de Rivera ultimately alienated practically every sector of the social, political and economic spectrum, including those who had supported his coup in September 1923. In 1926, however, he had not yet exhausted his credit with them, and even believed he could turn his regime into a permanent system which would continue after he himself had left power.

On the surface, General Primo de Rivera's Spain may have appeared quite calm and prosperous to Franco in 1926. Economic output and productivity had increased significantly by comparison with the beginning of the decade. An impressive programme of road, railway and hydraulic construction had been undertaken, which not only improved Spain's transport and energy infrastructure but also stimulated related industries and provided hundreds of jobs. Government controls had been introduced to discourage the consumption of imported goods and, so, to protect national production. Working and living conditions in an increasingly urban, industrialized society were improving slowly and the annual number of strikes had declined. Socially, too, certain areas – such as health, education and the incorporation of women into the labour market – had improved as a result of measures introduced by the dictatorship. At first glance, then, it may have seemed to Franco that General Primo de Rivera was achieving the harmony and stability he had proclaimed as the objectives of his regime.

A closer look, however, would have revealed many difficulties and unresolved problems. In the first half of the 1920s, Spain had benefited from economic recovery in the rest of western Europe. But the prosperity which filtered through to Spain – mainly through investment and trade – was heavily dependent on the state of the world economy. Thus, when the onset of recession began in Europe and the United States in the second half of the decade, Spain also felt the pinch. Moreover, Primo de Rivera's promotion of national enterprise was inspired by a protectionist, autarchic view of economic affairs, which ultimately choked off external trade and discouraged foreign investment. Consequently, the public works programmes could not be financed by revenue from these sources; nor was direct taxation a viable alternative, on account of the opposition it provoked among those who would be liable to pay. The 'solution' was massive public debt, which weakened the economy as a whole and attracted sharp criticism from the middle classes.

Primo's attempts to control every aspect of the economy alienated both employers and workers. The operation of the National Economic Council and its network of subsidiary bodies angered the capitalist entrepreneurs of Spain's industrial regions, who wanted a free hand in the manufacturing, commercial and financial sectors. This was particularly the case in Catalonia, where the rich, influential bourgeoisie was also strongly regionalist and deeply resented intervention from Madrid. On the labour side, the dictatorship had set up 'Parity Committees' which ostensibly provided a forum for negotiation in which workers and employers were equally represented. In fact, they were an exercise in class collaboration which denied or ignored the conflicts inherent in a capitalist economy. Controlled by the government, they presumed to take the place of genuine representation, as this had been expressed through class-based organizations such as the anarchist CNT and the socialist UGT, until the former's suppression in 1923 and the latter's partial cooption, partial subjugation by the dictatorship.

Politically, too, initial hopes that Primo would provide strong leadership and an end to the corruption and instability of the preceding parliamentary system gradually began to fade. For those who supported left-wing or liberal options, the dictatorship was simply repressive, forcing all dissent underground and making alternative views *ipso facto* subversive. For the conservative classes, Primo was not sufficiently authoritarian: in their view, the 'iron fist' should be used not simply to intimidate but to crush all manifestations of liberalism.

In an attempt to placate his critics, Primo de Rivera took a series of steps designed to temper the military nature of his regime, without returning to parliamentary democracy. Thus, he replaced the Military Directorate set up in 1923 with a mixed civilian–military body; announced the creation of a corporatist quasi-parliament, the General Assembly, which would draft a new constitution; and set up an organization entitled Unión Patriótica (Patriotic Union), whose principal task, in the absence of legal political parties, was to mobilize popular support for the dictatorship. Not surprisingly, given their piecemeal nature, these measures satisfied no one. The working classes were alarmed by the job losses, shrinking real wages and inflation of a worsening economic situation, and were exasperated by the repression of their political and trade union organizations. The middle and upper classes were irritated by what they saw as the dictatorship's excessive and wasteful 'prestige' spending, and incensed by the idea of income tax. Above all, they were frightened by the growing militancy of the working masses and indignant at Primo de Rivera's failure to stamp out the threat of popular mobilization. Significant sectors of the Army (particularly the élite troops of the Army of Africa) were disillusioned by Primo's decision to pull out of Morocco, disturbed by what they viewed as a chaotic political situation and increasingly disaffected from a king whom they believed to have abandoned the Army's professional interests. For their part, the political parties of the Right resented Primo's failure to provide strong leadership and stable government, while those on the Left were increasingly convinced that he could not and would not carry out the far-reaching reforms which Spain desperately needed.

By the time General Franco installed himself in Madrid in 1926, republicanism appealed to an increasingly wide range of people as an alternative to both military dictatorship and monarchy. Indeed, from the mid 1920s onwards, support for the idea of a republic grew not so much from genuinely republican convictions as from a widespread desire to be rid of both General Primo de Rivera and King Alphonso XIII. Thus, when Alianza Republicana (Republican Alliance) was formed in 1926, it grouped together an assortment of turn-of-the-century federalists, Centre-Rightist radicals, Leftist reformers, Catalanist liberals and independent intellectuals. As was the case with the anarchist, socialist and communist sectors of the political spectrum, Spanish republicanism was far from homogenous in its views and aims. This led to the existence of personal and ideological animosities within its own ranks which were to have important consequences for its development in the next decade.

The mood of the society to which Franco returned in

February 1926 was, thus, of apparent calm and prosperity which only thinly veiled the underlying currents of simmering discontent and growing pressure for change. Given that military intervention in politics was then a well-established tradition in Spain, that Primo de Rivera was himself a military man, and that military (as well as civilian) personnel occupied positions at all levels of the regime's administrative apparatus, it is inconceivable that the political situation was not discussed by the high-ranking officers who were Franco's professional companions. Yet both contemporary and later accounts of Franco's career at this time insist that he never talked about anything other than purely professional matters – 'especially the Legion and the Moroccan war'[21] – in the groups of officers with whom he met daily in one or another of the city-centre cafés where political discussion was the order of the day. Indeed, he must have been a rather tedious coffee companion, for, as his cousin and fellow-soldier, Francisco Franco Salgado-Araujo, relates, Franco Bahamonde always told his stories with exactly the same words, 'as though he were reading them'![22] Franco's 'Notes' for his autobiography suggest that his reticence was due, not to a sense of personal loyalty or professional discipline, but to an acute sense of timing. He felt himself destined for great things, but preferred to wait until he judged the moment propitious. 'When I was made a general at the age of thirty-three', he wrote, 'I was marked out to assume enormous future responsibilities . . . Although politics were repugnant on account of the degeneration of the party system, I was, because of my age and prestige, called to render transcendental services to the nation.'[23] But, in 1926, not yet awhile. He did not take part in an attempted coup in June of that year, nor in a meeting of officers in September, both of which were organized in protest against General Primo de Rivera's desire to reform the Armed Forces.

His fidelity was soon rewarded and his professional talents deployed in a post more challenging than the routine duties of a city garrison in peace-time. In 1927, he was chosen to be the Director of a new General Military Academy which was to be built in the city of Zaragoza, 320 kilometres to the north-east of Madrid. Its creation was part of General Primo de Rivera's reform programme, designed both to modernize the Spanish Army in the light of the lessons learned from the Great War and to try to eliminate divisive internal differences such as had given rise to the Junta movement. Until then, cadets from each of the five different army corps had trained in separate academies. Now, future officers would train together for the first two years of their career, irrespective of whether they were later to serve in Infantry, Cavalry, Artillery, General Staff or Service Corps units. As Director of the new Academy, Franco effectively had 'the direct control of all the future officers of the Army'.[24] This was an important position in military terms by any standards, but in the Spain of the early twentieth century it had a special significance, given the Army's conception of itself as the nation's social and political guardian.

While the Zaragoza Academy prided itself on teaching the most advanced military techniques of the day, it also aimed to imbue cadets with a particular kind of values, inculcating in them the 'ruthless arrogance of the Foreign Legion, the idea that the Army was the supreme arbiter of the nation's political destiny, and a sense of discipline and blind obedience'.[25] The Zaragoza ethic was encapsulated in 'ten commandments' drawn up by General Franco himself:

1. Love the fatherland and the king.
2. Show military spirit in vocation and discipline.
3. Profess unequivocally the qualities of a gentleman and guard your reputation zealously.
4. Fulfil your duties faithfully and to the letter.
5. Never grumble, nor allow others to grumble.
6. Make yourself loved by your inferiors and wanted by your superiors.
7. Volunteer for sacrifice, requesting the greatest risk.
8. Be a noble companion, sacrificing yourself for your comrade and rejoicing in his successes.
9. Love responsibility and be decisive in finding solutions.
10. Be courageous and unselfish.[26]

With the exception of point 2, there is nothing to indicate that this is a decalogue for soldiers, rather than for any other profession. In other words, these ten instructions not only represented Franco's recommendations for soldierly proficiency, but were also his guidelines for life in general. For him, there was no distinction between military and other kinds of human values; and these came from such essentially conservative concepts as hierarchy, duty, discipline, and self-sacrifice. Conversely, they did not encourage notions such as intellectual curiosity, the questioning of received truths, or each person's intrinsic right to liberty and equality, for such ideas were the stuff of liberalism and, therefore, anathema to Spanish conservatives.

As the Academy gained a reputation as a centre of professional and moral excellence, the identification between military, moral and political authority had the effect of enhancing Franco's social and personal prestige. More at home in the provincial atmosphere of Zaragoza, a town similar in size and character to El Ferrol and Oviedo, Franco and his wife attended the soirées and Sunday promenading of the Zaragoza aristocracy and upper middle classes, and rubbed shoulders with the pillars of local society. Although Franco's hagiographers have insisted on his preference for an austere life-style, and, as we noted earlier, he had not taken part in the social life of Madrid, he did not shun the attentions of the Aragonese nobility, nor the material comforts afforded by his position. On the contrary, his self-confidence was boosted by the respect and admiration of the local notables, who told him that they considered him a bulwark against any threat to the status quo. It is not hard to imagine how this kind of attention increased the sense of his own prestige and national importance which Franco had felt since his promotion to general.

The mood of impending disaster which prevailed in conservative circles in the second half of the decade sharpened as the crisis of the dictatorship deepened. Primo de Rivera had failed to introduce reforms which would, at least, have spared him the hostility of the political Left and contained the opposition of the anarchist – and socialist-led labour movement. At the same time, however, the failure of his repressive measures to stamp out that opposition and of his economic interventionism to prolong the prosperity of the war years frightened the ruling middle and upper classes. They had looked to him to stabilize the situation in 1923, and he had failed to do so. His domestic difficulties were compounded by the onset of world-wide economic crisis in 1929. By then, Primo retained only minimal support and the republican cause was gaining ground daily. A sign of the times was an anti-monarchical conspiracy hatched in January 1929 by conservative politicians, Alianza Republicana, the anarchist CNT, members of the artillery corps and some of the military men who had taken part in the attempted coup of June 1926. In the words of military historian Gabriel Cardona: 'Primo de Rivera had achieved something incredible: secured agreement between such heterogenous people.'[27] A further sign came in August 1929 when the PSOE, part of which had once favoured collaboration with the dictatorship, included a call for the institution of a republic in its party manifesto.

Although the 1929 plot was discovered, the conspiring continued. Indeed the harsh treatment meted out to the military men involved in that subterfuge served to alienate significant sectors of the armed forces even further from the dictatorship. By the beginning of 1930, the political relationship between General Primo de Rivera and King Alphonso was no longer tenable. In January the dictator asked the highest ranking members of the military establishment – the Captains General – whether they retained confidence in him, offering to resign if they did not. Their lukewarm response effectively obliged him to renounce power. In addition, two of his closest friends, the Director-General of the Civil Guard and the Captain-General of Catalonia, convinced him that there was nothing to be done. On 30 January 1930 General Primo de Rivera offered his resignation to the king. Alphonso, who had since 1928 been under pressure from the conservative Right to be rid of Primo, accepted it. The General exiled himself to Paris, where he died a mere six weeks later, on 17 March 1930.

There is not space here to analyse all the many and complex factors which contributed to the downfall of General Primo de Rivera, but we may highlight the most important of them. In the first place, the dictatorship failed to resolve the structural problems which had given rise to the 1923 coup: the upper and middle classes sought the guarantees of the rule of law and order against what they perceived as threatening changes. Secondly, Primo de Rivera failed to calm their fears because he repressed, but did not totally eradicate, the forces of liberalism, socialism, communism and anarchism; on the contrary, he had tried to secure their participation in an exercise in class collaboration. Thirdly, Primo's attempts to reform the armed forces were centred almost exclusively on the number, structure, procedures and privileges of officer ranks, many of whose members resented such interference with established practices and were not compensated by, for example, significant wage increases, better promotion prospects, or technological improvements. Fourthly, the king had compromised himself by acquiescing in Primo's assumption of power; the only way to avoid the monarchy being dragged down with the dictatorship's failure was to sever the connection. That in itself hastened General Primo de Rivera's political and physical end.

The demise of Primo de Rivera did not and could not resolve the impending crisis, for it did nothing to remedy the underlying social, political and economic problems. King Alphonso commissioned another general – Damaso Berenguer – with the formation of a cabinet, which would effect a gradual return to the 'constitutional normality' interrupted in 1923. But Berenguer was a soldier, not a politician, and he had no clear idea of his objectives, other than 'to temper spirits, attend to the administration and achieve much-desired juridical and constitutional normality'.[28] In any case, an attempt simply to blot out the Primo de Rivera years by reviving the 1876 constitution could never have succeeded, for too many people wanted decisive change. The National Assembly was dissolved, the CNT made legal again and political, even republican, proselytising allowed, to prepare the ground for a return to constitutional government. But Berenguer had inherited a poisoned chalice. In order to form a government, he had to resort to reactionary conservatives, for none of the liberal or progressive conservative forces would take part in what they saw as an attempt to return to precisely the situation which Primo de Rivera had sought to destroy in 1923.

Even if Berenguer could have mustered moderate

support, it is doubtful whether the monarchy could have survived, so strong and so widespread was the pressure for change. Clandestine pro-republican meetings and propaganda were known to be taking place in a large number of army barracks, while civilian political and trade union organizations also plotted to remove the monarchy. On the Right, some of the king's own erstwhile supporters called for his abdication, while others advocated an authoritarian approach and still others tried to find a middle-of-the-road solution. In the centre, as we have noted, the Republican Alliance had been formed four years earlier, in 1926. Now, one of its component groups (Acción Republicana – Republican Action) became a party and other republican parties quickly appeared in its wake, particularly in Catalonia, where Catalan nationalism and opposition to the centralist monarchy were almost synonymous among the middle classes. On the Left, socialists, anarchists and communists all wanted an end to the existing regime, although they were by no means unanimous as regards what form of state should replace it. In the summer of 1930, in the northern coastal resort of San Sebastian, a group of anti-monarchical politicians and intellectuals signed an agreement (known as the 'Pact of San Sebastian') in which they committed themselves to the overthrow of the monarchy and the institution of a Republic. Later that year, in October, the Socialist Party pledged its support for the Pact and a Revolutionary Committee was formed. At the same time, a Military Committee was created, whose leader was the *africanista* General Gonzalo Queipo de Llano.

In the self-sufficient world of the Military Academy, Franco made no public comment on the growing clamour for far-reaching change, nor on the king's inability to arrest the decline in his own support. Many years later, he was to write of 'the ingratitude of the Monarchy towards General Primo de Rivera' and of the 'injustice' done to the dictator,[29] but he voiced no misgivings at the time. His silence in 1930 may have been the prudence of the soldier who thought it was not his place to make political statements. It seems more likely, however, that, in such uncertain circumstances, he did not want to place his career in jeopardy by openly criticizing the regime to which he owed his livelihood and to whose principles he was sincerely loyal. By the end of the 1920s, Franco was approaching the age of forty. He had a wife and daughter to provide for, and, foreseeably, many more years in his profession to safeguard. The man of impulsive action that he had been in Morocco had all but disappeared, to be replaced by one who, like a chess player, silently worked out his strategy, trying to predict the final result before making a move.

He was, however, acutely aware of the republican conspiracies, for his own younger brother was heavily involved. Ramón Franco was the leading light of a clandestine organization, the Agrupación Militar Republicana (Republican Military Group) which, in the spring of 1930, circulated anti-monarchical literature around the garrisons. As a ploy to get him out of the way, he was offered a posting as military attaché in Washington, but he saw through the manoeuvre and turned the job down. Shortly afterwards, his elder brother, Francisco, tried to talk him out of what he perceived as the error of his ways. In a letter dated 8 April 1930, the General spoke of his desire to steer his brother away from 'the path upon which, without realizing it, [he had] embarked and which imperceptibly [was] dragging [him] towards disaster'. Defending the Berenguer regime as 'a legal government, which is restoring citizens' guarantees', Franco assured Ramón that all his conspiring was known to the authorities and that 'the Army will remain within the law and will at all times defend order, discipline and the throne'. Franco ended this paternalistic missive with a plea to Ramón to think how upsetting were his actions for their mother. Ramón was astounded by the letter and amazed that Francisco had so high an opinion of the monarchy. In his reply, he gave an impassioned summary of the flaws and failings of the monarchy and reproached his brother for his 'profound ignorance' of the real situation. 'If you descend from your general's throne', he wrote, 'and take a walk among the ordinary ranks of captains and lieutenants, you will see how few think like you and how close we are to the Republic.' Attributing Francisco's incapacity to understand that one could be both a republican and a patriot to his dealings with the 'aristocratic and wealthiest classes', Ramón ended his letter on a defiant note:

> I do and will continue to do what I want, and that's what I am told to do by my conscience, which is less aristocratic and more citizen-like than yours. If my career gets in the way of that, I shall not hesitate to give it up and earn my life as an ordinary citizen, devoting myself to the service of the Republic, which is to say the service of the Nation.[30]

Not surprisingly, in view of his brother's republicanism, General Franco was at pains publicly to show that he, at least, was loyal to the monarchy. When King Alphonso took the salute at the first passing-out ceremony at the Zaragoza Academy, in June 1930, Franco urged the cadets always to be conscious of the meaning of the colours of the flag: red, for the blood of many generations of soldiers, and gold, 'which represents the glory of Spain and of the monarchy'.[31] In October, Ramón Franco was arrested on charges of participating in secret, subversive meetings, arms smuggling, and bomb-making. At the request of the Director-General of Security, General Emilio Mola, General Franco had forewarned Ramón, but rumours of a general strike precipitated his arrest. His confinement served only to increase his popularity and to publicize his cause. Even more sensational than his arrest was his escape, in the early hours of 24 November 1930. At no point since his arrest had his elder brother made any attempt to intervene with Mola or Berenguer to persuade them to treat Ramón with leniency. Doubtless Ramón's April letter and his manifest determination to go his own way influenced Francisco's attitude.

While Ramón Franco went to ground on the outskirts of Madrid, the republican conspirators continued to plot. The plan was for a military rising to take place on 15 December 1930, followed immediately by a general strike. As a result of confusion over the date, a group of captains and lieutenants rose at the garrison of Jaca, about 150 kilometres north of Zaragoza, on 12 December. At first, it was rumoured that Ramón Franco was at the head of two columns of ill-equipped soldiers, marching south. In nearby Zaragoza, General Franco placed the Academy on the alert, ready to intervene. Later in the day, he sent four companies of cadets, armed with mortars and machine guns, to set up a road-block on the main road from Jaca to Zaragoza. In the event, this proved unnecessary, for the rebels were forced to surrender on 13 December, but 'Francisco Franco had once more shown his military efficiency and his proven loyalty to the Crown.'[32] The two principal leaders, Captains Fermín Galán and Angel García Hernández, were summarily court-martialled and shot on 14 December.

In Madrid, a group of aviators, which included Ramón Franco, tried unsuccessfully to launch a coup from the Cuatro Vientos airfield. Ramón himself flew over the royal palace with the intention of bombing it, but desisted when he saw some children playing near by. The 'Revolutionary Committee' had issued a manifesto, but the call for a general strike went unheeded by the trade unions and the moderate sector of the PSOE. The Committee members were rapidly arrested and the military conspirators fled to Portugal, where they were interned by the Portuguese authorities. To avoid extradition to Spain, Ramón Franco decided to escape to Uruguay. Desperate for money, he appealed to his family in Spain. Francisco sent him 2,000 pesetas and a letter reiterating the points he had made in his April missive: Ramón was wrong, led astray by the evil influence of others. He also made a judgement of Ramón's action which, in the light of Francisco's own subsequent career, appears charged with irony:

> what might have been appropriate to the circumstances of the middle of the last century is impossible today, when the reasoned evolution of ideas and peoples, becoming more democratic within the confines of the law, constitutes true progress for the Fatherland. Any extremist and violent revolution will drag [the Fatherland] down to the most hateful of tyrannies.[33]

He had either forgotten these words of advice or simply did not think them applicable to himself when, in July 1936, he rose against the legally constituted, democratic government of the day.

In April 1931 Franco formed part of the military tribunal set up to judge the Jaca rebels. In view of the wave of public protest which had followed the execution of Galán and García Hernández in January, a third death penalty was not carried out. Nevertheless, five life sentences and more than sixty other prison sentences were passed. Denying the political character of the rising, Franco called it a 'military crime, of a purely military essence, committed by military men'. This might seem to be an indication of how Franco interpreted the soldier's duty as strictly apolitical, but it was, rather, an example of his duplicity, for he did not openly condemn his brother's behaviour as a 'military crime'. Moreover, five years later, he viewed his own participation in a military rising not as a 'military crime', but as a legitimate political act.

The failure of the Jaca rising in no way strengthened King Alphonso's position. On the contrary, it gave the republican cause its first martyrs and strengthened the conviction of those on both Right and Left who believed that radical change was an urgent necessity. In an effort to contain the situation, General Berenguer promised that elections would be held. All the pro-republican political forces responded by announcing their intention of abstaining. Incapable of resolving the impasse, Berenguer resigned. He was succeeded by a senior naval officer, Admiral Aznar.

In the event, the anti-monarchical parties did not abstain when local government elections were held throughout Spain in April 1931. In the first round, on 5 April, the monarchist candidates obtained an overwhelming majority, but this was not enough to dispel the fears of the conservative bourgeoisie. On that same day, a group of Franco's Zaragoza friends told him that he was their only hope of salvation from the threat of revolution.[34] If they were worried by the fact that elections were taking place at all, their concerns turned to panic when the second round took place a week later. In the rural areas, the conservative, monarchist candidates carried the day, thanks in large measure to the underhand methods of local political bosses (*caciques*), who were able to rig the polls by threatening poor, often illiterate, peasants with eviction or redundancy if they did not vote for the 'right' candidate, or by falsifying the electoral roll to include the names of people who had been dead for years. In the cities, however, it was more difficult to manipulate the results, because of the higher cultural level of the electorate, its greater political awareness, and its mobilization by the parties of the Left and Centre. In the cities, the second round gave the victory to the republican candidates. General Franco considered marching on Madrid, but changed his mind when he discovered that neither the Minister of Defence, Berenguer, nor the Director-General of the paramilitary Civil Guard, General Sanjurjo, would mobilize the forces under their command in defence of the monarchy.[35] Thirty years later, Franco would condemn 'the lack of moral fibre and authority of those who exercised power . . . handing [it] over to the revolutionaries without firing a single shot in defence of legality'.[36] A member of King Alphonso's cabinet, Count Romanones, tried in vain to bargain for time with the Revolutionary Committee, in prison since December. Scenting victory, the Committee would accept nothing less than the departure of the king. With few exceptions, the cabinet was also in favour of abdication. Faced with such overwhelming opposition, King Alphonso decided on 14 April 1931 to leave Spain, in order, he said, 'to avoid a fratricidal civil war'. That same day, the Revolutionary Committee was released from prison and established itself in Madrid as the provisional government of the Second Republic.

Spain's first Republic had lasted barely a year (1873–74) and had ended with a military coup which ultimately restored the monarchy. This unpromising precedent did not dampen the spirits of those who, on 14 April 1931, celebrated the birth of the Second Republic with dancing in the streets of towns and cities all over Spain. They may not all have understood fully what the new regime meant, nor were they all conscious of the ideological differences between its partisans. What they did know was that they had lost patience with, and confidence in, King Alphonso's regime and looked to the new Republic to right all the wrongs they considered the monarchy to have committed.

. . .

NOTES

1. R. Carr, *Spain 1808–1975*, Oxford University Press 1982, p. 261.
2. Ibid., p. 261.
3. A. Balcells, *Historia contemporánea de Cataluña*, Barcelona: Edhasa 1983, p. 193 gives casualties as 113 dead, of whom nine were soldiers and 104 civilians, and 341 wounded, of whom 125 were members of the armed forces and 216 civilians; L. Suárez Fernández, *Francisco Franco y Su Tiempo*, (8 vols) Madrid: Ediciones Azor 1984, vol. I, p. 92 states that 1,725 people were arrested.
4. L. Suárez Fernández, *FFST*, vol. I, p. 92. For details of the 'Tragic Week' see J. Romero Maura, *La Rosa de Fuego*, Barcelona: Grijalbo 1974; and J. Connelly Ullman, *The Tragic Week*, Cambridge, Mass.: Harvard University Press 1968.
5. R. Carr, *Spain 1808–1975*, p. 519.
6. L. Suárez Fernández, *FFST*, vol. I, p. 109.
7. *La guerra de Africa*, RTVE Archive, Madrid, Ref. No 408, Roll 1.
8. J. Arrarás, *Franco*, San Sebastian: Librería Internacional 1937, p. 32.
9. Franco's official service record, quoted in L. Suárez Fernández, *FFST*, vol. I, p. 113.
10. J.P. Fusi, *Franco. A Biography*, London: Unwin Hyman 1987, p. 2.
11. It was not until a year later, in February 1918, that Franco was notified that he was not to be awarded the Saint Ferdinand Cross.
12. L. Suárez Fernández, *FFST*, vol. I, p. 134.
13. Ibid., p. 131.
14. F. Franco, *"Apuntes" personales del Generalísimo sobre la República y la guerra civil* (hereafter, *Apuntes*), Madrid: Fundación Nacional Francisco Franco 1987, p. 5.
15. J. Sinova (ed.), *Historia del franquismo* (2 vols) *Madrid: Diario 16* 1985, vol. I, p. 187.
16. Prologue to F. Franco, *Diario de una bandera*, Sevilla and Huelva: Editorial Católica Española 1939.
17. L. Suárez Fernández, *FFST*, vol. I, p. 145; F. Franco, *Apuntes*, p. 5.
18. P. Preston, *Franco*, London: Harper Collins 1993, ch. 2. Francisco Franco and Carmen Polo were finally married in October 1923.
19. J.P. Fusi, *Franco*, p. 3.
20. L. Suárez Fernández, *Franco. La historia y sus documentos*, (20 vols) Madrid: Ediciones Urbión 1986, vol. 1, p. 33.
21. F. Franco Salgado-Araujo, *Mi vida junto a Franco*, Barcelona: Editorial Planeta 1977, p.71.

22. Ibid.
23. F. Franco, *Apuntes*, pp. 5–6.
24. G.P. del Acqua, *Los grandes protagonistas de la II Guerra Mundial: Franco*, Barcelona: Ediciones Orbis 1985, p. 17.
25. P. Preston, *Franco*, ch. 2.
26. J. Arrarás, *Franco*, pp. 158–9.
27. G. Cardona, *El poder militar en la España contemporánea hasta la guerra civil*, Madrid: Siglo XXI 1983, p. 99.
28. *El Sol*, 29 January 1930, quoted in Cardona, op. cit., p. 105.
29. F. Franco, *Apuntes*, pp. 7–8.
30. R. Garriga, *Ramón Franco, el hermano maldito*, Barcelona: Editorial Planeta 1978, pp. 173–8.
31. Ibid., pp. 181–2.
32. Ibid., p. 198.
33. Ibid., pp. 209–10.
34. R. de la Cierva, *Franco*, Barcelona: Editorial Planeta 1986, p. 110.
35. R. Serrano Suñer, *Memorias*, Barcelona: Editorial Planeta 1977, p. 20; R. Garriga, *Franco-Serrano Suñer. Un drama político*, Barcelona: Editorial Planeta 1986, p. 16.
36. F. Franco, *Apuntes*, p. 7.

Chapter 3

THE SECOND REPUBLIC (1931–36)

In Zaragoza, General Franco's response to the declaration of the Republic was ambiguous. Having discounted a march on Madrid, he gave the order that everyone must 'cooperate, with discipline and virtue, in making peace reign and in leading the nation along the natural path of justice'. At the same time, however, he made it clear that he was no Republican, for he insisted on applying military regulations to the letter and would not hoist the new, Republican flag until he had received the order in writing. This was a carefully calculated gesture of protest, designed to make a point without incurring penalty. It was evident from the recent elections that, for the moment at least, the Republic had strong support in the urban working and middle classes; and the response given by Berenguer and Sanjurjo revealed that the military high command would not back armed intervention to reverse that result. It would, therefore, have been foolhardy for Franco to do anything more provocative. But it was uncertain how long the newly declared Republic would last; after all, the first one had been very short-lived and monarchism as a political ideal still had many followers in Spain, even if King Alphonso XIII as an individual did not. Franco therefore hedged his bets, writing a letter to the monarchical daily, *ABC*, on 18 April, in which his disaffection from the new regime was barely disguised, but, four days later, giving the promise of allegiance to the Republic which obliged him to serve and defend it. It was small wonder that, whenever it was rumoured during the Republic that a coup was in the offing, no one could answer the question 'What is Franco going to do?' He was a master at concealing his true intentions – a trait which was later to enhance the aura of mystique appropriate to a great leader with which he surrounded himself.

The provisional government of the new Republic was composed mainly of the representatives of moderate, bourgeois, republican parties, but its explicit commitment to establishing a democratic, egalitarian society immediately aroused the hostility of the social, economic and political forces which had sustained and benefited from the previous regime. In particular, the Republican reformers had to confront three powerful and deeply conservative forces: the Army, the property-owning élite and the Catholic Church. Because these three had come to identify their particular interests and values as those of the nation, they and their supporters viewed any attempt to change their own status quo as an attack on Spain itself. Thus, the protection of their particular interests and privileges from change was presented as the 'salvation' of Spain. According to this Manichaean logic, the representatives and supporters of the Republic were the agents of the destruction of Spain; they were 'anti-Spain'. Those who were against the Republic, by contrast, were 'patriots'. Thus, from the earliest days of the Second Republic, the country was potentially divided into two antagonistic camps. The development of the Republic between 1931 and 1936 was to turn that latent division into stark reality.

The Army was one of the Republic's prime targets for reform, for political, economic and technical reasons. The Minister for War in the provisional government, Manuel Azaña Díaz, was a liberal lawyer and intellectual, who had devoted considerable time to studying military matters during the Great War. He wanted to model the Spanish Army on its French counterpart, believing that, in a civil regime, the military should be politically neutral, intellectually competent and professionally efficient. The core of Azaña's reforms was in place by the autumn of 1931. They concentrated on reducing the excessively high number of officers, bureaucratic positions and regiments, and emphasized the Army's role as a defensive force against external attack. In this way, Azaña aimed to make the Armed Forces not only more economical and more efficient but also less inclined to see their role as that of guard-dog of the internal political situation. Azaña's measures were bitterly attacked by military and civilian conservatives, who accused the War Minister of trying to destroy the Army – a clear sign that he was 'anti-Spain'.

On the face of it, General Franco should have welcomed Azaña's measures. He was, before all else, a professional soldier and, as such, greatly admired the French Army. Moreover, the Zaragoza Academy prided itself on the excellence of its technical training, imparted in practical, rather than purely theoretical, courses. And Azaña's objective of reducing the size and dispersion of the army was perfectly in line with what General Primo de Rivera (whom Franco had admired) had tried to do before him. In practice, however, there were several reasons why General Franco could never have been Azaña's ally. In the first place, Azaña was a civilian politician and a liberal, both anathema to a conservative military man such as Franco. Secondly, Franco's conception of what were ideal military qualities (as laid down in his 1928 'decalogue') was at variance with that of Azaña: 'The mind, study, discipline, moral integrity, knowledge and aptitude for leadership . . . here are to be found the roots of the qualities which are appropriate to and excellent in an officer.'[1] Thirdly, Azaña's reforms abolished a number of military institutions which had until then given the military a certain degree of jurisdiction in civilian matters, thereby putting the Army in its place and asserting the supremacy of civilian rule. Fourthly, in June 1931, a review of promotions granted prior to April 1931 was initiated, which adjusted Franco's position as the top-ranking brigadier-general and left him much lower down the scale. Finally, and probably most importantly, as part of the drive to reduce the size, simplify the structure and democratize the nature of the Army, the government issued a decree on 30 June which closed until further notice four of the six military academies, including Franco's pride and joy, the Zaragoza General Academy.

Understandably, Franco was outraged and demoralized by this news, which deepened his belief that Azaña was 'anti-militarist and sectarian'.[2] In an impassioned speech at the passing-out ceremony on 14 July (the same day that the Cortes – Parliament – was reopened) Franco insinuated that the Republic was illegitimate and made veiled but bitter references to Azaña's military advisers, whom he held even more responsible than the minister for the military reforms. He harped on the need for discipline, which he extolled as 'that most excellent of virtues, indispensable to the life of any army', but declared that maintaining discipline was not worthy of merit when orders were welcome and obedience easy; it only attained its true value 'when our ideas advise us to do the opposite to what we are ordered, when our hearts are bursting to rise up in rebellion, or when the actions of those in command are arbitrary or erroneous'.[3] In other words, he was making clear that if he obeyed orders emanating from the Republic it was because he considered himself a disciplined professional, not because he felt any respect for the new regime. This time, 'those in command' decided that Franco had been too outspoken. He was formally reprimanded by the Minister of War and ordered 'in future, to abstain from making similar statements and to temper [his] conduct to accord with the most elementary demands of discipline'.[4]

But Franco was not a man who simply turned the other cheek when he felt he had suffered a personal slight or an injustice. Just as he had appealed to the king, in 1916, against the decision not to promote him to major, he now responded to the official reprimand with an exculpatory letter (dated 24 July) to the Chief of the General Staff of the Fifth Military Division (which included Zaragoza), for onward transmission to Azaña. In it, Franco expressed his 'regret for the erroneous interpretation given to the ideas in the speech' and at the Prime Minister's 'apparent assumption that there [was] something lukewarm or reserved' about his 'loyal commitment' to the Republic.[5] The reprimand remained on Franco's service record, but no more was heard of the matter. Notwithstanding the letter of 24 July, Azaña knew that Franco was hostile to the new regime and was wary of acting against him on account of his reputation among both the conservative classes and the officer corps of the Army. Even so, the closure of the Zaragoza Academy had given the anti-Republican forces a martyr. Conscious of the value of this to the opposition's cause, the government took the precaution of keeping Franco out of positions of strategic command. In February

1932, after a period of enforced inactivity spent in Asturias, he was posted to La Coruña, in his native Galicia, far from the military and political nerve-centres of Madrid. What was, effectively, banishment to a backwater added further professional resentment to the political hostility and moral anger Franco already felt towards the Republic.

As we have seen, the new regime speedily and decisively tackled the issue of the excessive size and influence of the Army. With similar urgency, but less success, it also confronted the second major source of potential threat: the land-owning élite.

Although a process of industrialization had begun in the 1920s, Spain was still primarily an agrarian society and economy in 1931. However, the vast majority of the people who worked the land did not own it. The more prosperous farmers rented tracts of land from the large landowners, which they then sub-let to small tenant farmers and share-croppers. Depending on the size of the plots and the quality of soil and irrigation, these farmers – located mainly in the north and east of the country – were able with difficulty to make a sparse living. Many others, however, did not have even those limited resources and were dependent for their livelihood on finding work as hired day-labourers. At the mercy of seasonal crops, climatic fluctuations and the personal whim of their employers, thousands of landless labourers in Andalusia, Extremadura, Castile and Aragon lived in abject poverty, while the handful of families who owned vast areas of land in those regions enjoyed enormous social, economic and political influence.

In every respect, agrarian reform was an extremely complex problem, but one which the first Republican governments were committed to resolving, not least because consolidation and expansion of popular support for the Republic would depend on their ability to satisfy the demands of the underprivileged classes whose material conditions they had pledged themselves to improve. However, they also wanted to avoid alienating completely the property-owning classes, some of whose interests were represented in the government: the leader of the first, provisional cabinet (April–June 1931), Niceto Alcalá Zamora, was a member of a liberal-conservative party, the Liberal Republican Right, and himself owned large estates in Andalusia. The government therefore recognized the right to private property, but also stipulated that the exercise of that right should be governed by the 'social function' of property. In order to make optimum use of the 'social function' of agricultural land, a compensated expropriation scheme was proposed, as a first step on the road to a more equitable distribution of productive land. The hostile reaction to the scheme among the landowners had the prevention of any agrarian reform as its specific objective; but it was also designed to weaken the Republic in a broader sense by undermining its overall credibility as a liberating social and political system. When the Agrarian Reform Bill began its passage through parliament in early 1932, it was persistently blocked by the conservative parties which represented the landowners' interests, such as Acción Nacional (National Action) and Derecha Regional Valenciana (Valencian Regional Right).

The Catholic Church, too, felt threatened by the reformist intentions of the Republic. Among the latter's proposed measures were the separation of Church and state, a divorce law, the creation of a nation-wide system of lay schools, freedom of religious practice for confessions other than Catholicism, and the abolition of all religious orders. All of these ideas were naturally met with hostility by those who considered Catholicism consubstantial with national identity. The idea of disbanding all religious orders provoked particular anger, for it was through the thousands of nuns, priests and friars who taught in schools, staffed hospitals and ran all kinds of cultural and charitable organizations, that valuable social tasks were performed and that the Church exercised a decisive influence over the hearts and minds of large sectors of society. Even some of the Republican politicians considered it excessively harsh and needlessly provocative. As a compromise, only the Jesuits were banned and the rest were allowed to stay. The other measures, however, were implemented, in spite of the indignation and disgust of thousands of families like the Francos, to whom such affronts to their most cherished values were tantamount to a personal attack and a vindictive attempt to destroy the very fabric of society.

Although the Republic's most open and virulent opponents were on the Right, it also faced problems on the

Left. The more radical elements, such as the members of the anarchist CNT, the left wing of the Partido Socialista Obrero Español (Spanish Socialist Workers' Party, PSOE), the socialist youth movement (JSU), and the socialist trade union (UGT), wanted the revolutionary transformation of Spain into a classless society. Even the more moderate members of the PSOE and the tiny Partido Comunista de España (Communist Party of Spain, PCE) soon began to feel impatient with what they saw as the slowness and timidity with which the largely centrist or centre-left government was approaching the issues of social and economic change. Two incidents in particular served to shake left-wing faith in bourgeois Republican government. In December 1931 Civil Guards shot dead one peasant and wounded two others, before being attacked themselves, after a peaceful demonstration at Castilblanco, in Extremadura. A short time afterwards, at Arnedo, in the wine-growing area of La Rioja, not far from Zaragoza, Civil Guards opened fire on a crowd of socialists, killing several and wounding many more. The parties and trade union organizations of the Left were outraged by the fact that the Director of the Civil Guard, General Sanjurjo, was not instantly dismissed. Castilblanco and Arnedo strengthened the view of those socialists who doubted the capacity or the will of bourgeois Republicans to institute change and sent a wave of revulsion through many who, not a year earlier, had danced in the streets to welcome the Republic. At the same time, such incidents and the conflict they sparked on the Left bolstered the fears of those on the Right who believed that the democratic Republic would sooner or later be taken over by Marxist or anarchist masses.

Manuel Azaña, who had been made Prime Minister as well as War Minister in May 1931, hesitated to dismiss Sanjurjo because he did not wish to increase conservative animosity towards the Republic by appearing to give in to left-wing pressure. In fact, Azaña's reaction to Castilblanco and Arnedo did nothing to improve the Right's opinion of the Republic. On the contrary, for the conservative sectors of Spanish society, staunch supporters of law and order that they were, the intervention of the Civil Guard had been no more than what was exigible in a right-minded state. Any slight merit which might have accrued to the Republic in the view of the Right on this occasion was annulled when it became known that Sanjurjo was to be transferred – demoted in effect – to the position of head of the Frontier Police, the *carabineros*. Azaña had found himself obliged to take this step to appease the Left and safeguard the parliamentary alliance with the PSOE which allowed him to govern. In doing so, however, he further irritated both the conservative Right and the Army.

It can therefore hardly have surprised the Prime Minister when, in August 1932, General Sanjurjo was involved in an attempted coup against the Republic. It was rapidly quashed in Seville, from where Sanjurjo had organised the plot, and in Madrid, where General Goded was the most prominent participant. As yet, such initiatives did not attract more than a handful of Army officers. Certainly, many military men and civilians felt no sympathy with the Republic, but they were sufficiently realistic to recognize that neither the return of King Alphonso XIII nor another Primo de Rivera-style dictatorship was a viable option.

At his post as military commander of La Coruña, General Francisco Franco was one of those officers who, although alarmed at what they saw as the country's slide into chaos, refrained from committing themselves to open opposition. Franco was aware of Sanjurjo's conspiracy. Indeed, Sanjurjo himself tried to persuade Franco to join it, but Franco remained adamant. His attitude was not due to loyalty to the Republic but to his lack of confidence in Sanjurjo's chances of success. Prior to the coup, he is reputed to have said, 'When I rise, it will be to win', and when he later visited Sanjurjo in prison, Franco told him that he deserved to die because his coup had failed.[6] For beneath the surface of Franco's (albeit grudging) obedience lay the instinct of self-preservation. He did not intend to sacrifice his past career or jeopardize his future prospects by subscribing to a purely testimonial act of rebellion, especially at a time when his previous promotions were still under review. Now he was beginning to show the hard, calculating side of his character which had been developing in Zaragoza, encouraged by the local gentry and spurred on by his wife, whose social and material ambitions were ultimately to reach legendary proportions.

In January 1933 the results of the promotions review were announced. Franco's promotion to colonel was challenged, although that to brigadier-general was maintained, as was his position half way down the seniority scale. A month later, he was appointed General Commander of the Balearic Islands, an area of increasing strategic importance on account of the Italian dictator Mussolini's aspirations to dominate the Mediterranean. In the wake of the First World War, pacifism was the keynote of foreign and military policies in democratic Europe – an attitude shared by Republican Spain. However, Italian ambitions and the accession to power in Germany of Adolf Hitler, in January 1933, advised defensive caution. Although Azaña considered Franco politically dangerous, he also knew him to be professionally competent. Franco's posting to Palma de Mallorca reflected not only the minister's concern that the General be kept away from the centres of military intrigue, but also his awareness that, should Italian and, especially, German bellicosity turn into armed conflict, Spain might find itself under attack or, at least, under pressure to assist its democratic European neighbours. In line with Azaña's objective of maximizing the efficiency of military deployments, he posted the man reputed to be the Army's best technician to what, in the contemporary European context, was Spain's key strategic area. Franco, however, was not pleased by his posting. His view that it represented professional exile reflected his burgeoning self-esteem and fuelled his growing hostility towards the Republic.

If there were unmistakable signs of polarization in Europe at the beginning of 1933, that year saw an organized Rightist revival in Spain, too. In February, an alliance of conservative parties was formed, entitled Confederación Española de Derechas Autónomas (Spanish Confederation of Autonomous Rightist Parties, CEDA) and, in March, radical Alphonsine monarchists created Renovación Española (Spanish Renewal, RE). The leader of the CEDA was José María Gil Robles, a pudgy, solemn-faced lawyer, whose sanctimonious air and vehement defence of Catholic, conservative values greatly appealed to those Spaniards who held the view that religion and middle-class respectability were being sacrificed on the altar of democratic liberalism. Politically, the CEDA maintained an ambiguous position, arguing that what form the state took was relatively unimportant, because it was merely 'accidental', whereas what really mattered was that its content should respect Catholic conservative values. There was no doubt that the CEDA was thoroughly conservative; indeed, Gil Robles' speeches and the coalition's press and propaganda clearly suggested that the CEDA aspired to mobilize right-wing sentiment on a massive scale in support of an authoritarian response to liberalism and socialism. However, the CEDA was careful not to overstep the limits of Republican legality. Its ambition was to take and enjoy power not by means of a *pronunciamiento,* which would leave it beholden to the Army, but with the juridical and political legitimacy afforded by mass support, freely expressed in democratic elections. That is to say, Gil Robles and his CEDA aimed to use the channels offered by a reformist, democratic system to reverse reform and possibly subvert democracy.[7]

The CEDA's combination of Catholic conservatism and legalistic tactics appealed to the landowners, industrialists, bankers, shopkeepers, tenant-farmers, civil servants, clerics and army officers who felt themselves threatened by the progressive aspirations of the Azaña government, but recoiled from the risks involved in taking drastic steps to strangle them. Sanjurjo's aborted coup had shown them that, at least for the time being, such steps were condemned to failure. For this reason, repeated attempts to launch an ultra-right-wing or overtly fascist party met with little success. Groups such as the Partido Nacionalista Español (Spanish Nationalist Party, PNE) or the Juntas de Ofensiva Nacional-Sindicalista (Committees for National Syndicalist Attack, JONS) were too extreme in their proposals and too raucous in their style for the anti-liberal and anti-Marxist but also anti-revolutionary sectors whose financial and moral support they, like the CEDA, were trying to recruit.[8] The sentiments of these sectors were to become more radical, and the political atmosphere more tense, in the course of 1933.

In January there were violent disturbances in a number of towns in Catalonia, Aragon and Andalusia. These were rapidly suppressed, but trouble quickly flared up again in rural Andalusia. A particularly gruesome incident occurred at Casas Viejas, a village in the southern province of Cadiz which literally belonged to the dukedom of Medina-Sidonia, one of the wealthiest families in Spain. On 11 January the local branch of the anarchist CNT declared the establishment of libertarian communism in Casas Viejas. A confrontation with the Civil Guard followed, the outcome of which was that the peasants fled the village, with the exception of a group of eight, who took refuge in a hut, surrounded by Civil Guards and Assault Guard reinforcements sent from Madrid. The peasants were clearly outnumbered but refused to surrender. On 12 January the Assault Guards set fire to the hut. Four men were burned alive; one man and one woman were shot while trying to escape. In reprisal for the death of two Civil Guards, fourteen villagers were then rounded up and shot.

This appalling episode reawakened the memory of Castilblanco and Arnedo and responsibility was once more laid at Azaña's door. The Republican government failed to give satisfactory explanations in the Cortes, but managed to defeat a motion calling for a parliamentary inquiry and a subsequent motion of censure against Azaña. On 16 March 1933 the government won a vote of confidence, but the whole affair had not only seriously damaged the Azaña government's authority and credibility, but had also added substantial fuel to the fire of those on the Right who claimed that the Republic was leading to chaos.

Under attack from both Right and Left, Azaña resigned in September 1933 when President Alcalá Zamora withdrew his confidence in the government. Azaña's successor, Alejandro Lerroux, leader of the Centre-Rightist Radical Party, formed a cabinet from which the socialists were excluded. After barely a month, Lerroux was forced to resign, following a socialist-led vote of no confidence. He was succeeded by his second-in-command, Diego Martínez Barrio, whose principal task was to prepare a general election. This was called for November. According to Franco's first biographer, Joaquin Arrarás, the main component of the CEDA, Acción Popular (Popular Action), offered Franco a place on its list of candidates for Madrid. Despite Franco's later contention that he had no public interest in politics, he was tempted to take up the

CEDA's offer, and only declined when friends assured him that he, 'in the Army, was the supreme, the definitive guarantee'.

Even without Franco among its candidates, the CEDA obtained 115 of the 470 parliamentary seats. The Radicals won 104 and the PSOE fifty-nine. Eighty-nine of the remaining seats went to Rightist parties or coalitions, sixty-six to Centrist candidates and thirty-five to the Left. In reality, the parties of the Left had obtained more votes than those of the Centre, and almost as many as those of the Right. But the Left's failure to form broad coalitions, together with the system of proportional representation, meant that the number of votes they had polled was not reflected in the number of seats they won. Contrary to his own expectations, the leader of the CEDA, Gil Robles, did not become Prime Minister because President Alcalá Zamora maintained that he was not the leader of a winning party, but of a coalition of parties. Instead, Alejandro Lerroux was again asked to form a government. Since he could only govern with the support of the CEDA, he agreed with Gil Robles a number of measures designed to reverse the policies of the previous government, starting with an amnesty for the instigators of the August 1932 coup.

The President initially rejected another of the proposals made by the new government with a view to consolidating its support among the military and the conservative classes, namely, that Franco be promoted to full general. Alcalá Zamora eventually relented, however, and the promotion was granted in March 1934. The Minister of War, Diego Hidalgo Durán, may well have been instrumental in changing the President's mind. When he first met Franco, in February 1934, Hidalgo was very impressed by how seriously Franco took his profession: 'a soldier who is totally devoted to his career . . . who never digresses . . . [who is] balanced when examining, probing and developing problems . . . his capacity for work, his clear intelligence, his understanding and his culture are always at the service of the army'.[9] These qualities convinced the Minister that 'if the Republic had to face the impending violent revolution, Franco was the person capable of saving it'.[10] As political tension grew, Hidalgo relied increasingly on Franco for assistance. In September Franco acted as the Minister's personal adviser during military exercises in the north of Spain, whose objective was as much to intimidate the miners of nearby Asturias as to rehearse the use of military force against them. When a revolutionary movement did break out in Asturias in October, Hidalgo, with CEDA support, summoned Franco to the Ministry of War to direct the military operations launched to repress it. Franco appears not to have been concerned that, in accepting this commission, he was effectively leap-frogging both the Chief of the Central General Staff, General Masquelet, and the General Inspector of Asturias, General López Ochoa. Hidalgo's willingness to defy the opposition of his Radical cabinet colleagues; the support of the CEDA; and the urging of José Antonio Primo de Rivera, leader of the fascist Falange Española de las JONS, persuaded him that there was more to be gained by accepting than lost by offending two colleagues.[11] Besides, both Masquelet and López Ochoa were Freemasons, which, in Franco's eyes, made them not only unworthy of respect but a threat to national security.[12]

The *October revolution* was the climax of a year of mounting left-wing exasperation and misgiving, in the face of deepening economic crisis, vindictive intransigence on the part of employers, and the increasing reliance of successive unstable Radical cabinets (three in the period December 1933–April 1934) on the CEDA, which was rapidly emerging as a powerful mass organization anxious for governmental control. Developments outside Spain also influenced the Spanish Left during 1934: the destruction of the labour movement in Germany and Austria; an attempted extreme right-wing coup in France; and the signature of an anti-fascist pact between French socialists and communists. The anarchists' long-standing rejection of bourgeois reformism seemed to be vindicated by the shift to the Right visible everywhere, while the moderates of the socialist movement were pushed aside by its increasingly numerous and vocal revolutionary sectors. December 1933 saw an attempt at concerted leftist action, with the creation of the 'Workers' Alliances', between socialists, anarchist splinter groups and some heterodox communist organizations. But, in reality, the Left could not overcome its internal differences and the forces of an exultant, if not wholly united, Right were more than a match for it. In December 1933 a badly organized, anarchist-led strike movement in Catalonia and Aragon was quickly broken by physical force. Six months later, in June 1934, the socialist agricultural union, the Federación Nacional de Trabajadores de la Tierra (National Federation of Land Workers, FNTT) organized a series of strikes which were harshly repressed by Civil and Assault Guards. Despite these setbacks, the socialist leader, Francisco Largo Caballero, threatened revolutionary action should the CEDA accede to power. Thus, when on 4 October 1934 Alejandro Lerroux formed his third cabinet and included in it three members of the CEDA, a general strike was called.

After a year of repression, aborted risings and worsening socio-economic conditions, the working classes were in no state to launch and sustain such an action. Moreover, the labour movement was deeply divided internally, with the anarchist CNT wanting no truck with the socialists or the Workers' Alliances. Consequently, the government had little difficulty in quelling the strike nearly everywhere it was attempted. In Madrid, the 'Revolutionary Committee' was arrested. In Barcelona, what started as industrial action rapidly became a separatist rebellion, with the leader of the governing Centrist party, Esquerra Republicana de Catalunya (Catalan Republican Left), Lluis Companys i Jover, declaring Catalonia an independent republic. For twenty-four hours, the streets of Barcelona were the scene of barricades, on-the-spot searches, demonstrations and violent confrontations between the partisans of Catalan independence and troops and Civil Guards obeying orders from Madrid. By 7 October the rebellion had been liquidated, with hundreds of people arrested, including the entire Catalan regional government.

The protest movement lasted longest in the mining valleys of Asturias. This was the only area in which the anarchist CNT had joined the Workers' Alliance movement. This, together with arms obtained by storming the military arsenal in Oviedo and explosives taken from the mines, and the isolated geographical situation of Asturias, made it possible for the strikers to resist much longer than elsewhere. Franco was already familiar with the terrain in Asturias, and with the miners and their political radicalism: his wife's family lived in Oviedo and he had been involved in the repression of the 1917 Asturian miners' strike. He was known to feel little sympathy for the Republic, but his opposition to left-wing ideologies was even greater and he believed the 1934 strike movement to be 'the first step towards the implantation of communism in our nation'.[13] In 1917 he had not played a leading role; this time, not only was he in charge, but he considered the task 'a war operation with all that that implied' and himself 'a specialist in such things'.[14]

First, he ordered the dismissal of a number of officers in the region of whose loyalty he was unsure. These included one of his own Lapuente Bahamonde cousins, with whom he had spent many summer holidays as a child in Galicia. Then, overriding an existing plan to send in troops from the neighbouring provinces of Burgos, Valladolid and Galicia, Franco deployed from Africa to Asturias a battalion of *chasseurs* (specialists in fighting in mountainous country), two units of the Foreign Legion and one of Moroccan Regulares. These were Spain's most battle-hardened forces and sending them to deal with a strike was, in operational terms, an unnecessarily extreme reaction. But, as Franco was well aware, the use of Moroccan troops conveyed a particular message, for Asturias had never succumbed to Arab occupation and it was from there that the Christian reconquest of the Peninsula had begun. For Franco, the repression of the Asturian rising represented both the subjugation of a hostile tribe and the salvation of the area in the name of Christianity. It was, he said many years later, 'a frontier war against socialism, communism and whatever attack[ed] civilization in order to replace it with barbarism'.[15]

The rebels put up extraordinary resistance for two weeks, but could not hold out indefinitely against overwhelmingly superior forces (some 18,000 soldiers and armed police). The ferocity of the reprisals taken by government forces, particularly the Legionnaires and Regulares, aided by members of the Falange and of the CEDA youth movement, exceeded anything seen thereto. In addition to approximately 4,000 fatalities, around 30,000 miners and other left-wing militants and sympathizers were rounded up and imprisoned. Many were brutally tortured. Even after the revolution itself had been crushed, 'cleansing operations' continued well into November, directed by a Civil Guard officer, Lisardo Doval, whose appointment as the government's 'special representative' in Asturias was due to Franco's influence on Hidalgo. So harsh was the repression organized by Doval that government embarrassment forced him to resign in December 1934. Hidalgo, too, resigned under pressure from the CEDA and an authoritarian monarchist coalition, Bloque Nacional (National Bloc, BN), which alleged that weak Radical government had allowed the events of October to occur.

By pressing for more authoritarian government than the radicals were prepared to countenance, the Right destabilized the situation even further. In November the Radical Ministers of War, State and Education were dismissed, in order to conserve Rightist parliamentary support for the government, while CEDA and BN *diputados* (members of parliament) and newspapers denounced the rebels as 'anti-patriotic' and howled for death penalties. Twenty-eight were passed, but the President, Alcalá Zamora, would not give his assent to more than two. When the CEDA ministers refused to sign the reprieves for the remainder, Alcalá Zamora suspended parliament for one month. But the authoritarian Right ultimately got most of what it wanted: when a new government was formed, in May 1935, it included five CEDA ministers. The coalition's leader, Gil Robles, was still not made Prime Minister, but he did secure the War portfolio. For the Left, this was worse than the 1934 cabinet that had triggered the revolution, but it was in no position to stage any further protest.

While the political representatives of the Right squabbled among themselves in the aftermath of October 1934, Franco was hailed as a saviour; the personification of the triumph of military strength over both liberal ineptitude and Marxist evil. He himself undoubtedly subscribed to this view, claiming that 'if the measures taken had not been taken, the revolution would have triumphed'.[16] His obsession with communism – paralleled only by his fixation with Freemasonry – had been growing since 1928, when General Primo de Rivera gave him a subscription to the journal of a Swiss-based organization, the Entente contre le Troisième Internationale, whose propaganda insisted that the 'civilized' world was under threat of communist takeover. In the spring of 1934, Franco renewed his subscription, at his own expense, in order to keep himself 'informed' of communist machinations world-wide.[17] His attitude towards the Republican Left was undoubtedly profoundly influenced by the material he received from the Entente, and the events of October 1934 'proved' to him that the information it contained was accurate. Thus, in organizing the repression of the Asturian rebellion, Franco felt that he was not only serving the public good in Spain, but striking the first blow in a universal mission to save Humanity. With such historic responsibility on his shoulders, it was small wonder that he did not risk his life by actually approaching the scene of the conflict. Not until it was all over did he go to Asturias. Then, with the Minister of War, he entered Oviedo, to the enthusiastic acclaim of the Asturian Right (which included his wife's family and friends), who greeted him as 'the saviour of the Republic'. This – and indeed the scale and brutality of the preceding military campaign – were tactics he would repeat many times in the future, when the failure of successive Republican governments to remedy the structural problems which had provoked the Asturian rising led, in 1936, to civil war.

In March 1935 Franco was rewarded for his part in the Asturian operation with the position of Commander-in-Chief of the Army of Africa. He was pleased by this posting, not only because it took him back to his beloved Morocco, but also because 'the Army of Africa was the most important military command on account of the number of its troops and the responsibility involved in such an extensive territory'.[18] At last, he felt, his worth was being recognized. His satisfaction was short-lived, however, for in May 1935, just as he was settling into his new job, Gil Robles became Minister of War and Franco was recalled to the mainland as Chief of the Central General Staff. His initial reaction was to refuse the appointment, for he was reluctant to become subject to the vagaries of political change. Ultimately, however, the high regard in which he held himself won out. Despite the satisfaction he derived from his position as Commander-in-Chief in Morocco, his previous posting to the Balearics still rankled with him; with the offer of promotion to Chief of the Central General Staff 'his amour propre had been satisfied',[19] and he accepted. With this confirmation of the Right's confidence in him, Franco became, by position and by reputation, not only the country's most important military figure, but also an increasingly significant political figure.

His principal objective was 'to correct Azaña's reforms and to return to the members of the army's units the internal satisfaction that had been lost with the advent of the Republic'.[20] This was perfectly consonant with the wider political aims of the Minister of War, Gil Robles. At the same time, Franco's continuing preoccupation with signs of communist agitation led him to set up a unit for 'communist intelligence and counter-espionage' within the Armed Forces. Determined, for the same reason, that the *October revolution* should not be repeated, he conducted exercises in Asturias which re-enacted the events of the previous year 'to study on the spot the improvisations and shortcomings' of 1934.[21] One particular lesson he had learned was the importance of rapid troop transportation, and he therefore planned the creation of two motorized units to eliminate the need to requisition private vehicles. These measures indicated that the authoritarian Right was determined to reaffirm the Army in its traditional role as a bulwark against *internal* threats to the established order. A programme of rearmament and the replacement of officers of known Republican sympathies were undertaken to ensure the Army's ability to fulfil that role. As Franco himself commented, years later: 'The officers who would one day be the mainstay of the crusade of liberation were appointed during this period and arms were redistributed in such a way as to enable them to respond in an emergency.'[22]

The strong political flavour of Franco's professional role was accompanied, perhaps inevitably, by the intensification of his personal interest in politics. As he himself commented, his work at the Ministry of War enabled him to see the internal workings of the party system.[23] It was also at this time that Franco came into contact with a conspiratorial, right-wing, military organization, the Unión

Militar Española (Spanish Military Union, UME). It had come into being in 1933, with the prime aim of protecting the professional interests of those soldiers (mainly middle-ranking captains and majors) who felt threatened by the policies of the bourgeois Republican reformers. By 1935, the UME had a representative in every military region and contacts with the political organizations of the authoritarian Right.[24] In July of that year, the movement's founding father, Barba Hernández, contacted Franco, whose non-committal response was entirely in character: he had refused to take part in the attempted coup of 1932 and had remained aloof from the plots hatched by a group of high-ranking officers in the wake of the *October revolution*.[25] Nonetheless, as we have noted, Franco's hostility towards the Republic was hardened by the events of October 1934 into the conviction that the Fatherland was under threat of Soviet takeover. Six months of close contact with the work of government entrenched further the twin ideas that the democratic party system was responsible for the growth of that threat, and that military intervention would be both necessary and legitimate to meet it. Franco maintained contact with the UME through Colonel Valentín Galarza, who kept him informed of the organization's state of preparation. 'This', wrote Franco, 'allowed one to look to the future with some confidence and to know that if one day the life of the nation should be in danger, there were those who would know how to defend it.'[26]

If Franco and the members of the UME were alarmed by 'the precipice over which the nation was throwing itself',[27] it was not because there was any real danger of left-wing revolution, but because the Right was in disarray. In September disagreement over revision of the 1931 Constitution and home-rule for Catalonia forced the resignation of Lerroux as Prime Minister. In October a fresh governmental crisis broke, which irreparably damaged the image of the Radical Party. This time, the motive was the involvement of Lerroux's nephew in a phoney roulette racket. A month later, Gil Robles withdrew his support, hoping to force President Alcalá Zamora at last to offer him the premiership. But the President trusted the power-hungry Gil Robles no more in 1935 than he had in 1933 and told him at the beginning of December that a general election must be held. He then asked an independent, Manuel Portela Valladares, to form a caretaker cabinet. When Gil Robles was replaced as Minister for War by General Molero, Franco was genuinely sorry to see him go, but disagreed with the opinion of Generals Fanjul, Goded and Rodríguez del Barrio (all of whom were UME members) that the Army should intervene to force Alcalá Zamora to hand power to the CEDA leader.[28]

Franco's response was based on his assessment that the point at which the success of a coup was guaranteed had not yet been reached. It is important to emphasize that this did not mean that he was against military intervention as a matter of principle. On the contrary, in conversation with the Spanish Military Attaché in Paris, Major Barroso, at the beginning of February 1936, Franco confided that he and other officers were worried; although the Left was not yet in power, they thought it soon would be and 'the Army had to be prepared. If the worst came to the worst, it would be [their] duty to intervene.' 'If you hear of me going to Africa', Franco told Barroso, 'you'll know we have decided there's no other way but a rising.'[29] Given that Franco was then at pains to avoid committing himself to participating in any conspiracy, his use of the word 'we' in that conversation supports the idea that it was not the principle, simply the details, that were not yet to his liking in the winter of 1935–36.

Parliament was duly dissolved on 7 January 1936, and the elections called for 16 February. In view of the electoral débâcle which had resulted from the disunity of the Left and Centre-Left in 1933, the leader of Republican Left, Manuel Azaña, had proposed the formation of a formal alliance with the PSOE in November 1935. The idea met, at first, with the opposition of the radical socialist, Largo Caballero, who feared that joining forces with the bourgeois republicans would enable moderate socialists to dominate the PSOE and allow rival parties such as the PCE and the revolutionary communist Partido Obrero de Unificación Marxista (Workers' Party for Marxist Unification, POUM) to capitalize at socialist expense on the growing militancy of the labour movement. Largo therefore insisted that the proposed alliance must also include the

PCE and the POUM, as well as the socialist trade union (the UGT) and the socialist youth movement. The title given to the resulting multi-party alliance was the Popular Front.

The socialist leader had, in fact, misread the strategy of the Spanish Communist Party for, in August 1935, the Seventh Congress of the Comintern had backed the idea of forming national 'popular front committees', composed of all the anti-fascist parties in each country. An alliance between the reformist Left and the PCE was entirely consistent with that strategy. The intentions of the PCE were also misinterpreted (or misrepresented) by the Right, whose representatives and sympathizers alleged that the creation of the Popular Front was a clear indication that a communist takeover was planned in Spain. This was soon to be used to 'justify' the reactionary backlash which followed the victory of the Popular Front in the 16 February elections.

The poll was conducted in an atmosphere of tense expectation, with thousands of people hoping for a Popular Front victory which would bring a return to progressive policies, and as many people counting on a right-wing triumph to safeguard the conservative status quo. At the end of the day, although the Right's candidates polled more votes than they had in 1933, the Left's tactic of unity paid off and the victory was theirs. Franco was convinced that this result meant 'the beginning of a fresh revolutionary process'.[30] Despite his consistent refusal to join insurrectionary plots led by military comrades, Franco now took steps which amounted to trying to launch a coup of his own. In seeking to clothe it with official support he remained true to form: minimizing the risks to his personal and professional position, yet maximizing the chances of enhancing both.

As though he were again directing the October 1934 operations, Franco started to organize what he thought should be the response to the Popular Front victory in the early hours of 17 February 1936. First, he sent a message to UME leader, Valentín Galarza, telling him to warn the organization's nationwide network of members to be at the ready 'in case of need'. Then he went to his office at the War Ministry from where he telephoned the Director-

General of the Civil Guard, General Pozas, informing him that 'the masses [were] on the streets' and that action should be taken to prevent matters getting out of hand. Pozas, however, was not moved by Franco's alarmism. Undeterred, Franco then tried to persuade the interim Minister for War, General Molero, that 'the best thing was to declare a state of war in the main cities and that with the civil authorities in a state of crisis the military authorities should guarantee public order'.[31] Molero resisted, but agreed to urge the Prime Minister to hold a cabinet meeting to discuss handing over power to the military. Franco wrote down for Molero what he was to say to Portela. Next, Franco used a military friend to get a message to the Chief of Police, (whom Franco did not know personally), asking him to contact Franco; and he asked another, politician, friend to persuade the Prime Minister that he should receive Franco urgently. In the meantime, Franco took soundings as to the willingness of certain Madrid units to intervene if called upon to do so. From these it was clear that it would be vital to have the support of the Civil Guard and the police, and that 'the orders should come from above'. In the light of this response, Franco tried once more to persuade General Pozas to mobilize the Civil Guard. Again he was unsuccessful.

When the cabinet met on the morning of 17 February, it was agreed to declare a state of alarm, but to keep the declaration of a state of war as a last resort. In spite of this, Franco took it upon himself to telephone the military commanders of Asturias and Barcelona – 'as the most sensitive regions' to tell them that martial law was to be established.[32] The ploy was frustrated when General Pozas confirmed to them that a state of war had *not* been declared. When Franco saw the Prime Minister later that day, he hinted that unless Portela took decisive action (i.e. gave the order to declare martial law), he would bear full responsibility for allowing communism to take power. To his credit, Portela resisted Franco's half-threatening, half-cajoling insinuations.

Franco's reaction to the 16 February election results reveals very clearly the limits of his much-vaunted belief in discipline and the call of duty. For him, these concepts had a particular political colour. Duty, discipline and obedience were owed when they coincided with the interests of the Right; that is to say, with his own interests. When they did not, it was legitimate not to obey orders. He had evidently forgotten, or was conveniently ignoring, his remonstrances with Ramón Franco in 1930, when he had told his brother that plotting against 'a legal government, which restores citizens' guarantees' was illicit. In fact, such duplicity lay at the heart of Franco's moral code and subsequently became part of the justification for the Civil War, of the basis for post-war repression, and, indeed, of the very fabric of Francoist government.

Although Portela resisted Franco's pressure, the Popular Front did not form a coalition government. In the first place, as Franco's reaction had indicated, there was every reason to fear that this would provoke military intervention which would attract massive support from the forces of the Right. Secondly, the personal animosity which existed between the radical socialist, Largo Caballero, and his more moderate party colleague, Indalecio Prieto, together with Largo's belief that the PSOE would soon be able to form a government on its own, impelled Largo to refuse to allow the PSOE to participate in a government headed by Manuel Azaña. Consequently, Azaña's liberal Republican cabinet was not a true reflection of the contemporary political map and was weakened by the absence of the socialist and communist Left.

As had happened on previous occasions, such attempts to placate the adversary not only failed to achieve that aim, but also led to the alienation of part of the home side. As in 1931, the hopes raised on the Left could not be fulfilled by a government hampered by its fear of upsetting the Right; and the Right was bent on placing its own interests before the Constitution, the authority of the government, the laws of the land, or the popular will. Faced with this dilemma, the Azaña cabinet chose to act against the most immediate threat, that of military intervention. On 21 February 1936 the generals who were known to be anti-Republican received postings away from Madrid and well away from each other, in the hope that this would prevent them from taking coordinated action against the Republic. General Goded was to go to the Balearic Islands and

General Mola to Navarre, in the north of the country. General Franco was given the most distant posting of all, to the Canary Islands, thousands of miles away from mainland Spain, off the Atlantic coast of Africa. He himself interpreted the posting as making him 'a prisoner in the Canaries'.[33]

In the event, geographical separation was ineffective as a deterrent. On 8 March a group of high-ranking army officers, including Generals Franco, Mola, Orgaz, Villegas, Fanjul and Varela, and Colonel Galarza, met in Madrid at the house of a member of the CEDA, José Delgado, to discuss the possibility of military intervention. Franco later claimed to have obtained from the others the agreement that 'the Movement should be for Spain, without any particular label' (i.e. that it should not be explicitly republican or monarchist).[34] In fact, he did not commit himself to the conspiracy at this stage and remained indecisive throughout the spring of 1936, while General Mola emerged as its leader, issuing instructions signed 'El Director' and coordinating a growing, secret network of military and civilian contacts. Franco's attitude irritated the rest of the anti-Republican military men, who dubbed him 'Miss Canary Isles 1936' in derisive reference to his apparent shyness. Perhaps, too, their sarcasm reflected annoyance at the fact that Franco had been ready to move very quickly on 17 February, but hung back when someone other than himself was directing operations.

In May, there was to be a re-run of the February election in Cuenca, a small town to the south east of Madrid. Disillusionment with the Army on Franco's part seemed to be reflected in the fact that he had allowed his name to be included in the list of candidates put up by the CEDA. In the event, he was persuaded to withdraw when José Antonio Primo de Rivera, who was also on the list, objected to Franco's candidacy because he considered Franco a reactionary (though this was not, of course, the reasoning used with Franco). At an electoral rally held in Cuenca on 1 May, the socialist leader, Indalecio Prieto, showed that, unlike Franco's own comrades in arms, he had no doubts about the General's potential as a threat to the Republic, singling him out as the man most likely to lead a rising:

> Among the military . . . there is a subversive ferment, an urge to rise against the Republican regime . . . General Franco, being young and gifted, and having a network of friends in the Army, is the man who at a given moment has it in him to lead such a movement with maximum probable success because of the prestige he enjoys.[35]

Prieto's analysis was soon to be proved correct.

For the time being, Franco played his cards carefully, alienating no one who might subsequently be in a position to make or break him. He maintained contact with the conspirators and tried, unsuccessfully, to find a way of returning to the Peninsula, in order (as he wrote) 'to be in closer contact with the garrisons, to be present in those places in which the Movement was in danger of failing'.[36] On the other hand, on 23 June 1936 he wrote a letter to the War Minister, Santiago Casares Quiroga, in which he warned that the Army's 'professional disquiet' and the concern 'of all good Spaniards about the Fatherland's enormous problems' was a dangerous combination.[37] Franco's admirers claim that the letter was a sign of his respect for legality, and Franco may well have wanted it to be interpreted that way. As we have seen, however, he believed the Republic to be illegitimate; he did not respect the lawful result of the 1936 elections; and he had not rejected the idea of a rising, he simply wanted to ensure that it would be successful. In writing to the Prime Minister, Franco was covering both his flanks. If the coup worked, he had given nothing away, so he would not have incurred the animosity of the conspirators. If it did not, however, the letter was 'proof' that he was loyal – so loyal that he had warned the Prime Minister of the impending danger. Either way, he would be on the winning side.

The danger to the Republic was real enough, but did not come from the Left, as implied by Franco. Contemporary accounts indicate that it was widely rumoured that a rising was being prepared, yet the government chose to ignore, or underestimate, the information provided by its own intelligence services and the leaders of the Popular Front parties. Incomprehensibly, even Manuel Azaña (who was invested as President of the Republic in May) referred sceptically to the reports as 'scaremongering', while Casares Quiroga, perhaps reassured by Franco's letter, boasted that the government was more than capable of dealing with any rebellion. This claim was very shortly to be put to the test. The government's complacency allowed the conspirators to elaborate their plans virtually unhindered. By mid-June Mola had circulated a series of 'instructions' for the planned rising (although the date had not yet been fixed); he had drawn up a blueprint for a civil-military dictatorship which would take power after the coup; and he had designated the chain of command in a number of areas. Despite his wavering, Franco was included in the last-mentioned of these, as he was presumably aware when he wrote to Casares Quiroga on 23 June.

The proposed rebellion still faced two major problems, however. The first was that the success of the venture was far from assured in three key places: Barcelona, Valencia and, most important of all, Madrid. There, it did not have the backing of the majority of the highest ranking officers; it was not known whether the Civil Guard would join the rebels or remain loyal to the government; and the political and labour organizations of the Left would undoubtedly mobilize effective civilian resistance. The second, related, problem was that, given these weaknesses, the conspirators could not afford also to be without the military strength of the Army of Africa, nor the professional skills and prestige of General Franco. General Sanjurjo, who was still in exile in Portugal, maintained that the coup would go ahead whether or not Franco joined it, but Mola knew that its chances of success would thus be severely handicapped. In the hope that he could eventually be persuaded, Franco was designated leader of the Army of Africa in Mola's plan at the beginning of July. At the same time, the owner of the monarchist daily *ABC* instructed the paper's London correspondent to hire a light plane, a pilot and two decoy passengers to fly from Croydon to the Canaries, ostensibly on a pleasure trip. When the rising was about to begin, the plane would be used to take Franco to Tetuan, in North Africa. The plane left England on 11 July and landed at the airport of Las Palmas de Gran Canaria three days later.

Franco was aware of the objective situation of the conspiracy and of his own strategic importance to it. As we have noted earlier, opposition from him had scotched plots in the past. This time, however, the political situation was more volatile than ever before and the plans further advanced. He could not be sure that pressure from Sanjurjo and other implicated officers would not precipitate the rising before he had decided whether or not to participate. If he did not, it was likely that the Army of Africa would not rise; and he might then be held responsible for the failure of the coup. If, however, it went ahead and was successful, he could not afford to be excluded. Nevertheless, on 12 July he sent a coded message to Colonel Galarza in Madrid, for onward transmission to General Mola, to the effect that he, Franco, was not going to join the planned rising. That same day, the atmosphere of gathering tension which followed the February elections had come to a violent head when a Rightist hit-squad killed José Castillo, a Republican police lieutenant of known socialist sympathies, in Madrid. Some of Castillo's companions decided to avenge his murder and, on the night of 13 July, kidnapped and assassinated José Calvo Sotelo, leader of the radical monarchist organization, Renovación Española. Calvo Sotelo had made no secret of his antipathy towards the Republic in general and the Popular Front in particular, and had made numerous impassioned and provocative speeches, condemning the Left and inciting the Right to take action. The action of the Assault Guards was not only an appalling act of premeditated violence, it was also doubly irresponsible. In the first place, it was carried out by members of a public body whose professional task was the maintenance of law and order. Secondly, Calvo Sotelo was a member of Parliament, a former minister under General Primo de Rivera, and greatly respected by a wealthy and powerful sector of the upper middle classes. Perhaps more than any other incident in the period 1931–36, Calvo Sotelo's murder discredited the Republic as a regime capable of guaranteeing public safety, thereby handing to its enemies on a plate the justification for its destruction.

The assassination of Calvo Sotelo almost certainly tipped the balance of Franco's indecision in favour of joining the anti-Republican conspiracy.[38] Franco had been warned in 1935 by the General Directorate for Security that, following his participation in the suppression of the Asturian strike, his name was among those on a Leftist 'hit-list'.[39] Since

Calvo Sotelo's name had also been on that list, the politician's murder may well have made Franco fear as much for his own life as for what he claimed was his prime concern, namely, the welfare of the nation. Be that as it may, the fact is that on 14 July, Franco sent another message to Galarza and Mola, reversing what he had told them two days earlier. Also on 14 July he began to write a manifesto, which was to be made public as soon as the rising was under way. As we have seen, however, the wheels for his participation had been set in motion before Calvo Sotelo died and, as early as February 1936, Franco's conversation with Barroso indicated his expectation that he would eventually take part in a rising. As we have also noted, the conservative sectors of the armed forces had been itching to step in at least since the autumn of 1934. The escalation in partisan violence which occurred in July 1936 gave them perfect cover for doing so. With socio-political tension at breaking point and both the authority of the government and the credibility of parliamentary rule reduced almost to nothing, military intervention would appear as the only way to prevent a complete breakdown of law and order. In fact, its objective was not the restoration of law and order, but, on the contrary, the overthrow of the Republic.

By now, the date had been fixed for 18 July. Everything was in position, except Franco, who was stationed on the island of Tenerife and had to get to Gran Canaria in order to board the private plane that was to take him to Morocco. That this was achieved was, as one analyst points out, 'the result of either an amazing coincidence or foul play'.[40] To make the trip from one island to another, Franco needed the permission of the Ministry of War. His application was refused. Then, on 16 July, the military commander of Gran Canaria died in what appears to have been a shooting accident. This was the second 'providential death' in Franco's career, for the ensuing funeral gave him a water-tight reason for going to Gran Canaria, which he did on 17 July.

Waiting in Las Palmas de Gran Canaria to set out for Morocco and thence to the Spanish mainland, he may have felt as he did in 1925, as he prepared to land on the beach-head at Alhucemas. In 1936, as in 1925, he was to lead the Foreign Legion in an operation in which the possibilities of success or failure, death or glory, were evenly matched. In 1925, however, he had had the authority and admiration of the government behind him; in 1936, he was committed to the overthrow of the government. Professionally and personally a disciplinarian, his love of authority and hierarchy now revealed its true colours of prejudice and self-interest. When faced with a choice between the advancement of his own class and political interests or respect for the legally established order, he opted for the former, fully conscious that his choice would entail the subversion, possibly even the destruction, of that order.

He also knew in mid-July 1936 that he had now taken the irrevocable step he had refused to take on so many previous occasions. If only to safeguard his own prestige and vindicate his past actions, this coup had to be a success. Franco had told Sanjurjo in 1932 that failure had earned him the right to die. Franco, who had been encouraged since childhood to succeed in everything he attempted, did not intend to suffer the same fate.

.   .   .

NOTES

1. M. Azaña, *Obras Completas*, Mexico: 1966–68, vol. II, pp. 90–8, quoted in G. Cardona, *El poder militar en la España contemporánea hasta la guerra civil*, Madrid: Siglo XXI 1983, p. 132.
2. F. Franco Salgado-Araujo, *Mi vida junto a Franco*, Barcelona: Editorial Planeta 1977, p. 104.
3. J. Arrarás, *Franco*, San Sebastian: Librería Internacional 1937, pp. 166–70.
4. Franco's official service record, pp. 82–3, quoted in L. Suárez Fernández, *Francisco Franco y Su Tiempo*, Madrid: Ediciones Azor 1984, vol. I, p. 229.
5. Franco to General Gómez-Morato, 24 July; Gómez-Morato to Azaña, 28 July 1931. Archivo Azaña, Ministerio de Asuntos Exteriores, Madrid, RE 131–1, in P. Preston, *Franco*, London: Harper Collins 1993, ch. 3.
6. R. Baón, *La cara humana de un caudillo*, Madrid: Editorial San Martín 1975, p. 110.
7. The contribution made by the CEDA to the destruction of the Second Republic is examined in detail in P. Preston, *The*

Coming of the Spanish Civil War, London: Methuen 1983, passim.

8. For an examination of the extreme Right during the Second Republic, see S.G. Payne, *Falange. A History of Spanish Fascism*, Stanford: University of Stanford Press 1961; H.R. Southworth, *Antifalange*, Paris: Ruedo Ibérico 1967; S.M. Ellwood, *Spanish Fascism in the Franco Era*, London: Macmillan 1987, pp. 7–28.

9. D. Hidalgo Durán, *¿Por qué fui lanzado del ministerio de guerra?*, Madrid: Espasa-Calpe 1934, p. 77.

10. L. Suárez Fernández, *FFST*, vol. II, p. 52.

11. José Antonio Primo de Rivera, eldest son of the late dictator, founded Falange Española (FE) in October 1933. In February 1934, it joined forces with another fascist group, JONS, to become FE de las JONS. In September 1934, Primo de Rivera wrote to Franco in Palma de Mallorca offering him Falangist support to put an end to 'rampant social indiscipline' and communist subversion. Franco did not reply. Primo de Rivera's letter in J.A. Primo de Rivera, *Obras completas*, Madrid: Ediciones de la Vicescretaría de FET y de las JONS 1945, pp. 623–6.

12. F. Franco, *"Apuntes", personales del Generalísimo sobre la República y la guerra civil*, Madrid Fundación Nacional Francisco Franco 1987, p. 9. Franco characterized Freemasons as 'atheists, traitors in exile, delinquents, fraudsters, unfaithful in marriage'.

13. Ibid., p. 11.

14. Ibid.

15. C. Martín, *Franco, soldado y estadista*, Madrid: Fermín Uriarte 1965, pp. 129–30, quoted in P. Preston, *Franco*, ch. 4.

16. F. Franco, *Apuntes*, p. 12.

17. L. Suárez Fernández, *FFST*, vol.I, pp. 268–9.

18. F. Franco, *Apuntes*, p. 13.

19. F. Franco Salgado-Araujo, *Mi vida*, p. 122.

20. Ibid., p. 122.

21. Ibid., p. 123.

22. F. Franco, *Apuntes*, p. 15.

23. Ibid., p. 14.

24. J. Busquets in D. Solar (ed.), *La Guerra Civil*, (24 vols) Madrid: Historia 16 1986, vol. 3, pp. 90–5.

25. P. Preston, *Franco*, ch. 4.

26. F. Franco, *Apuntes*, p. 18.

27. Ibid.

28. L. Suárez Fernández, *FFST*, vol. I, p. 300; J. Arrarás, *Franco* p. 198; J.M. Gil-Robles, *No fue posible la paz*, Barcelona: Ariel 1968, pp. 375–6.

29. G. Hills, *Franco. The Man and His Nation*, London: Robert Hale 1967, p. 210.
30. F. Franco, *Apuntes*, p. 24.
31. Ibid., p. 26.
32. Ibid., p. 30.
33. Ibid., p. 33.
34. Ibid., p. 33; see also G. Hills, *Franco. The Man and his Nation*, London: Robert Hale 1967, p. 219.
35. I. Prieto, quoted ibid., p. 221.
36. F. Franco, *Apuntes*, p. 34.
37. J. Arrarás, *Franco*, pp. 240–4.
38. Cf. J.P. Fusi, *Franco. A Biography*, London: Unwin Hyman 1987, p. 16; G.P. del Acqua, *Los grandes protagonistas de la II Guerra Mundial: Franco*, Barcelona: Ediciones Orbis 1985 p. 20.
39. F. Franco, *Apuntes*, p. 21.
40. P. Preston, *The Spanish Civil War, 1936–39*, London: Weidenfeld and Nicolson 1986, p. 49.

Chapter 4

THE CIVIL WAR (1936–39)

The garrisons of Spanish Morocco rose on 17 July 1936, a day earlier than planned. In the early hours of 18 July, Franco sent a telegram from Las Palmas to the eight regional headquarters of the army in mainland Spain and to thirty-one other garrisons. 'Glory to the Army of Africa', it began. It went on:

> Spain above all. Receive the enthusiastic greeting of these garrisons which join with you and the rest of our companions in the Peninsula in these historic moments. Blind faith in victory. Long live Spain with honour. General Franco.[1]

As in his letter of 23 June to Santiago Casares Quiroga, there was a certain ambiguity in this message, such that, had the rising failed, Franco might have argued that it was a gesture of solidarity towards the defenders of the Republic. Similarly, a manifesto issued by Franco and broadcast later that day by the local radio in Las Palmas left some room for manoeuvre, should it prove useful. Certainly, it justified the rebellion as a military duty, necessary to save the Fatherland from anarchy; but it did not say that the objective was the overthrow of the Republic.

Meanwhile, the local radio station in the capital of Spain, Unión Radio, gave out news of the insurrection in Spanish Morocco, confirming what everyone except the government had deemed imminent for months. The rising was not confined to North Africa, however. All over Spain, rebel officers put into action the plan they had been

72

elaborating since December of the previous year. In Andalusia, General Gonzalo Queipo de Llano occupied Seville on 18 July, while General Enrique Varela took the port of Cadiz and a long stretch of coast eastwards as far as Algeciras, close to Gibraltar. That same day, General Miguel Cabanellas rose in Zaragoza, from where he controlled a large area of territory stretching from the Pyrenees to the town of Teruel, in the east. In Castile, the heartlands of Catholic conservatism and the fascist Right, the rebellion triumphed with little difficulty, placing the principal towns of Burgos, Valladolid, León, Soria, Salamanca and Segovia in anti-Republican hands. In the north-west, too, in Galicia, the rebels quickly triumphed, thanks to the assistance they received from the Civil Guard in overcoming the resistance of loyal troops and civilians. The coup's 'Director', General Mola, rose in Pamplona, the capital of Navarre, on 19 July. His action triggered such a massive response from the Carlist movement that Mola had to ask its leaders not to send any more volunteers for the time being, because the Pamplona garrison had run out of rations. Undaunted, the Carlist militias – the Requetés – formed into columns and set out for Madrid, some 500 kilometres to the south, in buses, in trucks and on foot.

The original plan had been for a rapid take-over of military and political control in Madrid, accompanied by risings in the other main cities and the convergence on the capital of detachments from the provinces to consolidate the coup and force the transfer of power. In the event, this plan was only partially successful, for the rebels failed to achieve their objectives in Madrid; in the important commercial and industrial cities of Barcelona and Valencia; and in the mining and manufacturing provinces of Asturias and the Basque Country. The two main frontier posts with France – Irun-Hendaye at the western end of the Pyrenees, and Port Bou at the eastern extreme – remained in government hands, thus ensuring the Republic's surface communications with its European neighbours. The rebellion had failed to gain control of the Navy. The lack of a contingency plan for this eventuality left the all-important Army of Africa, together with its commanders, General Franco and Colonel Yagüe (who, under Franco's orders, had been in charge of the Legion during the repression of the Asturian revolutionary movement in 1934), stranded on the far side of the Straits of Gibraltar. Finally, the bulk of the Airforce had remained loyal to the government, as had the frontier police and the Civil Guard in Madrid, Barcelona and Valencia.

Given that so many crucial factors militated against the success of the rebellion, the government should have been able to overcome it. Instead of taking decisive action, however, the cabinet's reaction was at best ineffective and at worst irresponsible. Certainly, the Navy was ordered to blockade the Straits of Gibraltar but, otherwise, merely bureaucratic measures were used to try to bring the rebels to heel. Thus, decrees were issued ordering the dissolution of the rebel units, exempting troops from any duty to obey rebel officers, abolishing the state of martial law proclaimed where the insurgents had triumphed and dismissing rebel generals. Inevitably, such paper tigers had no effect on men who had embarked on so desperate a venture, especially when they had never paid more than lip-service to the authority of the Republican politicians. In addition to virtually dissolving the Army – a measure described by contemporary witnesses as 'completely crazy'[2] – the Prime Minister, Casares Quiroga, refused to distribute arms to the political and trade union organizations of the Left, evidently more afraid of the Republic's supporters than of its enemies. In response, the anarchist CNT called a nationwide general strike and started to form volunteer militias, as did the PSOE and the PCE.

Overwhelmed by the situation, Casares Quiroga resigned on 18 July and was succeeded by Diego Martínez Barrio, who had led a caretaker government in the autumn of 1933. Following an unsuccessful attempt to reach a peaceful agreement with the rebels, he, too, resigned after less than twenty-four hours in the job, to be replaced by José Giral, who, like Casares, was a member of Manuel Azaña's Republican Left party. Giral agreed to the distribution of arms to civilians, under the responsibility of the political and labour organizations. Thanks to this initiative, the attempted rising was put down in Madrid and Barcelona, though not without excesses and vandalism which did considerable harm to the Republican cause.

While the Republican politicians dithered and the more

violent partisans of the Popular Front vented their anger and frustration on people they considered to be right-wing, ecclesiastical properties and captured rebels, the insurgents entrenched themselves in the positions they had managed to take. There, with the assistance of volunteers from the Rightist political organizations, particularly the Falange, they undertook a brutal campaign of repression designed to rid 'their' territory of the last vestige of Republican support. Hundreds of people were arrested and imprisoned, or summarily executed, because their ideas or sympathies were considered 'wrong' by those who happened to be in local control.

With roughly half the country under the control of each side, a situation of stalemate had been reached. The key to its resolution lay in the Army of Africa. Without it and its leader, General Franco, the moral and military debilitation of the rebels might allow the government to gain the upper hand. With both in the Peninsula, however, the insurgents would have a major advantage. Franco landed in Tetuán on 19 July to a rapturous welcome from rebel officers. Despite his minimal role in the preparation of the rising, he immediately began to take executive action, raising the Legionnaires' wages by one peseta per day and broadcasting speeches over the radio. Most importantly, he set about resolving the problem of transporting his troops to the mainland. Although the rebels had begun an air ferry with six planes they had at their disposal, it was clear that the rate of transfer thus achieved was much too slow and that the only hope of improving it was to obtain more planes from outside Spain. Franco had spotted this possibility at an early stage: on arrival in Tetuán, he had authorized Luis Bolín (who had travelled with him from Casablanca) to purchase aircraft and armaments in Italy, Germany or Britain. Bolín set off for Rome on 19 July.[3] Meanwhile, Franco himself approached the Italian government and General Mola organized a delegation of monarchists, who saw the Italian Foreign Minister, Galeazzo Ciano, on 25 July. Initially, the Italian government declined to become involved, but Mussolini relented when he heard that his principal rivals in the Mediterranean, the French, were going to aid the Republic.[4] Accordingly, twelve Savoia-

Marchetti bombers were promised on 28 July. Nine arrived in Morocco two days later.

At the same time, Franco made a similar request (this time, for transport planes and crews) to the German government; and, initially, received a similarly negative response. While waiting for a reply, Franco decided to make a direct appeal to Hitler on the Nazi Party network, through certain members of the German business community in Morocco. Hitler agreed on 25 July to send twenty transport planes. He also sent six fighters, nearly one hundred pilots and a supply of machine guns. Thanks to the German and Italian aid, Franco was able substantially to increase the number of troops being transported daily from Morocco to Spain, while the Republic remained apparently unable to stop him. As in the 1920s, Morocco provided the scenario in which Franco appeared to be endowed with a special mix of luck and divine protection – *baraka* as his Moroccan soldiers called it.

Franco's success in obtaining German and Italian equipment greatly increased his political stock among the rebels. In barely two weeks (12–25 July), he had gone from being very reluctant to participate in the rising to being one of its main protagonists, and a vital interlocutor with Hitler and Mussolini. It was an enormous leap, which he was able to make by virtue of the professional competence and political significance he had built up over the preceding twenty years. His prestige was shortly increased still further. On 20 July he had discussed with General Yagüe the possibility of putting together a naval convoy to transport the Army of Africa across the Straits. With Italian and German bombers providing air cover, the convoy set out on 5 August, carrying some 3,000 men. On that day, a dense fog appeared in the Straits, through which, according to Francoist mythology, the Virgin Mary appeared to guide the rebel ships. In fact, the fog obliged the convoy to turn back at first, but it set out again later in the day and reached the Spanish mainland with little difficulty. Thus, by the end of the first week of August, between 8,000 and 9,000 soldiers had been transferred from North Africa to Seville, and the way was open for more to follow throughout the summer. This not only altered the strategic military balance in favour of the rebels, it also gave them an important psychological boost. With specific regard to Franco, he was now seen as militarily and personally indispensable to a rebel victory.

By August 1936 it was no longer appropriate to talk of a coup. The failure of the insurgents to secure the country's political and economic nerve-centres, the provision of German and Italian military aid and the resistance put up by the defenders of Republican legality had turned the insurrection into a war whose duration or outcome no one could foretell. It is important to understand that it was essentially a *political* war. It was, of course, a conflict fired by material interests; but it was, above all, a conflict about the ideas and opinions to which those interests gave rise. It was not, in essence, a struggle for territory; nor for religious supremacy; nor for independence; nor against external aggression; nor about the rights of minorities. These questions were, to a greater or lesser degree, part and parcel of the armed confrontation, in so far as each side had opposing views on them, but they were merely strands in the overall picture, not the underlying design. The salient features of that design could be summarized as follows.

For three years, between July 1936 and April 1939, two opposing forces attempted to settle by military means a dispute which had been going on since 1931 over what form the state should take in Spain. That is to say, whether it should or should not be a republic. Yet it was not a straightforward choice between republic or monarchy, but between a state whose political basis was liberal democratic parliamentarism, and some other kind of system whose legitimacy did not derive from the theory and practice of one person, one vote. In addition, there were a number of other conflicting relationships within this central (and here, much simplified) question, which affected and were affected by the course of the war as a military exercise. The Spanish Civil War was the result of the collapse of political and social coexistence among Spaniards; and, in turn, fashioned subsequent political developments, inside each of the opposing war zones which emerged in the summer of 1936, between them, and between them and the outside world.

That last factor – the outside world – was crucially

important. The Spanish Civil War took place at a time of growing tension in Europe, on account of the increasingly belligerent attitude of Hitler's Germany and the less bellicose, but also expansionist, intentions of fascist Italy. Since the political division of Spain corresponded closely to that of contemporary Europe, each of the Spanish camps looked to its European counterparts for assistance, which turned the Spanish war into an international, as well as a national, conflict. Indeed, the Spanish Civil War came to be viewed by some as the preface to the Second World War. Whilst it could only be considered such with the wisdom of hindsight, it was nevertheless seen at the time as a geographically limited episode of a much wider-ranging struggle. Recent research strongly suggests that an important factor in the inhibition of the western democracies towards the Spanish conflict was their concern not to provoke Hitler or Mussolini.[5] For the Republicans and their partisans, the broader struggle was between democracy and fascism. For the insurgents and their supporters, it was between conservatism and communism. For both, it was a conflict between two incompatible sets of ideological and political concepts. Once the process was set in motion, there could be no going back and no possibility of negotiation. It was a fight to the death; a fight for power, couched in stark terms of 'winner takes all'.

As the initiators of the final, armed, phase of the dispute, the rebels were, perhaps, more acutely, or more immediately, aware of the risks involved. The Republic had legality on its side and, at the beginning, it seemed inconceivable that the will of the majority, as expressed in the February 1936 elections, could succumb to the self-centred truculence of the minority. The rebels, by contrast, had no objective legitimacy to support their action. Moreover, they had revealed their game irrevocably this time and could expect no clemency if they lost. Consequently, they simply could not afford to lose. They had to achieve a total military victory in order also to impose the total political victory which would at once provide *ex post facto* legitimation for the rising and enable them to ensure that there would be no return to pre-July 1936 conditions.

It was not any supposed inherently violent trait in the

Spanish character, but this element of desperation which made the Spanish Civil War the brutally barbaric conflict it was. Death and destruction were meted out by both sides, but there can be little doubt that the rebels carried a greater burden of responsibility than the Republicans, for their repressive actions took a higher human toll and they, not the Republicans, had acted against legality. For the rebels, the war was a military enterprise with political motives; for the Republicans, it was a political question, whose resolution necessitated, but did not rest entirely upon, military intervention.

This difference of criterion as to the character of the conflict was reflected in the way power was handled on each side. In the Republican zone, power remained in civilian hands and democratic forms were maintained until the end. In the areas controlled by the insurgents, by contrast, martial law was immediately declared and power was, from beginning to end, vested in military men. Thus, on 23 July the rebels created a Committee for National Defence, composed of seven generals, whose role was that of an embryonic and, of course, illegal government. The following day, the Committee issued a manifesto expounding its justification for the rising, and appointed General Franco – who, it will be remembered, had been dismissed by the legitimate government of the nation – as chief of the Armies of Morocco and southern Spain. On 7 August Franco set up his headquarters in Seville, in a large house offered to him by a local aristocrat, the marchioness of Yanduri. This was the first of many palatial properties occupied by Franco over the next forty years – a tendency which is difficult to reconcile with his hagiographers' insistence that he was a man of austere tastes and habits.

By mid-August the rebel advance on Madrid from the south was well under way, spearheaded by two columns of Legionnaires and native Moroccan Regulares. As he had done in Asturias in 1934, Franco did not participate in the advance but coordinated its progress from a safe distance, ensconced in his headquarters in Seville. Despite the fact that he had not committed himself to the rising until the last moment, he was quickly consolidating the initiative he had taken in Morocco and was emerging as its sole leader. Thanks to a series of events which he had done nothing to bring about, other prominent figures in the anti-Republican camp had been permanently or temporarily removed. As we have seen, the prestigious ultra-Rightist politician, José Calvo Sotelo, had been assassinated on 13 July. The CEDA leader, José María Gil Robles, had been politically discredited by his electoral defeat of February 1936 and was now stranded in Biarritz, where he had been on holiday when the rising occurred. The Falangist chief, José Antonio Primo de Rivera, had been imprisoned in March and by August was under close guard in a Republican jail in Alicante. As for Franco's military colleagues, Goded and Fanjul were under arrest in the Republican zone. None of the other conspirators, such as Queipo, Yagüe, Varela, or Cabanellas, had Franco's prestige. Sanjurjo had been killed in an air accident on 20 July, on his way to Pamplona to assume the leadership of the rising. General Mola was inferior in rank and had less prestige among the military, but he did have two factors in his favour: he was the director of the conspiracy and he was in command of all the rebel troops in the northern half of the country, thus 'mirroring' Franco's command in the south. Moreover, although Franco had the political and military support of Hitler, Mussolini, the Falangists and the CEDists, Mola had that of the Carlists and the exiled King Alfonso and his supporters. Thus, at the height of the summer of 1936, General Mola was the only person who might be considered Franco's rival.

As the chief of the Army of the South, Franco's plan was to occupy the western provinces of Badajoz and Cáceres; link up with Mola's troops, which were driving south-westwards from Navarre; and advance eastwards on Madrid, following the natural line of penetration provided by the valley of the River Tagus. In principle, it might have been quicker to take the direct northward road through Andalusia and southern Castile. But this would have left a great swath of territory to the west in Republican control. Franco therefore preferred to employ the tactics learned in Africa, securing every inch of territory as he progressed by thoroughly 'cleansing' it of possible pockets of resistance. His approach to Madrid, via Extremadura, indicated that, while he wanted to take the capital as quickly as possible, he would not sacrifice thoroughness to speed.

By mid-August Franco's troops were poised to initiate the drive for Madrid. They were under the direct command of Lieutenant-Colonel Yagüe who, as an *africanista*, could be relied upon to conduct the campaign in the manner of the frontier war Franco himself believed it to be. Franco knew that Yagüe would show the enemy no mercy; that was why he had deployed Yagüe with the Legion in Asturias, in 1934, and that was why he repeated the tactic in 1936. Yagüe did not disappoint Franco's expectations. In the conquest of the town of Badajoz, on 13 and 14 August, Yagüe repeated and surpassed the repressive brutality which in 1934 had earned him the name of 'Hyena of Asturias'. For decades afterwards, Francoist supporters denied the carnage which took place in Badajoz, in spite of the overwhelming evidence of contemporary eye-witnesses, who saw hundreds of Republicans rounded up in the municipal bullring, heard the machine guns, and smelled the reek of bodies being burned in the cemetery. It was – as it was undoubtedly intended to be – a terrifying example of Franco's determination, to crush physically and morally, all opposition. It was (as I have written elsewhere) 'ironic that the war of which this slaughter was part had been initiated, allegedly, to save Spain from the "barbarity" of the "atheistic hordes" which were supposedly about to invade Spain from eastern Europe'.[6] By using Yagüe as his intermediary, however, Franco effectively distanced himself from the horror.

In the second half of August, the Army of Africa pressed towards Madrid, with the Republican forces falling back all the way. The latter, composed mainly of volunteer militias, lacked the arms, the training and the organization of the rebels, who, as part of their patriotic façade, had adopted the term 'Nationalists' to refer to themselves. In addition, although the Republicans knew that they were defending legality, they did not have the moral stimulus of winning battles which the insurgents had, and which (as we have noted earlier), derived in large measure from the desperate fanaticism of their enterprise. Also in contrast to the Nationalists, the internal differences which had so damaged the Republican camp prior to 1936 persisted even now, causing deep divisions between the Republican rank and file and their government, and between the political and trade union organizations of the Left. Finally, the Republicans did not receive the same level of external aid as their adversaries enjoyed. On 1 August France proposed a policy of non-intervention in Spain's internal affairs. By the end of the month, the resulting non-intervention pact had been signed by Britain, Belgium, Czechoslovakia, Germany, Holland, Poland and the Soviet Union, with the United States supporting the policy. The signature of the Soviet Union did not, in fact, prevent the despatch of Soviet diplomats and military advisers, nor the sale of Russian arms, to the Republic. However, this was more than counterbalanced by the amount of *matériel* and troops shipped to the Nationalists by Germany, Italy and Portugal; by the British and French prohibition on the sale of arms to the Republic; and by the fact that many of the Soviet arms purchases never reached the Republic because they were destroyed in transit by enemy action or were retained in France.

By the end of August, the territorial situation was of equilibrium. The Nationalists occupied most of the western half of the country, and the government most of the eastern half, plus the city of Madrid. The rebels held the ports of Andalusia and Galicia, but the Mediterranean and Pyrenean communication routes were still under Republican control. Finally, the insurgents were in possession of the principal agricultural areas (especially the vital cereal-producing lands of Extremadura and Castile), while the Republic retained the main industrial and political centres, plus the fertile horticultural areas of the south-east. The Republic, however, was on the defensive everywhere, and the relentless enemy onslaught on Madrid was draining its human, material and spiritual resources, as well as taking a heavy toll in political terms. In early August the Minister of War, General Castelló, had had to be relieved of his post, suffering from psychological exhaustion. Then, at the beginning of September, Prime Minister Giral was forced to resign by intense pressure from the Socialist and Communist Parties, whose leaders bitterly criticized what they saw as the Left Republicans' incompetent handling of the Republican war effort, accusing them of having lost control of the situation. When the socialist Francisco Largo Caballero became Prime Minister and Minister for War on

4 September 1936, the Army of Africa was less than 100 kilometres away from Madrid, advancing rapidly from the south-west.

Perhaps because they were suddenly aware that Madrid could fall to the rebels at any moment, or perhaps because they felt more confident with a government which now included representatives of all the Popular Front forces and the anarchists, the Republican troops rallied at that point and managed to slow down the Army of Africa's advance on the capital. With Mola still pushing towards the city on its northern flank, Franco realized that he might not be the first Nationalist general to enter Madrid. If Mola got there first, not only would he snatch that honour from him, but it might also mean the end of the war and his return to the relative anonymity of normal army routine. Finally, although the fall of Madrid at this stage might produce the capitulation of the Republican forces, it would not entail their annihilation. Badajoz had demonstrated that Franco wanted the latter. Thus Franco had powerful personal, professional and political reasons for wanting to avoid the immediate capture of Madrid at the beginning of September 1936. It was perhaps partly for this reason that on 21 September he ordered General Enrique Varela (who had taken over from Yagüe when the latter became ill) to make a detour to Toledo, to relieve what remained of nearly 2,000 Nationalists who had been besieged in the giant fortress – the *alcazar* – since the end of July.

Toledo was of no military value to the Nationalist advance, but it had considerable religious, historic and emotional significance, for it was the seat of the head of the Catholic Church in Spain and had once been the hub of the Spanish empire. Moreover, it was the location of the Infantry Academy where Franco himself and many of his fellow-rebels had been cadets. The resistance of the defenders of the *alcazar* was, for the anti-Republicans, symbolic of the whole Nationalist cause, with a minority of 'true' Spaniards taking up arms to defend the Fatherland and Christian values against the onslaught of the hordes of anti-Christ and anti-Spain. Franco was well aware that the deliverance from evil of so powerful a symbol would greatly enhance his standing among the Nationalist partisans. General Varela occupied Toledo at the head of Yagüe's three columns of Legionnaires and Regulares on 27 September 1936. The *alcazar* itself was relieved on the following day. In what was becoming his familiar style, Franco appeared on the scene on 29 September, when success had already been achieved. In spite of the fact that he had not set foot in Toledo throughout the entire operation, he was acclaimed as the saviour of the *alcazar* and received with smiles and gestures of obvious satisfaction the near-delirious attentions of the survivors of the siege. As we shall see, what had been a relatively minor military operation enormously enhanced Franco's position in the Nationalist power stakes and proved to be an important milestone along his road to power.

Meanwhile, in the north, part of General Mola's forces had taken control of the Hispano-French frontier at Irún, on the Basque coast. On 13 September they entered the one-time royal holiday resort of San Sebastian and, by the end of the month, were no more than 60 kilometres from Spain's largest centre of heavy industry and shipbuilding, Bilbao. By then, extensive areas of territory were under rebel control and the problems of financing the war, procuring arms and other supplies, and administering the civilian population, were in danger of overwhelming the limited resources and authority of the seven-man Committee for National Defence set up in July. In addition, the complexity of the purely military aspects of the conflict advised the appointment of someone to take overall command of the Armed Forces. While as professional soldiers immersed in a war the Committee members were primarily concerned with the military considerations, the fact that a general state of martial law was in force meant that whoever was appointed would effectively also exercise supreme authority over both the civilian and the military populace.

Franco was well aware of the practical need for a single commander-in-chief who would supervise the coordination of all the different aspects of the rebel war effort. He had discussed the matter in mid-August with General Mola, who (naïvely, in the view of his closest aides) was happy to allow Franco to take sole responsibility for arms procurement.[7] Franco's position of superior strength was consolidated further when, around 23 August, Germany and Italy decided to send all future aid to him, or to the places specified by him, and nowhere else. When they also indicated that they would prefer to have one central point of communication for their dealings with the Nationalist camp, it was clear that the question of leadership must be resolved at once.

On 21 September, at Franco's request, a meeting of the Defence Committee was called in Salamanca to discuss the military and political conduct of the war. On that same day, Franco ordered Varela to detour to Toledo. This may have been coincidence or, as we noted earlier, a deliberate ploy to enhance his own standing. Whatever the case, the fact remains that the Defence Committee voted almost unanimously to appoint Franco Commander-in-Chief of the Nationalist forces.[8] Perhaps because some generals (particularly Cabanellas and Queipo de Llano) were unhappy with this outcome, the Defence Committee did not immediately announce it publicly. On 28 September – the day of the relief of the *alcazar* – the meeting was reconvened for further discussion. This time, the chief of the Nationalist Airforce, General Kindelán, put forward the proposal that, for the duration of hostilities, the Commander-in-Chief of the Armed Forces should also have responsibility for 'all national activities: political, economic, social, cultural, etc.'[9] Kindelán's proposal was accepted by the Defence Committee, but when the appointment was published in the Committee's *Official Bulletin*, the reference to its temporary nature had disappeared. Franco had evidently crossed it out, thus making himself supreme chief (*Generalísimo*) of the Nationalist Armed Forces and 'head of the Government of the Spanish state'.[10] Franco believed that one of General Primo de Rivera's mistakes had been to establish the provisional nature of his regime at the outset. By removing any temporal limitation on his own mandate, Franco showed that he did not intend to suffer the same fate as Primo.

In addition to his growing aura of having a special providence, which was conveniently (or deliberately) fostered by the timely relief of Toledo, Franco's designation was secured by two factors. In the first place, his military pre-eminence was undisputed. But because military and political factors were inextricably mingled in this war, the appointment of a military leader was, at the same time, the choice of a political leader. Here was the source of the Committee members' indecision and the second of the factors which decided the matter in Franco's favour. On 18 July 1936 there had been no consensus on this question among those who joined the rebellion, beyond their unanimous desire to see the legitimate, democratically elected government removed from power. Two months later, the designation of a single leader was a means to that end, not an end in itself. In that context, Franco was the unifying common denominator, in that he was the only person acceptable to all the shades of political opinion present on the Committee, to the external powers whose political and material support were vital to the Nationalists, and to the Catholic Church, which had given its blessing to the rising as the defence of Christianity against communism. By placing Franco in overall command, the Nationalists made a quantum leap forward in their efforts to secure victory. No one was more aware of this than Francisco Franco. That he knew his position to be unassailable was reflected in the fact that he immediately began to refer to himself not as Head of Government, but as Head of State. The two positions were to remain merged in him until 1973.

For Francisco Franco, the war now had a new meaning. Or, perhaps, it had the meaning he had wanted it to have from the beginning: the meaning that had kept him out of coups led by others. It was not only the struggle to reverse the result of the 1936 election, nor even to stamp out Marxism in Spain. It was also a fight to consolidate his position within the insurgent camp. The achievement of all three aims would depend, to a large extent, on his ability to maintain the reputation for winning battles which had secured his appointment as military and political supremo. To that end he now turned his attention back to the military progress of the war.

Shortly after his election as *Generalísimo*, Franco relinquished direct command of the Army of Africa, which was incorporated into the Army of the North, whose overall chief was General Mola. With Queipo de Llano in direct command of the Army of the South, Franco retained supreme control over the Nationalist forces, but was not directly in charge of how operations were handled on the ground. In other words, he chose to conduct the war by remote control, distancing himself, as ever, from the brutality and the risks (including that of defeat), but preserving his stake in a successful outcome. The focus of the war now returned to Madrid.

The seizure of power in the capital had been the rebels' primary objective since 18 July. On 7 October they began an all-out offensive on the western flank of the city, with the columns of the erstwhile Army of Africa attacking from the Toledo direction, to the south-west, and further units of Mola's forces advancing from the north-west. While the fighting took place in open country, the Legionnaires and Regulares were in their element. Republican counter-offensives, launched by numerically, militarily and materially inferior Republican militias, were able to delay, but could not halt, the enemy advance. By 17 October Mola's troops were only 30 kilometres from Madrid, causing President Azaña to remove himself to the safety of Barcelona. By the end of the month that distance had been halved; and when, in the first week of November, Nationalist troops managed to cross the River Manzanares, which marked the city's western boundary, the rest of the Republican government decided that Madrid could not be defended. The cabinet left on 6 November for Valencia, on the Mediterranean coast, ostensibly to direct from there the continuation of the struggle after the expected fall of Madrid. But Madrid did not fall. There were a number of interacting reasons for this, not the least important of which was that the rebel leadership – including Franco – made a serious error of military judgement.

The Nationalist offensive against Madrid deployed the same tactics that its *africanista* commanders were accustomed to using against tribesmen in the Moroccan Rif: a series of columns attacking simultaneously at different points along an extensive front. To be successful, this required surprise, speed and weak enemy defences. Clearly, there could be no element of surprise, and although the rebel advance had been rapid until then, it had effectively been halted at the gates of Madrid. There remained the question of the strength of Republican defences. In principle, they were by no means impregnable, but the Republican Field Commander, Colonel Vicente Rojo, had concentrated as many as possible of his human and material resources on the city's western flank, and his troops had the advantage of a commanding position overlooking the river valley and familiarity with the urban terrain. The Republican militias were assisted in their efforts to defend Madrid by the discovery of a copy of the Nationalist plan of attack on the body of an Italian soldier; a substantial delivery of Soviet arms, munitions and aircraft; the arrival of the first contingent of International Brigade volunteers; and the tenacity of the civilian population. By 23 November Franco was forced to recognize that the head-on approach to the conquest of Madrid had failed.

He did not admit defeat or withdraw. He simply had his forces retrench while a new strategy was considered. Some of his advisers favoured a large-scale attempt at encirclement from the north of the capital. Franco, however, instinctively rejected the risks involved in an audacious operation and opted instead for the less ambitious objective of driving a wedge between the city and its northern line of defence, in the Guadarrama mountains, by severing the road and rail communications north-westwards out of the city, towards La Coruña. The first attempt did not succeed; mainly, in the view of military historian Gabriel Cardona, because Franco failed to realize that the conquest of a large city like Madrid required massive and concentrated artillery attack, with coordinated and sustained support from the air, not African-style cavalry charges followed by rapid, but unsupported, infantry attack.[11] A second attempt, made on 14 December, was also unsuccessful. When the Nationalists launched their third attack, on 3 January 1937, their forces had been reinforced considerably, especially by Italian and German aircraft, including the German 'Condor Legion', despatched to Spain at the beginning of November and allowed by Franco to use the Spanish war as a practice ground for devastating new techniques of destruction and terror. The fact that more than 70,000 men were now concentrated on the western flank of Madrid (compared to 14,000 deployed in October) bore witness to Nationalist determination to take the capital. The main Madrid-La Coruña road was finally cut on 13 January, but other roads to the Guadarrama mountains remained in Republican hands. Even though 30,000 lives had been lost and massive amounts of *matériel* consumed on both sides, Madrid did not fall to the Nationalists. For once, Franco was not victorious.

Had the war ended with the collapse of Madrid in November 1936, the Nationalists would have had considerable difficulty in improvising the governmental and administrative apparatus necessary to sustain a new regime. The Nationalist high command had disrupted the normal functioning of the country's political, economic, cultural and social life, but had given no thought to the construction of alternative infrastructures and super-structures on their own organizational patterns. Without adequate groundwork, there was no guarantee that any regime installed at the end of the war would not collapse very quickly. In the autumn of 1936 Franco set about preparing the political foundations of his 'New State', in anticipation of what he thought was his imminent entry to Madrid.

Perhaps recalling General Primo de Rivera's ill-starred attempt to rule, initially, through an all-military committee, one of Franco's first steps was to replace the exclusively military Committee for National Defence with a mixed, civilian and military, Technical Committee. While this organ could and did assume the executive functions of a provisional government, its creation did not resolve two crucial problems: what roles were the existing political parties and the mass of the population to play in the New State.

Notwithstanding the two occasions on which he had been tempted to abandon the Army for politics, and the cordial relations he had maintained with the CEDA, Franco was disdainful and suspicious of politicians. In this, he was typical of the Spanish officer class of his day, which harboured a deep-seated resentment against what it considered the neglect of its legitimate claims to attention by inept and uncomprehending civilian governments. It was for this reason that no civilians had been formally involved in the spring 1936 conspiracy, and that the Committee for National Defence had issued a decree on 25 September 1936 which prohibited 'all political activity' for the duration of hostilities.[12] It was for this same reason that

José Antonio Primo de Rivera, while supporting the military rising, had harboured serious doubts as to what might be the fate of his party in the event of a triumph by the military.

There were a number of factors which made it ill-advised, and indeed impossible, to ignore completely the presence of political organizations in the Nationalist rearguard. In the first place, they had lent vital paramilitary support to the rising and continued to be a crucial source of committed volunteers on the battle fronts. Secondly, they assisted the Army and Civil Guard in tasks of rearguard control and repression. Thirdly, they were a source of ideological arguments which would legitimate what, otherwise, would appear to be simply another military rising organized by discontented soldiers. Finally, when the war was over, the political groupings which had given the Nationalists their moral and material support would not only not disappear, but would expect to be duly recompensed and might even expect to take over the legislative and executive control of the New State. The question, therefore, was how to satisfy the aspirations of the political groupings, without allowing them to gain the upper hand; how to make use of their mobilizing capacities, without these being used to ends other than those approved by the Commander-in-Chief, *Generalísimo* Franco.

In a radio broadcast on 1 October 1936, the day he was officially invested as Head of State, Franco hinted at how he envisaged the organization of the as yet non-existent state of whose equally non-existent government he had just been made leader. 'Spain', he said, would be organized 'within a wide-ranging totalitarian concept of unity and continuity'.[13] This was a shrewd declaration. All four of the major political forces supporting the Nationalist military effort subscribed to some form of totalitarianism, while references to 'unity' and 'continuity' suggested that a return to the status quo prior to 1931 was envisaged. Thus the partisans of the Falange, the CEDA, Renovación Española and the Comunión Tradicionalista could each imagine that Franco specifically meant them. In this way, Franco could secure their cooperation for as long as the war might last.

However, this still left the question of how the

'totalitarian concept' would be implemented. There were two possible answers. The first was that Franco intended to create a party for himself. This, in fact, was the option favoured by his secretary-brother, Nicolás. The *Generalísimo*, however, was not convinced that this was the ideal solution. In the first place, far from eliminating the kind of inter-party competition he believed to be the fatally debilitating flaw of liberal democracy, it would add another participant to the contest. Secondly, it might arouse the hostility of some of his comrades in arms, on the grounds that he was using the war to further his own political ends. Thirdly, this solution was too reminiscent for his liking of the unsuccessful Unión Patriótica (Patriotic Union), an artificial creation which had failed to provide Primo de Rivera's dictatorship with the spontaneous popular support it had needed to survive.

The second option was to make one single party out of the existing political organizations. In this way, inter-party friction would be eliminated, while, at the same time, the new organization would still be able to draw on the mobilizing capacity of the old parties. Moreover, far from excluding anyone, this would be a way of including the existing membership of the individual groupings. Finally, such an all-embracing solution could be presented as based on national, rather than personal, interests, for it appeared to represent everyone, not just certain social or economic sectors. It was this second scheme that Franco was inclined to favour and whose realization he began to turn over in his mind in the autumn of 1936.

While one part of his armies laid siege to Madrid and another pressed westward along the north coast towards Bilbao, Franco studied the idea of uniting the Falange and the Carlist Comunión Tradicionalista. He reached the conclusion that such a move would be relatively simple, on the grounds that the two organizations had much in common. It was true that both were rabidly anti-Marxist, anti-separatist, nationalist and, above all, intent upon the destruction of the Second Republic. The Falangists, however, were not monarchists and their rhetoric, if not their ideology, was revolutionary, whereas the very *raison d'être* of the Carlists was monarchism and they were totally opposed to all revolutionary notions. Any attempt to unite them would, therefore, have to be carefully planned if it were to win the acquiescence of the parties involved. Alternatively, if their agreement could not be achieved, it would have to be effected by force. Franco began to prepare the ground, starting with the Falange.

In the absence of its national chief, José Antonio Primo de Rivera, the party had become divided into a number of factions whose mutual animosity was only kept in check by their common interest in a Nationalist victory in the war. A provisional executive committee had been set up, whose chairman Manuel Hedilla Larrey, was a former member of Acción Española. Hedilla believed that he was head of the party, but other members of the committee and their respective coteries considered that Hedilla was no more than 'first among equals' and that, in any case, his authority was only provisional. The parallel between Hedilla's situation and Franco's is striking. Each was temporarily leader of his respective peer-group and power-base, but each had less than unanimous backing, especially in the long term. Consequently, each could be strengthened by the support of the other. Cooperation between them was possible and necessary, but it was implicit that each would use the other to further his own ends. Until then, Franco had never shown any interest in the Falange, and the party had made no attempt to recruit him. In the autumn of 1936, however, they needed each other and accordingly made an effort to conceal their mutual distrust. Following Franco's example, Hedilla had transferred his headquarters from Burgos to Salamanca in October, and was thus able to see Franco quite frequently. Their relations were always cordial and, in his memoirs, Hedilla recounts how they often talked of politics. Their discussions included the merger of the Falange and the Traditionalist movement and they went so far as to commission a draft document outlining the project.

Although Franco seemed well on the way to having Hedilla in his pocket in late October, Falangist support for merging with the Traditionalists was not yet guaranteed. Primo de Rivera was still alive and there could be little doubt that he would be opposed to the idea, for, even before the rising, he had warned against the danger of becoming the puppets of the military. The Falangists had made a number of attempts to rescue Primo de Rivera from prison, all of which had failed. In fact, unbeknown to them, Franco had played a crucial role in the failure of what turned out to be the last of these, in September 1936, shortly before his elevation to the position of Head of State.[14] Clearly, Franco would stop at nothing to retain his hegemonic position. Some two months later, on 20 November 1936, Primo de Rivera was executed in Alicante prison, leaving the Falange under the disputed leadership of the malleable Hedilla. As with Calvo Sotelo and Sanjurjo, the intervention of 'fate' had removed another of Franco's possible rivals.

The Traditionalists were less easy to tackle. Their opposition to the idea of fusion with the Falangists was foreseeable, as we have noted, on account of their immovable monarchical and counter-revolutionary ideals. Certainly, the Comunión, too, was split into two main factions, but, in contrast to the Falange, its organizational structure was intact and its top men were in the Nationalist zone. Moreover, the movement's supreme leader, the Pretender Don Francisco Javier de Borbón, was alive and well and living in Biarritz. The Nationalist cause needed the Carlists' paramilitary support, and the Carlists wanted a Nationalist victory, but Franco was not their only possible military champion. It was widely believed, at the time of the rising, that General Sanjurjo had intended to assume the leadership of the Traditionalist Communion as well as of the military rising. As a sign of this, a statue of Sanjurjo in Pamplona was adorned with one of the red berets which were part of the Carlist uniform. With Sanjurjo dead, General Mola was the Carlists' immediate interlocutor, for it was with him that the Carlist leadership had negotiated the Traditionalists' active support for the rising. Since the Carlists were unlikely to accept any kind of power-sharing arrangement, it was less a question of making a political pact with them than of imposing the desired situation on them and limiting as far as possible their capacity to reject it.

The first practical step towards reducing the potential threat of the autonomous power of the political organizations was, in fact, military in nature. In December 1936 a decree was issued which made all volunteer forces subject to military jurisdiction. Up to that point, the

Falangist, Carlist, monarchist and CEDA militias had been covered by civilian law and ultimately responsible to their political leaders. The December decree annulled that situation, placing the party militias fully under military control. Furthermore, any attempt on the part of the political organizations to use their militias independently of what military GHQ disposed would be tantamount to a crime against the state and would merit the severest of penalties.

Franco made no mention of the creation of a single party after November 1936. By then, not only had the Nationalist seventh Division failed to enter Madrid, it had also failed in its first attempt to isolate the city from its northern defences in the Sierra de Guadarrama. There was no longer, therefore, any urgent need to prepare the political as well as the military take-over of the seat of national power. Nevertheless, the issue was discussed publicly in the winter of 1936–37, when Carlist and Falangist newspapers published articles about it in December 1936 and January 1937. According to Hedilla, 'the idea began to take shape that the *Generalísimo* would decide to unify the Falange and the Requeté'.[15] In view of this possibility, both the Carlists and the Falangists decided to forestall an imposed unification by negotiating their own, spontaneous merger. A tense power-struggle now began to unfold, for, in both parties, there emerged two different concepts of what such fusion would mean. For one group of Carlists and one of the Falangist factions, the new party would be the political organ of a regime headed by Francisco Franco – a party whose leader would be appointed by the *Generalísimo*. For a second group of Carlists and the Falangists closest to Hedilla, the new party would elect its own leader and would have a status and role independent of the regime, whilst sharing power with the government. During the first two months of 1937, Carlists and Falangists tried, unsuccessfully to reach an agreement on a coalition while, internally, the gap widened between the different factions. In March Hedilla had talks not only with members of the Comunión Tradicionalista, but also with some of the supporters of the Alphonsine dynasty, whose political future also depended on the outcome of what was becoming a bitter, subterranean confrontation within the main conflict against the Republic.

By then, the war had again reached stalemate. Yet another unsuccessful attempt to isolate Madrid, this time by severing its road link with Valencia, was made in February 1937. The battle of the Jarama valley occasioned appalling casualties on both sides. Some 16,000 men lost their lives in three weeks of intense fighting. When the battle ended, on 23 February, both sides were exhausted and neither could claim victory. Madrid and the road to Valencia remained in Republican hands, but the Nationalists had pushed the front line forward a few kilometres and were dangerously close to the Madrid-Valencia road.

Barely two weeks after the Jarama carnage, Franco launched what was to be the last Nationalist attempt to take Madrid, with an attack to the north-east of the city, in the province of Guadalajara. In this battle, the key element was the leading role given to a contingent of Italian infantry, which formed part of the volunteer forces sent by Mussolini in increasing numbers in the winter of 1936–37. Franco had been grateful to receive Italian planes in July and August, but he was not happy with the massive despatch of foot-soldiers, partly because Mussolini had the temerity to send more than had been agreed, and partly because the *Duce* insisted that they were not deployed as part of the Spanish Army, but formed an independent corps, with their own officers. The Italians had brought with them a battalion of tanks, a company of armoured cars and another of motorized machine guns, all designed for the kind of fast-moving warfare that Mussolini wanted to see in Spain and which was inimical to Franco's preferred *modus operandi*.[16] The Corpo di Truppe Volontarie (CTV) had taken part in the occupation of Malaga, on the south coast, in the first half of February, but Franco had refused to allow them to continue their advance eastwards, towards Valencia. He was instinctively sceptical of the Italian *guerra celere*, wary of finding himself politically beholden to Italy in return for military aid; opposed to the occupation of Valencia – the seat of the Republican government – by anyone other than Spaniards; and desirous of prolonging the war. As he explained on 13 February to the Italian Chief of the General Staff, Colonel Emilio Faldella, he wanted the slow occupation and thorough 'cleansing' of the territory, not just quick military victories.[17] Nonetheless, Franco agreed that the Italians could spearhead the attack on Madrid from Guadalajara, as part of an ambitious Italian plan to tighten the circle round the capital by advancing in a south westerly direction towards Alcalá de Henares, where they would meet up with Spanish troops marching north-eastwards from the Jarama, across the Madrid–Valencia road.

The attack began on 8 March and went well for the Italians at first. But their troops were badly trained and inexperienced and rain and fog turned the ground into a quagmire, which prevented the use of their aircraft and impeded the advance of their lorries and tanks. By mid-March the operation was literally bogged down in mud and confusion, allowing the Republicans to mount a counter-offensive. Despite the agreed battle-plan, Franco did not move any of his forces up from the Jarama front and twice refused the request of the Italian Commander-in-Chief that his troops be relieved by Spaniards. The battle ended in defeat for the Italians on 22 March. Franco's failure to assist them undoubtedly contributed to that result and had been calculated in political rather than exclusively military terms. Strategically, the Guadalajara débâcle made little difference to either side. Politically, however, it meant that Franco had asserted his authority *vis-à-vis* Italy, for both Italian and Nationalist consumption. He evidently considered that gain to be worth the negative propaganda value of a militarily minor defeat, especially as it was portrayed as a defeat for the Italians, not for the Nationalists.[18]

The failure of the Guadalajara offensive marked the end of a period of change discernible in Franco's military tactics. Until November 1936, the leitmotiv of his campaign had been speed, with the rapid conquest of Madrid as the prime objective. During the winter of 1936–37, the impossibility of isolating Madrid began to impose a change of tactic, and the slow, relentless erosion of the Republican defences became a necessity which was presented by Franco (for example, in his conversation with Faldella in mid-February 1937) as a deliberate choice. By the end of March this had been 'refined' further: from then onwards, Franco's war of attrition was both a military inevitability and a punishment for the Republic's resistance.

At the same time, having failed to take Madrid, Franco

needed a victory elsewhere to revitalize and reassert the military prowess which had led to his election as supreme military and political leader. The most obvious targets were the remaining northern provinces of Vizcaya, Santander, Gijón and Oviedo, cut off from the rest of the Republic in three directions by Nationalist troops and on the fourth side by the sea. Franco had decided to launch his next offensive in the north even before the battle of Guadalajara had concluded, and gave orders to that end on 23 March 1937. On 29 March, the Italian ambassador in Salamanca, Roberto Cantalupo, reported to Rome that Franco had told him how, in the wake of Guadalajara, he was aware of 'the urgent need to satisfy his Spain and to humiliate the reds. Hence the idea of making a sudden attack in the direction of Bilbao.'[19] The commanding officer of the Army of the North, General Mola, had some 40,000 men at his disposal for the campaign, including a mixed Hispano-Italian unit, the Black Arrows, created after the battle of Guadalajara. In addition, ground troops were to be supported by Italian aircraft and, most importantly, by the German Condor Legion. This was to be the first time in history that aircraft were used for ground attack, as an integral part of an operation carried out by ground and air forces.

Mola had estimated that it should take about three weeks to conquer the coastal area as far west as Santander. Even so, Mussolini was becoming impatient. Cantalupo was pessimistic about the likelihood of a rapid Nationalist victory and even thought that the Republican defence of the north might not collapse, as the Nationalists expected. He believed that it was possible to 'foresee this war of positions between the two Spains lasting a long time', unless there occurred 'the intervention of internal political factors (revolution in one of the two Spains) or external political factors (mediation or a more active form of intervention by the Powers)'.[20] In order to avoid what Cantalupo termed a situation of 'paralysis' in Spain, Italian diplomacy sought to arrive at a political solution in the Basque Country.

Towards the end of March, the Italian Consul in San Sebastian, the Marquis of Cavaletti, contacted the President of the autonomous Basque government, José Antonio Aguirre, and proposed that Italy should act as the mediator between Franco and the Basque government, in order to achieve a negotiated end to the war in the north. Aguirre was favourable to the idea, provided that Italy would guarantee the conditions once agreed. When told of Cavaletti's initiative by the Italian embassy in Salamanca, Franco reacted favourably at first, but later began to raise objections.[21]

The northern offensive began on 31 March 1937. Despite the failure of similar tactics on the Madrid front, it had been planned as another Moroccan-type, head-on attack along the first line of Republican defences, with the aim of breaking through at two points, advancing as far as the second line of defence and laying siege to Bilbao from there. In this way, the Nationalists hoped to force the Basques to surrender. After four days of unrelenting attack, including aerial bombardment of civilian targets, the Nationalists had managed to break through the Basque lines but were unable to push on as they had planned. The Nationalist leadership had underestimated the strength of Basque resistance, as they had miscalculated that of the *madrileños* (inhabitants of Madrid) four months earlier. Realizing this, Franco stepped up his arguments in favour of a slow campaign, justifying it as a political necessity. Thus, when he explained his view of the campaign, and of the war as whole, to Cantalupo on 4 April, he claimed that he was waging war slowly, in order to avoid unnecessary destruction and to consolidate the 'liberation' (which, he said, was not the same as the mere 'conquest') of one area before going on to the next. He had no intention of hurrying; that, he implied, with as much hypocrisy as lack of tact, was what foreigners wanted, not good Spaniards like himself.[22]

Franco's thinly veiled reference to a difference of opinion with his Italian and German collaborators was an understatement of the truth. In particular, the Commander of German forces in Spain, General Sperrle, and the Chief of Staff of the Condor Legion, Lieutenant Colonel von Richthofen, were becoming increasingly perplexed and irritated by Franco's reluctance to intensify the northern offensive. On 11 April General Sperrle asked Franco to send reinforcements to the northern theatre. Franco not only did not do so but, on the following day, requested

Sperrle to send any spare aircraft he might have to the Madrid front. In view of this, Paul Preston questions how fully Franco understood the German strategy.[23] In this writer's view, Franco's response showed that he understood it well enough, but behaved as though he did not in order to avoid direct confrontation with the Germans and, at the same time, to slow the war down. As a strategist, Franco wanted the local victory in the Basque Country which would help him to win total victory in the whole of Spain. As a believer in the centralized, indivisible unity of Spain, he wanted to crush *separatists* such as the Basques. As a Catholic, he wanted revenge for the Catholic Basques' 'betrayal' of the Nationalist cause. As a committed and intransigent military man, he wanted an unequivocal victory, with no conditions. Finally, as an incipient autocrat, he would not tolerate any interference, or 'mediation', wherever it came from, but especially if it came from foreigners. The week of 12–19 April provided decisive proof of the last of these considerations.

On 12 April (the day that Franco made his disconcerting request for aircraft to Sperrle), the Italian government formally approved Cavaletti's mediation project, which offered the possibility of raising Italy's profile internationally and, especially, of improving relations with Britain, whose many and lucrative economic interests in the Basque Country were eyed longingly by Italy. That same day, San Sebastian was the trysting place of a series of people whose principal concern, apart from winning the war, was the achievement of a political union 'which would have the appearance of spontaneity'.[24] The Falangist leader, Hedilla, met with a group of Alphonsine monarchists which included José María de Areilza, erstwhile right-wing parliamentary candidate for Bilbao, clandestine messenger between some of the military conspirators and nephew of the man who had propitiated the contact between Consul Cavaletti and the Basque president, Aguirre. Later that same day, and still in San Sebastian, Hedilla met with two Falangist comrades, who worked in the party's press and propaganda office there. The central theme of all these conversations was the same: 'the advisability of uniting the Falange and the Requeté and of constituting a single party'.[25]

Given that San Sebastian was then a hive of intrigue and rumour; that there were multiple connections between the parties involved; and that they had a common interest in retaining political initiative in their own, civilian hands, it seems not impossible that the Falangists and Carlists were aware of the negotiations between Cavaletti and Aguirre. Perhaps the discussions of the Falangists, Carlists and Alphonsines envisaged Italian mediation not just to end the war in the north, but to end it everywhere, and to install a new regime under Italian tutelage. The urgency which imbued the comings and goings of the party men and, particularly, the rapidity with which Franco acted in the week following the San Sebastian meetings, certainly suggest that there existed a serious potential threat to the latter's military and political plans, emanating from the political sectors of his own camp.

On 12 April, while Cavaletti prepared to arrange negotiations between Aguirre and Franco, and Hedilla discussed the spontaneous creation of a single party with Alphonsine monarchists and Falangists, Franco was taking steps to impose his full control on all political activity in the Nationalist camp. That day, he received three members of the moderate Carlist faction in Salamanca, and informed them of his intention of fusing together Falange and the Traditionalist Communion.[26] Although it is not clear whether the Falange leader was notified at the same time, the indications are that he was aware of Franco's decision, for he called an extraordinary session of the party's National Council, in order to elect a permanent party leader. Before the meeting could take place, an incident occurred between two rival factions of Falangists, in which two Falangists were killed. On 18 April, in an atmosphere of great tension, Hedilla was elected as the national chief of Falange Española, but, the same evening, Franco made a radio broadcast in which he announced the immediate fusion of the Falange and the Communión Tradicionalista. Moreover, he intended to take on himself the national leadership of the party thus created, which would be called Falange Española Tradicionalista y de las Juntas de Ofensiva Nacional Sindicalista (FET y de las JONS). Decree number 255, published in the 20 April edition of the state gazette, gave the form and force of law to what Franco had said in his speech. In addition to the merger of the two main parties, the other Rightist parties (such as Renovación Española and the CEDA) were to dissolve themselves and their members automatically be absorbed by FET y de las JONS. Franco had effected a master-stroke which rendered irrelevant plots to achieve spontaneous unity and inter-necine struggles to occupy the position of national leader. As far as the negotiations between Italy, the Basque government and the Nationalists were concerned, Franco's *coup de main* had eliminated all but himself as valid interlocutor in the anti-Republican camp.

By resisting Sperrle's request for aircraft on 11 April, Franco had caused a temporary hiatus in the progress of the northern campaign while he focused his full attention on its internal political aspect. As soon as the political problem was resolved, he released military operations from their state of suspended animation. On 18 April – the day of the unification – Franco ordered Sperrle to continue and, on the day that the decree of unification was published (20 April) the second phase of the Basque campaign began. In the space of ten days, Franco had demonstrated unequivocally that he was in complete control, militarily and politically. The point was hammered home by the arrest of Hedilla, when he refused to accept a position on the Party Political Committee (appointed on 22 April); by the conditions for negotiation communicated by the Nationalists to the Basque government via Cavaletti, which made it abundantly clear that Franco did not want a 'separate peace' but total surrender; and, finally, by the *blitzkrieg* bombardment of the Basque market town of Guernica, historic cradle of Basque nationalism, on 26 April 1937. This appalling act of terror and destruction was carried out 'by aircraft of the Condor Legion and the Italian Aviazione Legionaria under the overall command of Richthofen' who, in turn, was in regular contact with General Mola, and ultimately responsible to Franco.[27] There can be little doubt, therefore, that 'the bombing was undertaken at the request of the Nationalist high command in order to destroy Basque morale and preclude the defence of Bilbao'.[28] In all three instances – Hedilla, the Basque government, Guernica – Franco was politically responsible, but employed his by now familiar 'long-handled spoon' tactic, keeping his own hands clean by using others to impose his will.

In the ensuing weeks, the Basque and Santander fronts collapsed under the weight of the Nationalist offensive. Neighbouring Asturias fell in October. By early autumn 1937 the war in the north had ended, with a victory for the Nationalists, which was to say, for Franco. He was all the more able to claim the triumph for himself in view of the fact that General Mola, leader of the Army of the North and 'Director' of the 1936 conspiracy, was killed in an air crash on 3 June 1937. Yet again, Destiny had stepped in, removing the last of Franco's potential rivals.

While Franco's energies were focused on the military progress of the war, he devoted little attention to its political aspects. Consequently, once the northern campaign was resumed, on 20 April, the task of political reorganization came to a temporary halt. The party Statutes of FET y de las JONS were published on 4 August, but the principal consultative organism, the National Council, was not created until October of that year and did not hold its first meeting until December. The unification of parties had served its immediate purpose of cutting short independent political initiatives in the Nationalist rearguard. Once this had been achieved and the victory in the north assured, nothing mattered to Franco so much as the final victory.

This was, in fact, still many months of fighting away, but with the loss of the northern territories, the die was all but cast for the Second Republic. In part, this was due to the military superiority of the Nationalists in both *matériel* and organization, assisted as they were by massive support from Germany and Italy. This in itself gave them also the advantage of a better fighting morale than the Republicans, whose desperate defensive efforts were unable to stop the implacable advance of their adversaries. In part, too, the Republicans' weakness was political in origin. Whilst the crisis which led to the unification was brewing in the Nationalist zone, a similar struggle for internal control was under way within the Republican ranks. The Nationalist denouement came in the third week of April, and the Republican at the beginning of May, in a week of violent confrontation between communists and anarchists in

Barcelona. But whereas General Franco's rapid and decisive action resolved at a stroke the problem of order and the underlying political question, the use of force to suppress anarchists and revolutionary communists in Barcelona only exacerbated the Republic's political difficulties and thereby seriously undermined its capacity to offer united resistance to its attackers.

The spring of 1937 was a political watershed on both sides of the lines, which the Nationalists navigated successfully and the Republicans did not. To a large extent, from the summer of 1937 onwards, the war was the military confirmation of that fact. For the Republicans, it was a defensive struggle for democracy, against increasingly unfavourable odds. For the Nationalists, it was an offensive war of attrition to eradicate every last vestige of liberal democracy, in which they were winning all the way. There were, of course, exceptions. In July 1937, when the war was one year old, the Republicans briefly seemed to gain the upper hand in an offensive they launched on the Madrid front, at a village called Brunete; but the Nationalists rallied and the Republicans were unable to chalk up even a partial victory. A year later, in the summer of 1938, the Republicans again launched a desperate attack, this time in eastern Spain, in Aragón. In this campaign too – the battle of the River Ebro – the government forces had the initial advantage of surprise, but their much depleted physical and military strength made them unable to turn it to their permanent advantage and they were eventually pushed back to their original positions. Both engagements illustrate Franco's obsession with retaking lost territory, even where this was strategically unnecessary, regardless of the cost in terms of *matériel*, time and human suffering.

By then, the Republicans were deeply divided on the utility of continuing the fight. Some, including the President, Azaña, believed that it was useless to do so. Others, such as the Prime Minister, Juan Negrín, advocated struggling on, in the hope that the situation in Europe would degenerate into an open conflict with Hitler and Mussolini, and that this, in turn, would oblige the western democracies to come to the defence of the Spanish Republic. What they did not seem to perceive was that non-intervention in the Spanish conflict was part of the policy of appeasement then being followed by the western powers, or that, even if a European war began before the Spanish conflict were settled, the European democracies would be reluctant to take on extended commitments, especially if this meant running the risk – as they saw it – of assisting communism on Europe's southern flank.

In truth, as testimonies from both sides bear witness, the combatants felt that the outcome of the conflict was irreversibly decided in favour of the Nationalists in the winter of 1937–38, when Franco's forces gained control of the town of Teruel, in southern Aragón, and were thus poised to launch an offensive on Catalonia and Valencia. In preparation for the final victory which he believed would be his, Franco nominated his first cabinet in January 1938. It contained representatives of the three Armed Forces and of all the political currents supporting the Nationalist cause. The formation of a coalition government is normal political practice in a situation of war but, in the case of this first Francoist government, there were two reasons behind this choice. In the first place, a cabinet which represented no one current in particular and all sectors in general reflected and reinforced the idea of a political system in which distinct and different options had been eliminated and replaced by one single channel for political activity. This, in turn, strengthened the image which Franco wished to convey of the rising, the war and his nascent regime, as representing not individual interests, but the *national* interest.

There was also a parallel with Franco's theories of military organization. During the Spanish Civil War, he had introduced the concept of the 'mixed battalion' into his Army. This meant that, instead of being composed entirely of separate infantry, cavalry, motorized, engineering, supplies and medical units, it also contained battalions each of which had its own infantry, cavalry, motorized, etc. sections. Such battalions had the flexibility and versatility of self-sufficiency, whilst the Army as a whole lost no cohesion. On the contrary, it was more cohesive because the mixed battalion system overcame the divisive effects of the strong corporatist sense developed by units composed only of one kind of soldier. This same levelling principle had been behind the creation of the Zaragoza Military Academy and was now applied to politics. By taking representatives from various political sectors, his cabinet had the diversity which would allow his political line to adapt to different internal and external circumstances and, at the same time, he assured himself of the allegiance of all the forces present in his camp. His was not simply a negative strategy of 'divide and rule'. His purpose was not only to prevent his own partisans from uniting to oust him, but also to use the fact that there were differences between them to strengthen his own position.

The government appointed in January 1938 remained in office for the rest of the war. Its principal task was to lay the foundations for the governmental structures of post-war Spain, so that, when the end of the war should finally come, the political transition from the Republican to the Francoist state could be effected without any hiatus. The 'New State' was to be the continuation, in peace-time, of a system set up, illegally, during and thanks to a war. There was to be no pause for reflection, nor – much less – for a changeover from military to civilian rule. Thus, the war was not a no-man's-land between, and distinct from, two different regimes. It was the preparatory phase of the 'New State' and, as such, should be seen as an integral part of it. It was the bridge between democracy and dictatorship; the road along which Franco walked, in the rearguard of his armies, to attain total power.

The fighting dragged on for another year, during which time the Nationalist armies occupied Catalonia and the ever-precarious unity of the Republican political forces collapsed. When Barcelona fell to General Yagüe's troops on 26 January 1939, it was clear that the Republic could not turn the tide in its favour. By the end of February, France and Britain had recognized Franco and his cabinet as the legitimate government of Spain, and President Azaña had resigned. In spite of the hopelessness of the Republic's situation, the Prime Minister, Negrín, and the communists argued that resistance was still possible. In the first week of March, in what was effectively a coup against Negrín, a National Defence Council was created in Madrid, with the aim of negotiating an end to hostilities. Franco, however, had already shown clearly that he wanted total victory and now indicated that he would contemplate nothing short of unconditional surrender. Talks between Republican and Nationalist representatives were initiated on 23 March but were abruptly curtailed by Franco two days later. On 26 March he announced that his armies would begin their final advance and Republican forces should show the white flag on all fronts. In Madrid, the rebels' objective since July 1936, the end came on 27 March, when the chief of the Republican Army of the Centre surrendered to the leader of the Nationalist forces on the Madrid front, General Espinosa de los Monteros. In the last week of March, the remaining areas of Republican territory in the south and east of the country were taken over by the Nationalists. With Republican resistance decimated, General Franco unilaterally declared the war to be at an end. On 1 April 1939 he wrote and signed the final war bulletin: 'On this day, with the red army captive and disarmed, the Nationalist troops have attained their final military objectives. The war has ended.'

It was significant that this terse declaration spoke only of the military aspects of what had been above all a social and political conflict. It was true that Franco had achieved his 'final *military* objectives', but, as far as his social and political objectives were concerned, the military victory was simply the beginning. In those areas, as we shall see, the war was far from ended.

. . .

NOTES

1. L. Suárez Fernández, *Francisco Franco y Su Tiempo*, Madrid: Ediciones Azor 1984, vol. II, p. 52.
2. F. Escofet in D. Solar (ed.), *La Guerra Civil*, Madrid: Hostoria 16 1986, vol. 4, p. 116.
3. L. Bolín, *España. Los años vitales*, Madrid: Espasa-Calpe 1967, pp. 45, 102; F. Franco Salgado, *Mi Vida junto a Franco*, Barcelona: Editorial Planeta 1977, pp. 175–6.
4. P. Preston, *Franco*, London: Harper Collins 1993, ch. 6.
5. This is part of the theory informing E. Moradiellos, *Neutralidad benévola*, Oviedo: Pentalfa 1990; see also E. Moradiellos, 'The Origins of British Non-Intervention in the Spanish Civil War: Anglo-Spanish Relations in Early 1936', in *European History Quarterly*, Vol. 21, 1991, pp. 339–64.

6. S. Ellwood, *The Spanish Civil War*, Oxford: Basil Blackwell 1991, p. 44.
7. P. Preston, Franco, ch. 6.
8. General Cabanellas abstained. None of the contemporary accounts indicate for whom Franco cast his vote, but, since Cabanellas's was the only abstention and there is no evidence of anyone having voted for an alternative candidate, the logical conclusion is that he voted for himself.
9. A. Kindelán, *Mis cuadernos de guerra*, Barcelona: Editoria Planeta 1982, p. 109.
10. R. Garriga, *La España de Franco. Las relaciones secretas con Hitler*, Puebla, Mexico: Editorial José M. Cajica Jr. 1970, p. 73; R. Serrano Suñer, *Memorias*, Barcelona: Editorial Planeta 1977, p. 163.
11. G. Cardona, 'La batalla por Madrid', in D. Solar (ed.), *La Guerra Civil*, Madrid: Historia 16 1986, vol. 9, pp. 19–24.
12. *Boletín Oficial del Estado*, 28 September 1936.
13. L. Suárez Fernández, *FFST*, vol. II, p. 111.
14. For details of this episode, see S. Ellwood, *Spanish Fascism in the Franco Era*, p. 37 and refs.
15. M. Hedilla Larrey, *Manuel Hedilla. Testimonio*, Barcelona: Ediciones Acervo 1972, p. 414.
16. G. Cardona, loc. cit., p. 46.
17. Ibid., p. 52.
18. J. Coverdale, *La intervencíon fascista en la Guerra Civil española*, Madrid: Alianza 1979, p. 229.
19. R. Cantalupo, *Embajada en España*, Barcelona: Luis de Caralt 1951, pp. 184–5.
20. Ibid., p. 217.
21. Ibid., p. 186.
22. Ibid., pp. 191–5.
23. P. Preston, *Franco*, ch. 9.
24. M. Hedilla Larrey, *Manuel Hedilla. Testimonio*, p. 441.
25. V. Cadenas, *Actas del último Consejo Nacional de FE de las JONS*, Madrid: private edition 1975, p. 69.
26. M. García Venero, *Historia de la unificación*, Madrid: Distribuciones Madrileñas 1970, p. 189.
27. P. Preston, *Franco*, ch. 9. The best account of the bombing of Guernica is H.R. Southworth, *Guernica! Guernica! A Study of Journalism, Diplomacy, Propaganda and History*, Berkeley, Los Angeles and London: University of California Press 1977. See also A. Viñas, 'La destrución de Guernica' in A. Viñas, *Guerra, dinero, dictadura*, Barcelona: Crítica 1984.
28. P. Preston, *The Spanish Civil War*, London: Weidenfeld and Nicolson 1986, p. 142.

Chapter 5

'FRANCO'S PEACE' (1939–42)

While in some ways the Civil War of 1936–39 was a parenthesis in the course of Spanish history, it undoubtedly marked a watershed; 'before' and 'after' were clearly distinguished from each other, in people's minds and in reality. Throughout the war, *Generalísimo* Franco's insistence that he would be satisfied only with total victory and the ruthlessness with which he pursued that objective had made it clear that, if the Nationalists won, there would be no forgiving or forgetting. Three years of bloodshed and misery could not be justified if the outcome were a return to the pre-Republican status quo. Besides, although Franco later blamed Sanjurjo and others for the advent of the Republic, he himself had made no attempt to save the monarchy. It would hardly have been consistent to bring it back now. Finally, Franco simply did not want to relinquish his position. He had reached the pinnacle of his military career and held supreme political power. Someone with greater political vision might have seen the end of hostilities as the right moment to substitute civilian for military leadership. Franco, however, would not delegate because he saw himself as the only person capable of carrying out the mission of maintaining a united Spain. In his terms, this meant a country in which plurality and diversity were replaced in every sphere, especially the political, by uniformity and conformity. The imposition of this Procrustean model necessitated preventing the resurgence of the liberal democratic ideas and values which had informed the Republic and, at the same time, managing the diverse forces which composed the

Nationalist camp. Both were essential to ensure the stability of the regime. They were also closely linked, for provoking or allowing the return of Republican 'chaos' and, therefore, the disintegration of the nation, was the ultimate, awful responsibility to be pondered by putative dissenters in the Francoist camp.

Such was the message put across by Francoist propaganda in the months following the end of hostilities. In reality, it was virtually impossible for the supporters of democracy to rally. Thousands had died on the battlefields, in rearguard bombing raids and in repressive purges. Many thousands more, including the Republican government and most of the leading political figures, had fled Spain for exile in Europe, the Americas and the Soviet Union. Of those who remained, thousands were rounded up and imprisoned. Those who had been in the Republican Armed Forces during the war were automatically placed under arrest at the time of the Republican surrender in April 1936, while police, Civil Guards and Falangist agents hounded those they suspected of pro-Republican sympathies. They were often assisted by ordinary Spaniards who, having fought on the winning side, now took the law into their own hands to wreak vengeance on their fellow-citizens. A sixty-year-old woman who was made to sweep the streets of her village with a placard reading 'I am a red' pinned to her back, because her son had been an active communist prior to 1939, was a typical example of how Spaniards continued to be bitterly divided.[1]

Such acts of individual retribution, however brutal, were easily surpassed by the collective cruelty of the dictatorship's official repressive machinery. In a very real sense, post-war repression was the continuation of the war. Indeed, Franco envisaged the war largely as a matter of internal order, in which the Armed Forces played the role of policeman: 'The defence of internal peace and order constitutes the sacred mission of a nation's Armed Forces and this is the mission we have carried out.'[2] Consequently, he saw the social and political organization of post-war Spain mainly as a question of the imposition of authority. In his view, as the victors, the Nationalists had acquired the right to exercise that authority, whilst the Republicans, as the vanquished, had lost all rights and must simply obey. It was the wholesale application to civilian society of the one-way chain of command learned from the military milieu into which Franco was born. It was no coincidence that Franco always referred to the exercise of political power as '*el mando*' – 'command'.

Totally consistent with this view of the Army's responsibility for maintaining law and order was the notion that justice should be administered by soldiers in military tribunals. In November 1939, with prisons and camps brimming with political detainees, military courts were created 'to try all civilians and all Republican Army personnel charged with any crime of a military or other nature'.[3] These courts continued to function until 1943 and sentenced thousands of Spaniards to execution or imprisonment. It is impossible to say how many participated in this operation simply because they were following orders, as obedient soldiers, and how many because they shared Franco's belief that their role was that of the 'saviours' of Spain. None was ever brought to trial for war crimes. It must also be said that they were not alone in their efforts to secure the Francoist state against those it branded as 'anti-Spain'. The official party, FET y de las JONS, set up its own intelligence brigade, which acted in parallel with the secret police run from the Ministry of the Interior. The Party's tentacles reached into every nook and cranny of people's lives, leaving them little room for manoeuvre and none whatsoever for criticism of the regime. In the rural areas, every village had someone who acted as the Party boss and who, in collaboration with the Civil Guard, kept the local populace under observation. In the towns and cities, every block of flats had a Party representative, who reported to an area controller, who, in turn, was responsible to a district officer. In this way, everyone spied on everyone else, in a vast network of internal surveillance. In effect, it was the mass application of a tactic Franco was frequently to apply in the political arena: divide and rule.

The military courts, the police forces and the intelligence services were assisted in their grim work by the foresight of the regime itself. In the first year of the Civil War, whenever the Nationalists had entered a town or a village in Republican territory, they had simply ransacked official buildings and premises used by left wing-parties and trade unions. By 1937, however, with Franco in possession of supreme military and political power, they had realized that the 'New State' could make use of documentary evidence of Republican sympathies to incriminate its adversaries. Consequently, after that date, the Nationalist forces began to seize party and union records found in newly occupied territory. So thorough was this exercise in data-collection that even children who had participated in union-organized picnics and outings were listed. The documents obtained in this way were stored in an archive in Salamanca (where they remain to this day) and, after the end of the war, were constantly referred to by the military courts trying suspected Republicans. The Franco regime was able to condemn thousands of people on the strength of the Salamanca files. Franco himself admitted in the mid-1940s that there were some 26,000 political prisoners in Spain – a figure he clearly considered normal and acceptable. What dismayed him was the 'infamous' allegation that there were more. Even Himmler was shocked by the scale of the repression he saw when he visited Spain in 1940.

There were other ways, too, in which ordinary people were made to conform with the regime's desire for order and control. In order to obtain such vital things as a ration card or a job, it was necessary to be able to provide evidence of loyalty to the regime, by means of an official certificate or a letter signed by a person who was, in turn, accredited as 'approved' by the regime. In a system like this, in which people's fate did not depend on merit nor on the fulfillment of objectively defined conditions, but on the arbitrary decision of a Party official, a neighbour, a local priest or some other 'authorized' citizen, bribery and corruption were soon rife. Their inevitable companion was fear: of discovery, of failure to satisfy the demands of those in positions of authority, of hunger, of death. For the destitute, the impoverished, the sick, the hunted and the bereft, life was intolerably precarious. For the regime, the fact that it presided over a cowed, debilitated populace enhanced its ability to remain in power.

Although, as an exercise against Republican democracy, the military rising of 18 July 1936 had had the backing of all who had sympathized with the Nationalist cause, there were many who felt that the result of the war – a military dictatorship – was not what they had intended. Some of those who had supported the 1936 rising had done so in the belief that the objective was the overthrow of the Popular Front, but not of the Republic itself. Others were specifically anti-Republican, and had sided with the conspiracy in the hope that the outcome would be the return of monarchy. None had foreseen the assumption of absolute power by one of their own number. Indeed, when Franco was made head of government in September 1936, it was as much because all the other candidates had important flaws as in recognition of his merits. Acceptable to all shades of political and military opinion, as well as to the Catholic Church, fascist Italy and Nazi Germany, yet not identified exclusively with any one of them, Franco was the common denominator on which they could all agree, for as long as the war demanded that particular interests be subordinated to the overall objective of defeating the common enemy.

Once the war was over, however, the diversity of the Nationalist camp resurfaced, as each group sought to promote its own cause. Paradoxically, what was potentially a threatening situation for Franco in fact strengthened his position. First, internecine rivalries ensured that his opponents would never join forces to oust him; for that reason alone, they would be allowed to continue, though never to reach a point at which they might get out of hand and overwhelm him. In addition, those rivalries enabled him in peacetime to go on playing his wartime role of common denominator; the arbiter who remained detached from conflicts of particular interests; the provider of unity. Thus, by allowing the divisions within his camp to exist and, at the same time, constantly insinuating that, without him, pre-war 'chaos' would return, Franco succeeded in creating the belief that he was not just indispensable to political stability, he was consubstantial with it. His survival in power for over three decades was due in no small measure to the endurance of that fiction. But that, in turn, owed as much to the readiness of the Spanish conservative classes to believe it as it did to Franco's skill in propagating it. Indeed, it could be said that the secret of his success lay not so much in his ability to use to his advantage the divisions within his own forces as in his perception of conservative Spain's deep-seated desire for a leader who would restore and conserve the country's identity as a great world power.

As we have seen, the seed of the idea of Franco as the providential saviour and guardian of the 'true' Spain had been planted in his and his admirers' minds during his time as the Director of the Military Academy in Zaragoza. Nurtured by his part in the suppression of the *October revolution* in Asturias, in 1934, it took root definitively when his troops crossed the Straits of Gibraltar from Africa in August 1936, thereby saving the day for the anti-Republican insurgents. The ensuing war saw the myth consolidated militarily and politically. By the end of the conflict, Franco was seen as having triumphed, single-handed, but for occasional instances of divine intervention, over evil.

The pomp, ceremony and popular jubilation accompanying his arrival in Madrid at the end of the war were, naturally, what befitted a conquering hero. Franco was assisted in the orchestration of this propaganda exercise by a convenient coincidence of the calendar. Although the final war bulletin had been signed on 1 April 1939, Franco did not enter the capital until 18 May, which was Ascension Day that year. Mounted on a white horse, he rode into the city which had for so long defied and denied him. It was, as Preston observes, as though he were a crusading warrior, El Cid or Don John of Austria.[4] Hundreds of cheering people lined the route to catch a glimpse of the man who, like those champions of 'true', Christian Spain, had put the infidel to flight. On the following day, Franco took the salute at a victory parade which took five hours to pass the towering dais on which he stood, flanked by military officers, Party officials, Church dignitaries and government ministers. Before the parade started, General Varela pinned on the *Generalísimo*'s chest Spain's highest military award for bravery, the Saint Ferdinand Cross with Laurels. Twenty one years earlier, Franco had been denied this decoration. Now, as head of the Armed Forces, he had approved its award to himself. The climax of these celebrations was reached on 20 May, when Franco attended a Te Deum celebrated by the Primate of all Spain, Cardinal Gomá, at which Franco offered the Nationalist victory to God. Again, the dual imagery of the victorious general and the holy saviour appeared: virtually everyone wore full military or party uniform, and the steps up to the basilica of Saint Barbara were lined with people carrying the palms they had bought for Palm Sunday, six weeks earlier. The tall fronds seemed to form a guard of honour for His Excellency as he entered the church.

Although Franco's position seemed unassailable in May 1939, the state of the Spanish economy constituted a potentially disastrous hole in the dyke. When the war ended, the most pressing need was to provide food and fuel. At that time, Spain was predominantly agricultural and the interruption of normal activity during the war had resulted in serious shortages of foodstuffs. Spanish agriculture was incapable of producing any surplus; indeed, production had sunk to nineteenth-century levels. Moreover, the bankruptcy of the Spanish Treasury precluded the import of foodstuffs from abroad. The Francoist government responded with a measure appropriate to a wartime economy, issuing ration-cards for all basic necessities, such as bread, potatoes, eggs, meat and milk. Coal and petrol were also rationed. In the rural areas, people could scrape by, thanks to what they grew themselves, but, in the towns, the queues for food and fuel were endless and often unrewarded. The quality and nutritional value of what little food was available was very low, but there were few alternatives. Some of the working- and lower-middle-class people who made up the bulk of the urban populace had relatives in the villages, but transport to and from the countryside was erratic and there was always the danger that food-parcels sent in from the villages would be intercepted and confiscated. Almost immediately, a flourishing black-market in foodstuffs sprang up which allowed those with money, influence or access to scarce goods to have a slightly better standard of living at the expense of those with none of these commodities. Corruption among the Party officials who ran the system of supply and distribution of goods became one of the major sources of conflict between the senior generals and the

Party. The first decade of the Franco regime was appropriately known by people on both sides of the political divide as 'the hungry years' ('*los años del hambre*').

The regime's spokesmen and its official propaganda machine blamed the war for the inadequacies of the economy and laid responsibility for both at the door of the Republic. Franco's own approach to the problem of starvation was ludicrously naïve. According to his brother in law, Serrano Suñer, Franco appointed José Luis Arrese as Minister Secretary-General of the Party in 1940 because Arrese had come up with the idea of 'relieving the hunger problem with dolphin sandwiches'.[5] There is nothing in Serrano's testimony to suggest that Franco did not take Arrese's idea seriously. The war had, of course, done considerable damage to Spain's productive capacity, but it had not occasioned total collapse. That the economy did not show signs of recovery once hostilities had ceased had more to do with the political choices made by the Franco regime than with the economic structures themselves. Franco made clear what those choices were in a 'National Programme for Resurgence' which he personally drew up and passed to his ministers for action in October 1939. His 'Basis and directives for a Plan for economic recovery, in harmony with our national reconstruction' viewed the fundamental problem as the Spanish trade deficit, which he proposed to eliminate by massive state intervention to stimulate exports and reduce imports. This was very reminiscent of General Primo de Rivera's economic policies of the period 1923–30, with the same basis in political nationalism. In 1939, as in the 1920s, any imports that could conceivably be replaced by nationally produced goods had to be reduced to a minimum or stopped altogether, even if the result were a reduction in quality. Imported cod, for example, could be replaced by *corbina*, from the Spanish Saharan fishing grounds. It was, admitted Franco, 'of poorer quality', but it was 'usable and an excellent food for the lower classes'.[6] We may reasonably assume from Franco's portly appearance throughout the 'hungry years' that dolphin sandwiches and low-quality fish did not constitute *his* staple diet. It was not only food imports that were to be substituted in Franco's plan. Scrap metal was to be used more efficiently to eke out imported steel and scrap, and the shortage of fuel oils would be resolved by resorting to bituminous slate and lignites which, according to Franco, existed 'in fabulous quantities' in Spain. In addition, exports were to be stimulated and 'the reconstruction of Spain' would require a programme of public works, defence spending, social and cultural projects, industrial expansion and agricultural investment. Ministers were to work out what the plan would need in their respective areas of responsibility and the Ministry of Industry would subsequently devise the necessary 'practical solutions'. The plan contained no hint of tax revenues to pay for all this and made only passing reference to budgetary requirements and credit policy.

Franco's 'Plan for economic recovery' recognized that, in order to feed the population, what was most urgently needed was 'to increase the amount of land under cultivation' through 'the creation of large areas of irrigated land and the improvement of those already in existence'. As we saw in Chapter 3, the attempts made by reforming governments during the Second Republic to carry out such reform were one of the principal causes of right-wing hostility to the Republic. In 1936 the property-owning classes had given their moral and financial support to a military rising which they hoped would halt the reforming process. Consequently, the Franco regime could not institute a programme of land reform without arousing the hostility of the landowners. To do so would have threatened the stability of Franco's position and was, therefore, out of the question. On the contrary, even before the war ended, the property-owners began to reap their reward. Not only was the Republican programme of land reform halted, it was reversed. Sanctioned by the Falangist Minister of Agriculture, Fernández Cuesta, and, ultimately, by Franco, thousands of hectares expropriated during the Republic were returned to their former owners. They, by contrast, did not have to return the money they had received in compensation from the Republic. In this way, Franco bought the continued support of the property-owning élite at the expense of his own blue-print for economic recovery. More significantly, he put his own continuation in power before the needs of a starving populace.

There was a second political reason for favouring the regime's agrarian interests. Their geographical location tended to coincide with those areas in which the 1936 rising had been successful. Spanish industry, by contrast, was situated almost entirely in areas which had remained loyal to the Republic. The policy of withholding funds for investment in the reconstruction of the Basque Country, Catalonia and Asturias was a deliberate, punitive gesture, as well as a precautionary measure, lest too rapid or too successful economic recovery should lead to agitation for the political autonomy to which they had aspired – and, in the case of the Basque Country and Catalonia, enjoyed – under the Republic. For the 'national unity' which Franco considered it his mission to create could not brook anything but centralized government. In his view, the devolution of power to regional governments was tant-amount to the dismemberment of Spain. It was an aberration permitted under the rule of 'anti-Spain' which would not, could not, be tolerated by a 'truly' Spanish regime. The statutes of self-government granted to the Basque Country and Catalonia had been rescinded during the war. Now, to political and economic repression in these areas was added cultural suppression. All manifestations of their indigenous cultures were outlawed. The Catalan and Basque languages were compulsorily replaced by Castilian Spanish for all public purposes (including speech outside the home, teaching, the press, literature and drama) and the music, dancing and folk songs traditional in those regions were proscribed. It was even illegal to baptize children with names other than those which appeared in the Castilian version of the Catholic calendar of saints. This kind of repression was especially harsh in the Basque Country, for this was traditionally a strongly Catholic region and its support of the Republic had surprised many. With his deeply ingrained Catholic convictions and his belief in his role as God's warrior, Franco could not tolerate what he considered to have been a religious and moral, as well as a political, betrayal.

In a sense, repressing all that was deemed to be inimical to the regime was the 'easy' part of the task of consolidating the result of the Civil War. All it required was the moral and political will, and control of the physical means. Franco had all three. Controlling his own forces required more subtle tactics, for they could not be dismissed as 'anti-Spain' and their part in his victory and elevation gave them a claim on his gratitude and on how post-war Spain would be shaped.

Because of his debt to his followers, Franco knew that a certain free play had to be allowed within the regime, but he was determined that he alone would control its limits and what was permissible within them. During the war, he had laid the foundations of his unipersonal command. In the summer of 1939 he consolidated the edifice further. On 8 August Franco signed a law vesting in himself total power over the administration of the state. This meant that, if he chose to, he could make and unmake laws without the ratifying sanction of any legislative or judicial body. On the following day, a cabinet reshuffle was announced. The new Council of Ministers included some of Franco's closest wartime collaborators, such as Generals Yagüe, Varela and Muñoz Grandes, and his brother-in-law, Ramón Serrano Suñer, on whom Franco had come to rely very heavily for his political knowledge and skill. At the same time, mindful of the need to reward his partisans while controlling the distribution of influence, he allotted at least one ministerial position to each of the socio-political groupings in his camp. Thus, military men were appointed to five of the fourteen posts; the Falangists received three portfolios; the Carlists one; and assorted Catholic conservatives the remaining five.

The differences of opinion which characterized the regime's political 'families' were not limited to domestic issues. While all could be said to be right-wing, their sympathies were not identical where other countries were concerned. Broadly speaking, they fell into two groups: those who identified with countries where right-wing totalitarianism was in power, such as Germany, Italy or Portugal; and those who revered the kind of conservatism they most readily associated with the United Kingdom. The Falangists fell mostly into the first category, while Great Britain was the model society for those for whom monarchy was the ultimate political goal. When Franco composed his first post-war cabinet, in August 1939, he was aware that confrontation was imminent in Europe, so his choices also reflected a desire to balance these conflicts of external sympathies.[7] Eight of the new ministers were admirers of fascist Italy and/or Nazi Germany; seven were not. Franco's concern with internal equilibrium was also reflected in the occupants of what were arguably the two most important cabinet posts. It was logical enough that the Minister for the Army should be a soldier, General Varela; but the choice of another military man, Colonel Juan Beigbeder y Atienza, rather than a diplomat, as Foreign Minister gives a revealing insight into how Franco thought foreign policy should be conducted. Finally, the mix of pro-fascist and pro-democratic elements was an indication that, in international as in domestic affairs, Franco's preferred tactic was to keep all his options open until it became clear which side was going to win.

Franco's concern not to risk backing the wrong side in a European war was also reflected in Spain's official position with regard to the conflict when it finally erupted in the autumn of 1939. On 4 September, three days after Germany invaded Poland, and the day after France and Britain declared war on Germany, Spain declared itself neutral. This did not reflect a desire to be impartial, but recognition that Spain's objective economic and military weakness precluded any other option at this stage. Moreover, neutrality favoured the internal political stability which, as we noted earlier, was of prime concern to Franco. There had already been some friction with the head of the Catholic Church in Spain, Cardinal Gomá, and with General Queipo de Llano; the monarchists disliked the Falange, as did many military men; and some Falangists harboured resentment over the 1937 unification of parties. Not wishing to risk increasing instability, Franco adopted a familiar tactic: he did nothing until the panorama became clearer. In so doing, he avoided committing himself too early externally and, at the same time, remained above the fray at home.

For the first months of the war, therefore, Franco proceeded with caution as he sought ways of using the conflict to Spain's and his own advantage. On the one hand, Germany was provided with vital supplies of minerals it needed for its war industries, such as wolfram and lead, and with facilities for repairing and refuelling its submarines. At the same time, the Spanish press, rigorously controlled through the Ministry of the Interior, printed lengthy and enthusiastic reports of the prowess of the Axis armies. Indeed, successive British ambassadors Sir Maurice Peterson and Sir Samuel Hoare were convinced that German agents in Madrid virtually wrote the Spanish newspapers directly. On the other hand, while Franco was selling strategic minerals to Hitler, he was also selling them to the Allies, precisely because he did not want Spain to become the economic satellite of Germany.[8] Similarly, in the spring of 1940, he assured the French Head of State, Marshal Pétain, that Spain would remain neutral, while he also assured Ciano that although Spain was materially unable to participate in the war, he was not indifferent to it and believed in the victory of the Axis. To back up the latter statement, Franco deployed reinforcements to the Pyrenees, the Campo de Gibraltar, the Balearic Islands and Spanish Morocco in April 1940. He had a second reason for doing this, which was that he hoped thereby to put pressure on France and Germany to hand over to Spain part of French Morocco. This was, in fact, the key to Franco's foreign policy throughout the Second World War: he viewed it primarily in terms of an opportunity to realize his own expansionist aims in Morocco.

As Paul Preston's authoritative biography of Franco demonstrates, there is no real evidence to support the notion, amply diffused by Francoist propaganda after 1945, that Franco skilfully kept Spain out of the conflict. It is true that Spain's only military contribution to the fighting was the despatch of volunteers (the 'Blue Division') who fought on the Russian front as part of the German Army, and that Spain did not declare war on any country. However, this was not due to any genuine belief in pacifism; Franco, after all, believed that war was the normal human condition.[9] Nor was it in order to spare Spaniards more suffering. The adoption of nationalist policies which subordinated economic need to ideological and political dictates deprived Spaniards of many basic necessities which would otherwise have been imported. Franco wanted to take part in the war and repeatedly assured Hitler and Mussolini of his desire. The question was not 'whether' but 'when'.

Yet, in a sense, it was also 'whether', for Spain's ability to play the part of a European military power was necessarily conditioned by the parlous state of the Spanish Armed Forces and economy. Consequently, it was also dependent upon the willingness of Germany and Italy to strengthen both sufficiently to make Spanish participation worthwhile for the Axis. The Allied powers realized early on that if the strategically crucial Rock of Gibraltar were to remain accessible to them, Spain would have to be persuaded to remain neutral; and that her economic needs could be a useful bargaining chip to achieve this. For the duration of the war, British and American diplomats performed a nerve-racking balancing act, providing just enough credit and material aid (especially grain and petroleum) to prevent Franco from going over completely to the Axis, but not so much as to enable him to become strong enough to dispense with maintaining relations with them. Franco knew well what the Allied game was, but, in view of Axis reluctance to give generously, he had little alternative but to play it. For him, this meant giving master classes in duplicity in order to keep both Axis and Allies in play for as long as he needed to achieve his economic, military and, above all, territorial objectives.

By way of indication of the direction he intended to take, on 14 June 1940 Spain invaded and occupied the internationally administered Moroccan city of Tangier. On the previous day, it had been announced that Spain's status would, henceforth, be 'non-belligerent' rather than neutral. The Tangier initiative demonstrated that Spain would not interpret this as a passive state. It was followed, on 18 June, by a letter from Franco to Hitler, in which the *Caudillo*[10] indicated that he was prepared to enter the war on the Axis' side, once the latter had recognized Spain's right to a portion of territory in North Africa and had provided sufficient economic and military aid to enable the Spanish Army to be placed on a war footing.[11] Hitler must have found it difficult to believe what he was reading. He, then the most powerful and feared man in western Europe, was being pressured by someone who was the less-than-firmly-established leader of one of the poorest, weakest states in Europe; who considered Nationalist Spain had done the Axis a great favour in beating communism in the Civil War; who appeared to have forgotten the extent of

German aid in achieving that victory; who offered to contribute next to nothing to the German war effort; and who, to crown everything, expected to receive military supplies and territory in return, at best, for vague promises. By any standards, it was a tall order.

There is, however, no reason to think that Franco was anything other than sincere when he stated his terms in this way. As his biographer Suárez Fernández admits, 'Franco never cultivated the art of paradox.'[12] The *Generalísimo* was thoroughly imbued with the idea that Spain had a right to territory in North Africa. His entire professional career had been based on that premise. The fall of France, in June 1940, appeared to him to present the ideal opportunity for the redistribution of her overseas possessions. On the second point, Franco had been reliably informed by his senior generals that without an extensive programme of externally-provided rearmament, the Spanish Armed Forces would not be capable of fighting a war. What Franco failed to take into account, however, was, first, that Germany had its own designs on French Morocco; second, that Hitler did not want to provoke Free French/Allied resistance in North Africa which would oblige him to open a new military front far away from what was then his principal concern, namely the invasion of the British Isles; and, third, that Hitler was not convinced of the need or utility of Spanish military help. At most, he wanted access to Gibraltar, but not at any price. A month after he had written to Hitler, in a speech made on the fourth anniversary of the 1936 rising, Franco demanded that Gibraltar be returned to Spanish sovereignty. Hitler, however, was unmoved for he was then fully occupied with his plans to invade the British Isles.

Failing to get from Hitler the assistance he needed, Franco signed a commercial agreement with the United Kingdom and Portugal on 24 July 1940. This might have seemed odd, coming as it did less than a week after Franco's bellicose public references to Gibraltar. Such was the concern of the Allies to prevent Spain from gravitating further towards the Axis that they were prepared to swallow Franco's blatant duplicity to achieve that aim. In a manner reminiscent of his seemingly indecisive attitude first towards the Republic and later towards the anti-Republican conspiracy, Franco courted both sides throughout the summer of 1940. Thus, the radically Falangist General Yagüe was sacked as Air Minister, but Franco appointed an enthusiastically pro-Axis ambassador to Berlin; and at the same time as he accepted Allied economic aid, he wrote letters of warm support to Hitler and Mussolini, and granted Germany and Italy access to military facilities in Spain.

Allied misgivings as to what might be the real meaning of Spanish 'non-belligerence' were deepened by the way Spain appeared to be moving closer to the Axis in the autumn of 1940. Judging the moment of British surrender to be very close and believing that this would bring the war to a close, Franco sent his confidant and Minister of the Interior, Serrano Suñer, to Berlin with a letter for Hitler, in which he repeated Spanish support for the Axis cause. In fact, on the very day the letter was delivered, 17 September, Hitler postponed *sine die* the invasion of Britain. Undaunted by this or by Hitler's discouraging response, Franco wrote again on 22 September, reiterating Spanish solidarity, but also Spanish demands, as outlined in June. Again the Spanish proposals were turned down.

It might seem odd that the Minister for the Interior, rather than the Foreign Minister, Beigbeder, should be entrusted with the mission of parleying with Hitler. However, by then, Beigbeder was known to be against Spanish entry into the war and Serrano's Axis sympathies were more appropriate to dealing with Hitler and more in tune with Franco's own preferences than the anglophile leanings Beigbeder had developed. Serrano's new role as Franco's personal representative to Hitler was, at once, an indication of the direction in which Franco wanted the regime to appear to be moving, of the importance he attached to relations with the Axis, and of the confidence he placed in Serrano. This was confirmed on 17 October 1940, when Serrano replaced Beigbeder as Foreign Minister and the Falangist Demetrio Carceller took over from the anglophile Luis Alarcón de la Lastra at the Ministry of Industry and Commerce. At Serrano's suggestion, Franco assumed the Interior portfolio himself, although the Ministry was effectively run by Serrano's close collaborator, José Lorente Sanz. A further indication of the growing strength of Hispano-Axis relations came on 20 October, when the German police chief, Heinrich Himmler, arrived in Madrid for talks on police collaboration between Spain and Germany.

Important though this visit was as a political signpost, a far more decisive meeting was to follow. On 23 October 1940, with France effectively under German control and Mussolini's troops about to invade Greece, Franco and Hitler met on the Hispano-French border, at the railway station in Hendaye. Franco is said to have arrived an hour late for his appointment with the Führer. According to some versions, this was a deliberate indication of Spain's refusal to jump to attention at Hitler's least whim. For others, the delay was due to the appalling state of Spanish railways. Serrano Suñer, who accompanied Franco on the trip, denies that there was any delay: 'Good God, no!' he said, in an interview given in 1988.

> That's a ridiculous story. At that time, when Hitler was master of Europe, such discourtesy would have been more than enough to irritate him. Imagine Hitler waiting an hour! He wouldn't have waited an instant. He'd have ordered the division he had with him to advance and enter Spain via Hendaye or Vitoria, just like Napoleon did.[13]

Certainly, this seems more plausible than the story of Franco's late arrival, which was almost certainly invented later as part of the propaganda campaign to present him as the powerful statesman for whom even Adolf Hitler would wait.

At Hendaye, Franco stated personally what had already been said in his letters and through his ministers and officials: Spain was committed to helping the Axis, but could only do so when she was materially equipped for war and assured of her 'rightful' territorial claims in North Africa. Hitler could barely contain his irritation at the audacity of Franco's claims and the pomposity of his discourse, but did not lose his temper. A few days earlier, Mussolini had told him that, in his view, Spanish non-belligerency was preferable to Spanish intervention. Hitler had come to Hendaye to weigh this up for himself, not to conclude a specific agreement with Franco. Consequently, the Hispano-German 'summit' resulted in no more than a secret protocol which confirmed the Spanish intention to enter the war on the Axis' side, but allowed Franco to decide when the right moment had arrived to do so.

Perhaps to impress upon Hitler that Spanish claims on Morocco were in earnest, Tangier was incorporated as part of metropolitan Spain on 3 November 1940. In fact, this was probably counter-productive. Hitler was in no doubt as to the seriousness of Franco's aspirations in Africa, but he was increasingly disinclined to sacrifice French collaboration there and in Europe, or Germany's own expansionist plans, on the altar of Franco's imperialist ambitions.

Franco appears to have failed to grasp the broader picture of Hitler's strategy, either because of lack of vision, or of hispanocentric insularity, or both. This raises serious doubts about his qualities as a statesman. On 3 November he wrote to Hitler an effusive letter in which he heaped praise on the Axis' conduct of the war and reiterated his conviction that victory would be theirs, but insisted yet again that Spain would be able to contribute only when fully rearmed and assured of its rewards. Essentially the same arguments were presented by Serrano Suñer when he met Hitler and Ribbentrop at Berchtesgaden on 19 November; by Serrano to the German ambassador, Stohrer, on 29 November 1940 and 27 January 1941; by Franco in December 1940 and January 1941, in response to German suggestions that Germany fix the date for Spanish entry, in his meeting with Mussolini at Bordighera in February 1941 and in a further letter to Hitler, also in February 1941. Each time, the Spaniards harped on the need to resolve their economic difficulties as the only obstacle to backing verbal expressions of support for the Axis with military action. By the end of February 1941, however, Axis interest in the Spanish offer had subsided considerably: Hitler's attention was focused on the Soviet Union; Ribbentrop had instructed Stohrer to desist from his attempts to secure active Spanish participation; and Mussolini had reached the conclusion that there was nothing to be gained by pressing Spain further.

What was later presented by Francoist propaganda as a demonstration of immense political skill on Franco's part was, in fact, essentially a non-meeting of minds. Franco, together with some of his generals and ministers and the Falange, wanted to join in the war, but only in return for the prior supply of the items on a substantial shopping list. Hitler and Mussolini wanted Spanish participation, but not at any price and certainly not on the terms Franco was offering. Nor was it the case that Franco made deliberately excessive demands, in the knowledge that the Axis would be unwilling to meet them. He genuinely believed that this was the least the belligerents could do in return for the 'sacrifices' made by Spain during the Civil War. Moreover, the problems affecting Spain's Armed Forces, industries, agriculture, services and people could only be remedied with outside help. Franco was well aware of this, in spite of the imposition of autarchic principles for ideological reasons. His crab-like approach towards relations with the Axis and, in particular, towards intervention in the war, was partly dictated by internal political considerations. To hold the regime together, and maintain himself at its head, he manoeuvred not only to maximize his chances of material and territorial satisfaction, but also to avoid alienating from himself any of the factions within his regime, while, at the same time, bolstering his own hegemony by ensuring the persistence of competition between them.

As early as December 1939, angered by Franco's decision to declare Spanish neutrality in the European war, a group of radical Falangists had plotted to oust him. They had tried to involve one of Franco's comrades in arms, General Yagüe, for he was known to have strong Falangist sympathies. Informed of the conspiracy, Franco's reaction was, at first sight, surprising, but entirely in keeping with the behaviour of a man whose responses were always based on strategy, never on emotion. He summoned Yagüe to his presence and, in a well-calculated blow below Yagüe's military belt, appealed to his *esprit de corps* as a soldier and a veteran of the Moroccan campaigns. Yagüe caved in, confessing his knowledge of the Falangist conspiracy. His acceptance of Franco's 'absolution' was given in the knowledge that if he engaged in further subversive activities, it could be at the risk of his career. His political inclinations got him into trouble again in 1940, however. He was sacked from his ministerial post in June for criticizing what he saw as Franco's lack of commitment to the Axis cause. Franco reacted in this way not because Yagüe's attitude posed any real threat to his position, but because it represented indiscipline.

Astonishing though it may seem, it was during this period of external and internal tension that Franco found the time and tranquillity necessary to write a novel, which was later converted into a film script. *Raza* ('Race') portrayed the history of Spain from the Cuban 'disaster', in 1898, to the end of the Civil War, in 1939, as experienced by a provincial, middle-class, Spanish family. The 'Churruca' family was fictitious, but bore a strong resemblance to Franco's own. It was composed of a dignified and long-suffering mother, a seafaring father (who, however, did not possess the errant ways of Franco's father) and their four children, who were clearly identifiable as Francisco Franco and his siblings. At the same time, the characters embodied Franco's personal and ideological values. 'Pedro Churruca' – wayward child, self-seeking politician, defender of the Republic and bringer of pain to his mother – represented a mixture of Ramón Franco and Francisco's detestation of politicians and of the democratic ideals which inspired the Second Republic. 'Jaime' and 'Isabelita Churruca' were, like Nicolás and Pilar Franco, characters who remained in the background but, nonetheless, were exemplary Spaniards and Catholics. 'José Churruca' was the boy in whom his father saw 'either a great soldier or a saint' and the man who, as an army officer, fought heroically for the Nationalists (at the head of a unit of Legionnaires) in order to save the Fatherland from chaos and destruction. The parallel with Francisco Franco scarcely needs pointing out.

Raza was an idealized dramatization of how Franco viewed his own life and his role in history: as hero and martyr, warrior and defender of the faith. By writing this story virtually as a film script and having it turned into a film very soon afterwards, Franco made it clear that *Raza* also represented what he wanted to be the popular, mass vision of him. It was an extraordinary piece of self-propaganda, dressed up as culture and presented under the pseudonym of 'Jaime de Andrade' (a name taken from Franco's mother's family). That he should write it at all was a measure of his egocentrism. That he wrote it in the winter of 1940–41 gave an indication of the insecurity which underlay his apparent aloofness. *Raza* was a reminder to Falangists, monarchists and others of why they had fought the Civil War and what they owed to Francisco Franco.

By the beginning of 1941 it was the monarchist lobby which seemed most in need of this reminder. They were feverishly engaged in anti-Francoist conspiring, partly because many monarchists were opposed to Franco's gestures of support for Hitler and Mussolini, and partly because they resented the national and international prominence given to Serrano and the Falangists Serrano had chosen as his closest personal and professional associates. Monarchist feeling flared in January 1941, when the exiled King Alphonso XIII abdicated in favour of his eldest son, Juan. The former king's death, a month later, removed any cause for divided loyalties among Bourbon supporters, thereby strengthening the monarchical cause. Moreover, Don Juan's sympathies lay with the Allies, which contributed to making his followers in Spain believe that they could look to the Western democracies in general, and to Great Britain in particular, for support. The British Ambassador in Madrid, Sir Samuel Hoare, rapidly appreciated the potential value, for pursuing the Allied objective of Spanish neutrality, of the monarchists' increasing opposition to the Falange, Serrano Suñer and the pro-Axis policies they supported. However, there was no question of assisting them to attempt to overthrow Franco, for the Allies had no interest in destabilizing Spain politically, thereby running the risk either of German invasion or the return of a left-wing Republican regime. When the most active of the monarchist conspirators, General Aranda, claimed that he could muster a small force capable of effecting a coup against Franco, he drew no response from Britain.

Franco was fully aware of the monarchists' discontent. His comrades in arms had made their views known to him quite openly and, in any case, he could not have remained ignorant in a country so full of informers, police and intelligence services as Spain then was. He also knew that these tensions could be turned to his advantage, for their existence provided an internal 'threat' which fully justified his permanence as guarantor of the nation's stability and integrity. For Franco, the key to survival lay in keeping the pot simmering, but never allowing it to boil over. When the critical point was reached in mid-1941, he acted quickly to turn down the heat.

Franco had relied heavily on Serrano Suñer for political advice and ideas since the arrival of the latter in the Nationalist zone during the Civil War. Serrano was widely regarded as the architect of the unification of political parties in 1937 which gave the Franco regime its political and ideological framework, and Franco regularly sought and accepted Serrano's judgement when making high-level political appointments. He was virtually the only cabinet member who really had Franco's ear and, until October 1940, had been responsible, as Minister of the Interior, for such nation-wide networks of social and political control as the police forces, the press, censorship, propaganda, cinema and radio. Serrano had not been a member of the Falange prior to 1937, but he had been a close personal friend of José Antonio Primo de Rivera and, after the war, became a fervent advocate of his ideas. This made Franco uneasy. So, too, did the fact that Serrano had acquired a following of radical Falangists who, though few, were strategically situated in sectors such as the press and the trade union organization. Part of their mission was to mobilize popular support for Franco, but who was to say that Falangist purists might not mobilize it against him? Franco interpreted as threatening anything that escaped his personal control, and by May 1941 he had begun to feel that Serrano and his collaborators were doing just that.

On 5 May 1941 the appointment was announced of General Valentín Galarza Morente as Minister of the Interior. Franco had nominally held this post himself since October 1940, but, for all practical purposes, the Ministry had been run by José Lorente Sanz, one of Serrano's trusted protégés. The appointment of the monarchist Galarza was clearly designed to quell the criticism emanating from that sector of the regime by reducing the area of influence of the pro-Falangist Serrano. A second appointment confirmed Franco's concern to retain the support of the military: Captain Luis Carrero Blanco became Undersecretary to the Presidency of the Government.

Since Franco himself was head of government, this effectively made Carrero his Private Secretary. The assumption by Franco of the chairmanship of the Party Political Committee, occupied until then by Serrano, further reduced the latter's ability to influence domestic affairs.

A full cabinet reshuffle two weeks later seemed, at first sight, to be designed to appease the Falangist sector, for it included the creation of a separate Ministry of Labour (it had been covered by the Ministry of Agriculture thereto) and placed a hard-line Falangist, José Antonio Girón de Velasco, at its head. On closer examination, however, it was immediately clear that Franco did not trust the Falangists in the areas most closely related to the exercise of real power (i.e. to the control of the force of arms): all three defence Ministries were in the hands of military men well known for anti-Falangist political sympathies. Only the Foreign Ministry, still occupied by Serrano Suñer, retained its position as a pro-Falangist stronghold, for the continued dominance of the Axis in the European war advised maintaining a pro-Axis stance in external affairs.

The course followed by Franco in foreign and domestic policies in the second half of 1941 was a classic example of his use of apparently contradictory tactics to disconcert friends and foes and, thus, stay ahead of the game. Having made significant political concessions to the pro-Allied monarchist and military 'families' in the first half of the year, while repeatedly stalling on entry to the war on the side of the Axis, from June to December 1941 he showed open and sometimes vehement support for the Axis, ignoring the criticism of his senior generals and their suggestions that the time had come to consider restoring the monarchy. For Franco knew that if the pro-Allied military men had been unable to secure active Allied support for an anti-Francoist coup when negotiations with the Axis for Spanish entry were at their height, their chances of success dwindled even further after June, when Hitler invaded the Soviet Union and the focus of the war moved away from Europe's southern flank. Moreover, Franco had seen in this development an aspect he could exploit for the reinforcement of his image as deliverer of the nation from evil. On 1 July 1941 it was announced that

Spain's position was of 'moral belligerence'. Thereafter, Franco began to make a rhetorical distinction between the war against the United Kingdom and the United States, in which Spain took no part, and the war against the Soviet Union, which, in Franco's view, was a new crusade against communism, of which Nationalist Spain had already fought the first battle during her Civil War.

The internal divisions which seemingly threatened, but actually assisted, the political survival of General Franco continued into 1942. Ever-present tension between the military and the Falange, and the military and Serrano, was accompanied, in March, by fresh rumours of a monarchist conspiracy against Franco (organized by Orgaz, Kindelán and the erstwhile ambassador to Berlin, Espinosa de los Monteros), and, later, by open talk in political circles of a possible restoration. By June, relations between Franco and Serrano Suñer were very strained; as they also were between Serrano and the Minister Secretary-General of the Party, José Luis Arrese. Even Serrano was beginning to toy with the idea of a monarchist restoration, albeit under Falangist tutelage. Franco responded with characteristic duplicity, giving the advantage of his favour to all and, thus, to none. In speeches delivered by him during a four-day visit to Catalonia in January, he called for unity and solidarity; yet, at the same time, he himself kept the in-fighting going by distancing himself from Serrano while cultivating Arrese. Similarly, he assured the American ambassador, Carlton Hayes, that Spain wished to remain neutral, while allowing German submarine detector stations to be built on the south coast. In the summer of 1942, however, Franco's ability to remain *au dessus de la mêlée* was put to its most serious test yet.

In August 1942 a violent clash occurred between a small group of armed Falangists and a crowd of Carlists attending a memorial mass for the latter's war-dead. Several people were injured, of whom two later died. The incident was not reported in the press and probably would have gone no further than the arrest and trial of the Falangist aggressors, had not protests from Generals Galarza and Varela (who was present at the mass) threatened to turn it into a major governmental crisis. The prime target of their discontent was Serrano, for he had intervened with Franco in an attempt to obtain clemency for the Falangists involved in what Galarza and Varela were presenting as an attack on the Army as an institution. This time, Franco did not leave the warring factions to fight among themselves. Like a ringmaster cracking his whip to bring squabbling lions to order, his intervention was rapid and decisive, demonstrating at once that he would not tolerate insubordination and that this applied to everyone. Varela and Galarza were dismissed; the leader of the Falangist agitators was tried by court martial and shot; and Serrano Suñer was told that he would no longer occupy the post of Foreign Minister.

.   .   .

NOTES

1. Personal testimony of the woman's daughter, given to the author in Madrid, 1986.
2. F. Franco, *Discursos y mensajes del Jefe del Estado, 1955–1959*, Madrid: Dirección General de Información, Publicaciones Españolas, 1960, pp. 170–1.
3. R. Salas Larrazabal, in J. Sinova (ed.) *Historia del franquismo*, (2 vols.) Madrid: Diario 16 1985, Vol. I, p. 19
4. P. Preston, *Franco*, London: Harper Collins 1933, ch. 13.
5. H. Saña, *El franquismo sin mitos*, Barcelona: Grijalbo 1982, p. 147
6. F. Franco, 'Fundamentos y directrices de un Plan de saneamiento de nuestra economía, armónico con nuestra reconstrucción nacional', reproduced in *Historia 16*, No. 115, November 1985.
7. Ciano had warned him in July of a possible German attack on Poland; X. Tussell and G. García Queipo de Llano, *Franco y Mussolini*, Barcelona: Editorial Planeta 1985, pp. 38–9.
8. D. Smyth, 'The Moor and the Moneylender: Politics and Profits in Anglo-German Relations with Francoist Spain 1936–1940', in M-L Recker (ed.) *Von der Konkarrenz zur Rivalität: Das britische-deutsche Verhältnis in den Ländern der europaïschen Peripherie 1919–1939*, Stuttgart: 1986.
9. P. Preston, *Franco*, ch. 17.
10. The Spanish equivalent of *Duce*.
11. D. Smyth, loc. cit., p. 127.
12. Suárez Fernández, *Francisco Franco y Su Tiempo*, Madrid: Ediciones Azor 1984, vol. V, p. 270.
13. R. Serrano Suñer, in *Panorama*, No. 48, Madrid, 2 May 1988.

Chapter 6

WEATHERING THE STORM
(1943–49)

With the wisdom of hindsight, Franco's admirers later pointed to Serrano's ouster as proof of the *Caudillo*'s keen political judgement. It came, they said, because Franco could see that the Axis was going to lose the war, so he wanted to distance the Spanish regime from Germany and Italy. There is little or no evidence to support this argument. Personally, the new Foreign Minister, General Gómez Jordana, was less pro-Axis than his predecessor. Professionally, however, he was a soldier, an *africanista*, and entirely subservient to Franco. When Jordana informed Ambassador Hayes in November 1942 that an Allied landing in French North Africa would be considered an act of aggression against Spain, he was undoubtedly expressing Franco's, not his own, view.[1] After the Allied landings took place, that same month, Franco's controlled press continued to assure readers that the Axis still had the upper hand, and the Spanish Foreign Ministry drew up a plan entitled 'Bases for Political Negotiations with Germany'. Even when Hitler was forced to beat a retreat for the first time, on the Russian front at the end of December 1942, Spanish support did not waver. In January 1943 Party Secretary Arrese discussed political organization in Berlin with his German counterpart. The following month Spain and Germany signed a secret protocol in which Spain pledged to repel any Allied invasion. These were hardly signs of a significant anti-Axis shift in Spanish foreign policy.

At the same time, the Spanish regime was not actively hostile to the Allies, for it needed to obtain from them vital supplies of rubber, petroleum, cotton and wheat. Yet German setbacks did not make Franco rush to embrace the Allied cause. As he had so often done during the Civil War, he sat behind the battle lines, watching through his binoculars as the two sides fought it out. Franco's immobility in 1942–43, his smiles first to one side, then to the other, were not the sign of an astute politician, but of the conservative strategist, determined not to risk anything by an impulsive action. Unsure where to place his bet (or, indeed, whether he wished to bet), he held his hand; on the alert, but immobile.

Other observers of the international situation did not share Franco's preference for inaction. For the anti-Nazi sectors of the Spanish political class, the defeat suffered by Hitler's forces at Stalingrad in February 1943 signalled the turning point in the war and, therefore, an opportune moment for the Spanish regime to change tack. In the course of that year, they appealed to Franco on four occasions to restore the monarchy before the war ended in the defeat of the Axis. In March the heir to the throne, Don Juan de Borbón, wrote to Franco suggesting that power be transferred to him. This proposal was repeated in June, shortly before the Allied landings in Sicily, in a collective letter written to Franco by twenty-five members of the regime's socio-political élite. In August Franco was pressed by Don Juan, Generals Orgaz and Aranda, a number of prominent Carlists and a group of lieutenant-generals. A month later, after the Allied liberation of Italy, eight senior military men presented a petition inviting Franco to consider the opportunity of the moment for restoring the monarchy.

Franco politely but firmly rejected the suggestion made in Don Juan's March letter; however, he gave no direct response to the pressure brought to bear in August. His reaction to the June letter was vintage Franco: a mixture of authoritarianism and blackmail. First, he sacked those signatories who held official positions. Then, on the anniversary of the July 1936 rising, he appealed to the Captains-General for unity in view of an international masonic plot which would destroy Spain. The restoration of the monarchy, he said, would bring back the communism and anarchy which had threatened to take over the country before the Civil War. It was clever use of classic ploys: the evocation of a common external enemy and of a stark choice between Franco and the abyss. Having thus fended off three challenges to his leadership, Franco felt sufficiently confident to deal summarily with the fourth, simply picking off the signatories of the September petition one by one.

The monarchists' proposals were doomed to failure a priori because they did not take into account a number of crucial factors relating to the *Caudillo*. First, he saw himself as charged with a mission (that of maintaining peace and unity) which he could not simply renounce by an act of free will. Second, he considered himself responsible only 'before God and History' and, therefore, exonerated from accountability to mere mortals, especially when, as in this case, he considered them hierarchically inferior. Third, when Franco dispensed with the services of the pro-Axis Serrano Suñer at the end of summer 1942, it was an indication that he felt very self-confident and that, consequently, he was unlikely to yield to pressure to withdraw.[2] Finally, he and his immediate circle, including his wife, were enjoying their privileged position; like many autocrats before and after him, Franco found the exercise of absolute power addictive.

As well as miscalculating Franco's personal ambitions in 1943, the exiled Pretender and his supporters in Spain also misjudged the international situation and its implications for Spain. Encouraged by their contacts with the British government and by the latter's efforts, through Ambassador Hoare, to coax Franco away from the Axis, the monarchists believed that the Allies would actively support a change of regime in Spain. They did not seem to realize that the Allies' prime concern was the neutrality of Spain, and that any interest they might have in the nature of its political regime existed as a function of that concern. If enemy access to the western Mediterranean could be prevented with Franco as head of the Spanish state, then the Allies had no reason to want his demise. On the contrary, his direct line to Hitler and Mussolini placed him in a better position than the monarchists to deal with Axis pressure. Whereas Hitler might hesitate before invading a fellow-member of the Anti-Comintern Pact, he would be unlikely to do so if liberalism returned to Spain, aided and abetted by his enemies. Failure to take all these factors into account resulted in the monarchists' excessively optimistic view of the likelihood of an imminent restoration.

Although Franco exploited to the full his position at the head of a non-participant and strategically important European state, he knew that the war would not last for ever. If, as seemed increasingly likely after liberated Italy had declared war on Hitler's Germany in October 1943, the Allied powers were to emerge victorious, then Spain's links with the defeated Axis would count more against it than its passive 'defence' of the western approaches to the Mediterranean would count in its favour. A slow process of *rapprochement* therefore began in the autumn of 1943. Franco conducted it on his own terms, however, which meant that it was so gradual as to be barely perceptible at times, and designed to show him in the most favourable light possible. On 3 October 1943 Spain had announced its return to 'neutral' status but, in fact, continued to export wolfram to Germany and to allow German agents to operate in and from Spain. When the Allies protested, Franco distanced himself from personal involvement and promised that something would be done. But nothing was. At the end of January 1944 the United States suspended its supplies of petroleum to Spain and advocated a full embargo on exports. This was a serious threat to a country so dependent on outside supplies but, in the same way that the divisions between the Francoist 'families' strengthened Franco's own position, the *Caudillo* was now assisted by a difference of opinion among the Allied powers.

Whereas the United States was in favour of taking a tough line, Britain argued that economic aid should not be stopped. Franco was quick to exploit the lack of unity in Allied attitudes to Spain, accusing the United States of intransigence and ingratitude and stating defiantly that Spain would not curtail its aid to Germany under Allied duress. The pressure of Spain's economic difficulties ultimately forced Franco to agree, on 2 May, to a reduction in wolfram exports, but he had weathered the storm. The regime's press and propaganda machine presented the issue as a triumph for the *Caudillo*, who, according to the officially manufactured version, had preserved Spain's freedom of action by agreeing to reduce exports to Germany, but not to stop them altogether, and had made two major powers negotiate with, rather than dictate to, him. When, on 24 May, in a speech before the House of Commons, Churchill acknowledged the Allies' debt to Spain for keeping open the Straits of Gibraltar, Franco naturally interpreted this as endorsement of his regime and, therefore, another international victory.[3]

In view of waning Axis fortunes in the summer of 1944 it seemed curious that when the Spanish Foreign Minister, Jordana, died in August he was replaced by Spain's ambassador to occupied France, José Felix Lequerica Erquiza, a man of known Axis sympathies. By then, Soviet forces were advancing into central Europe and Hitler's forces were falling back all the way. On the western flank, Allied troops had landed in northern France and were rapidly approaching Paris. The writing was clearly on the wall for Hitler; indeed, Lequerica's appointment came barely two weeks after an assassination attempt on the Führer. To place foreign affairs in the hands of a man whose sympathies lay with the losing side seemed both out of character for Franco and politically inept. The explanation was two-fold. First, Franco still held out hope of a late Axis victory, believing – astonishingly – that Hitler possessed and would soon deploy secret weapons and 'cosmic rays'. Secondly, Lequerica's ambivalent political make-up chimed perfectly with Franco's duplicitous strategies at home and abroad. His pre-Civil War sympathies for the national-syndicalist JONS and his membership of Falange from 1936 onwards had made him a natural choice for the post of ambassador to Vichy. As such, he had shown unflagging support for the Axis cause. His appointment as Foreign Minister was not, therefore, likely to irritate Hitler. But Lequerica was also a monarchist, and thus acceptable to the pro-restorationists in Spain. At the same time, he was totally loyal to Franco and unlikely to seek Allied aid to bring back the monarchy. Finally, and most significantly, he was not a military man, but a lawyer and former conservative politician. His professional experience was thus appropriate to what even Franco must have realized would soon be post-war diplomacy.

The immediate task entrusted by Franco to Lequerica was to secure for the Spanish regime the approval of the western democracies without, as yet, severing its links with Nazi Germany. The tactic employed was not simply, as in the past, to cultivate each side simultaneously, but actively to stress the compatibility of the Spanish and Allied regimes, without making any explicit condemnation of the Axis. On the one hand, Franco reiterated his belief that the common enemy was communism while, on the other, he insisted that the system he had instituted in Spain was neither Nazi nor fascist, but a unique and original synthesis which transcended both fascism and anti-fascism. Despite the fact that his previous attempts to draw the western democracies away from the Soviet Union had borne no fruit, Franco wrote to Churchill on 18 October 1944 to propose an anti-Bolshevik alliance and to state his belief that Spain should take part in any post-war peace conference. That same month, a large group of anti-Francoist guerrillas entered Spain from France through the Val d'Aran, in the Pyrenees. Although the 'invasion' was rapidly repressed by the Army, it suited Franco's purposes perfectly, for he was able to use it to support his theory that communism was an ever-present threat. Soon afterwards, and before he had received a reply from Churchill, Franco gave what was his first foreign press interview as Head of State. 'Spain', he told the United Press correspondent, 'has never been fascist or Nazi, and is fully capable of participating in all the political decision-making processes of the present moment.'[4] It is difficult to decide whether this reflected cynical disregard for foreign public opinion or gross political *naïveté*. Either way, Churchill's response to Franco's October missive made very clear that the British government would not swallow the *Caudillo*'s attempt to rewrite history in his own favour. Undaunted, Franco next approached President Roosevelt, only to receive a similar rebuff. However, it was also evident from both Roosevelt's reply and from the absence of western democratic support for the Val d'Aran attempt that there would be no outside intervention in Spanish domestic politics. Thus, even if Franco did not have the explicit or active alliance he sought with the Allies, he had their acquiescence.

Franco was, therefore, unperturbed by the manifesto issued by Don Juan in Lausanne on 19 March 1945. He knew that the Pretender's words were not backed by solid political or social support from inside or outside Spain. He also knew, however, that if, as now seemed inevitable, Germany were defeated, it would be even harder for Spain to survive economic isolation than it had been hereto. As the Second World War entered what was to be its final phase, Franco therefore stepped up his efforts to court Allied favour. In April 1945, as Allied forces closed in on Hitler and Italian resistance fighters prepared to capture Mussolini, it was announced that Spain no longer maintained diplomatic relations with Japan. On 8 May (VE Day), diplomatic relations were broken off between Spain and Germany. If Franco thought that these gestures would be sufficient to change the policies towards Spain of governments whose democratic principles he despised and violated, he was shortly disabused of the notion. When the United Nations Organization was created in June 1945, Spain was debarred, thanks to a proposal made by the Mexican delegation to the effect that countries whose regimes had been assisted by anti-democratic states should be excluded from membership.

At the end of the Civil War, Mexico had taken in thousands of Republican exiles, some of whom had had a hand in the drafting of the proposal. For Franco, its acceptance by acclamation was proof that the enemies of Spain were still active and it was therefore necessary to keep a constant vigil, lest their conspiracy to destroy Spain should succeed. Yet again, he preyed upon the sensitivity of all Spaniards to the spectre of renewed civil war and upon the Right's deeply-rooted fear of democratic values, to make the idea of his own indispensibility prevail. At the same time, he – or his more perspicacious advisers – knew that the critical state of the Spanish economy would not allow Spain indefinitely to deny or defy the predominance of democratic regimes in the western world. Ideologically, he would not shift his ground; politically, however, he began to tack to the prevailing wind, giving his regime an appearance of popular, constitutional legitimacy, and gradually taking over and presenting as his own the idea of reinstating the monarchy.

The *Fuero de los Españoles* (Spaniards' Charter), drawn up in June 1945, nominally defined the rights of all Spaniards; but there were no juridical mechanisms to guarantee those rights and they were, of course, posited on acceptance of the regime. Dissent was not a fundamental right of Spaniards, nor was freedom of expression. Like the Cortes, opened in 1943, the *Fuero de los Españoles* was designed to give the appearance of a certain free-play but, in reality, always within the Procrustean confines of the Francoist system. Not surprisingly, the publication of the Charter did not sway the western democracies. The resolution adopted in June by the newly-founded United Nations was ratified by the Potsdam Conference in July.

The timing of this rejection was unfortunate for Franco, for nothing would have suited him better than to have been able to announce Spanish membership of the international winners' club on the morning of the ninth anniversary of the 18 July rising. Instead, readers of the Spanish press had to make do with the news that Franco had reformed his Council of Ministers.

The keynote of the reshuffle was the dilution of the Falangist predominance visible until then. Since there was no longer any need to make diplomatic gestures in the direction of right-wing totalitarianism, Lequerica was replaced at the Foreign Ministry by Alberto Martín Artajo y Alvárez, a man well known and much respected in Catholic circles at home and abroad. The Party Secretariat ceased to have ministerial status, but, in reality, both it and the vast bureaucracy it controlled continued to function exactly as before. The three most important ministries in terms of mass control – Interior, Justice and Labour – continued to have Falangist ministers, while the economic ministries – Treasury, Agriculture, Commerce and Industry – were to be run by men committed to state interventionism and national self-sufficiency. Thus, it was clear from the composition of the new cabinet that, while foreign policy might follow a new direction, domestic policy would not change at all. That much must also have been clear to contemporary foreign observers. Yet the western democracies held to their policy that there could be no intervention in Spanish internal affairs and that if the Spanish people wanted to be rid of Franco, they must achieve this by their own efforts alone. Even Churchill, who repeatedly acknowledged the Allies' 'debt' to Franco for his 'neutrality' during the Second World War, recognized the absurdity of this pious hope.

Franco, too, knew that as long as he kept the lid of repression screwed tightly down on the Left, his fiercest opponents would never be able to constitute a serious threat. He was also aware that constant allusions to the awful consequences of not keeping the lid screwed down would bring to heel, like so many Pavlovian dogs, those within his own camp who hankered after some form of leadership other than his. Year after year, for the next three decades, Franco harped in innumerable, interminable speeches to the National Council, to the Cortes, to the Armed Forces and to the nation, on the need for unity and solidarity around him, against the divisive forces of anti-Spain. For as long as it seemed remotely relevant, the tactic never failed; and it was easy enough to make it seem relevant in the atmosphere of international hostility of 1945. In a sense, Franco had the United Nations to thank for consolidating his regime at the end of the Second World War. Non-intervention did as much to allow him to win the peace as it had done to assist him to victory during the Civil War.

Franco refused to adopt a conciliatory attitude towards the Allies in the summer of 1945. In the first place, he despised parliamentary democracy as a system of political organization and distrusted liberalism as the root of his perennial *bêtes noires*: Freemasonry and Marxism. Moreover, since his political authority was based partly on the myth of his personal infallibility, he could not eat humble pie before the Allies without causing people to question both. That is to say, he could not admit he had made a mistake in siding with the Axis, without jeopardizing his continuation in power. His response, echoing what he had so often done on the battlefield, was first to sit tight and then to try to turn an apparently negative situation to his advantage. The first opportunity to do so was offered precisely by the Potsdam Communiqué. On 5 August he made a statement in which he said that Spain 'was not begging for a place in any international organization and would certainly not accept any such place unless it were commensurate with her historical importance, size of population and her services to peace and culture', including neutrality during the Second World War.[5]

In the autumn of 1945, Franco was sitting fairly pretty. The western democracies might have condemned his regime, but they were clearly not going to intervene to overthrow it. This, in turn, weakened both the Republicans in exile (who, in any case, were bitterly divided among themselves) and those in Spain (who, moreover, could do little to avoid the repressive clutches of the regime). Franco's own forces were similarly, if less virulently, shot through with internal rivalries and disagreements; but if confronted with a choice between the status quo and the risk of 'the reds' returning, they would all opt for the former. Finally, the three mainstays of Franco's power – the Catholic Church, the Armed Forces and the Party – were sufficiently loyal in the main to make the occasional critical voice as of one crying in the wilderness. Thus, when in September 1945 Ramón Serrano Suñer suggested that a national government be formed and Falange Española allowed to recover its pre-1937 autonomy, Franco refused. To have agreed would have meant addressing the question of a return to political pluralism, an idea which was anathema to the *Caudillo*. He would allow the existence of different ideological currents, but they must be bound by the common rules of play imposed by him.

That Franco would tolerate political diversity only as long as it offered no real competition to his hegemony was revealed by an incident which occurred in February 1946. In that month, Don Juan de Borbón moved from Lausanne to ⸱ Estoril in Portugal. Nearly 500 prominent Spanish monarchists sent him a collective letter of greeting and welcome, which was published on 13 February. Franco was beside himself. The Cortes had been opened in 1943 to ensure that 'the contrast of opinions' remained within certain limits, but this was an action far exceeding those limits. It was a demonstration of what would happen if Franco were not there to impose order. But he was; and he did. Just as he had made an example of earlier insubordinates, such as Hedilla, Varela, Galarza and Yagüe, now the monarchist Kindelán, who had been a stone in Franco's shoe since 1936, was arrested and exiled to the

Canary Islands. When Don Juan declined an invitation – which was really a summons – to go and meet Franco, the *Caudillo* broke off relations with him.

Franco was also faced with challenges on other fronts. Four days before the publication of the monarchists' letter to Don Juan, the United Nations issued a condemnation of the Franco regime, following the execution in Madrid of ten Leftists accused of anti-regime guerrilla activities. As if in defiance of the United Nations and to confirm Franco's confidence in his regime's rectitude, Cristino García, a former Republican exile who had reached the rank of lieutenant-colonel in the French resistance movement, was executed in Barcelona on 21 February 1946. In protest, France closed its southern border and proposed that the situation in Spain be discussed in the UN Security Council. The proposal foundered on British and American fears that the Soviet Union wanted, for its own purposes, to provoke another civil war in Spain and that it would seek to manipulate any Security Council debate to that end. As a compromise, on 4 March the British, French and United States governments issued a joint Note in which they expressed their rejection of the Franco regime and urged Spain to seek democratic government. But the Note also made clear that the western democracies would not intervene to bring about the change of regime they advocated.

Franco was irritated by the Tripartite Note but, ultimately, it reassured him. He could not expect the support of the Allies, but, more importantly, neither would he face active hostility. The guaranteed absence of external intervention left the regime a free hand to continue its repressive domestic policies. One by one, European doors began to close on Franco's Spain, as the closure of the French border in March was followed, in April, by the breaking of diplomatic relations with Romania, Yugoslavia and Bulgaria. Franco remained unperturbed, even satisfied. For Churchill had made his famous 'Iron Curtain' speech on 5 March, and these were countries which lay beyond that barrier. That they should sever contact with Spain strengthened its anti-communist credentials and supported Franco's theory that his regime was compatible with the western democracies. And for domestic consumption, nothing could be better than such external 'provocation'. It allowed Franco to play the nationalist card more blatantly than ever, using his public appearances to recall the horrors of the Civil War and to present himself as both martyr on the altar of Spain's liberation from communism and guarantor of the continued existence of Spain as a coherent socio-political entity. 'I am the sentry who is never relieved', he said at the opening of new rooms at the Military Museum in Madrid on 7 March 1946,[6] conveniently overlooking the fact that several unavailing attempts had been made to relieve him since 1939. In a speech to the Cortes, two months later, he referred to his regime as 'providing the authority to keep in check the Spanish tendency to "egotism and anarchy" '.[7] This was a cynical hint that, if Spain had an authoritarian regime, it was because the Spanish people were ungovernable otherwise. This line of argument was often and successfully used by the dictatorship; its absorption by many Spaniards contributed in no small measure to the duration of the regime.

So, too, did international reluctance. At the end of May 1946 a UN Subcommittee report opined that the Franco regime was 'a potential threat to international peace and security' but advised against interference from outside. The report did recommend that members be called upon to break off relations with Spain, but there were serious divisions among them about the efficacy of such measures. Thus, as Franco was strengthened by the internal divisions of his followers at home, he was assisted by the disagreements of his opponents abroad. He reacted with a mixture of self-righteous indignation and complacency, safe in the knowledge that his detractors were impotent to dislodge him and that he commanded the loyalty and obedience of large numbers of his countrymen and women. The Party could always be relied upon to orchestrate the massive demonstrations whose purpose was to cow those who doubted Franco's strength and silence allegations that the regime was not legitimated by popular support. Thus, even when, on 12 December 1946, the UN General Assembly adopted a resolution which excluded Spain from all UN bodies and recommended members to withdraw their ambassadors from Madrid, the *Generalísimo* showed no sign of being ruffled. The next day, a huge crowd gathered on the esplanade in front of the Royal Palace in Madrid, carrying placards rejecting the UN announcement. Franco appeared on the balcony to receive the acclaim of his supporters. This exercise, organized and stage-managed by the Party, was presented by the official press and propaganda machine as a spontaneous demonstration of popular backing for Franco and, by extension, as 'proof' that the Spanish regime did not need validation from outside. Besides, no economic sanctions were to be implemented; military intervention was not contemplated; and diplomatic relations were not to be totally broken off. Franco was confident that alliances could be sought elsewhere. In Argentina, for example, Juan Domingo Perón had been elected President in February, and neighbouring Portugal was still ruled by another Right-wing dictator, Antonio Oliveira de Salazar. Thanks to these two countries and the absence of UN-imposed sanctions, Spain would survive economically, albeit at the cost of enormous hardship to the populace. Moreover, there had been six votes against the resolution and thirteen abstentions. Finally, the western democracies were soon to be preoccupied by new threats. On 19 December 1946 the leader of the indigenous forces in Vietnam, Ho Chi Minh, initiated the rising against French colonial occupation, which was eventually to lead to the bloodiest and politically most crucial local war this century.

As Paul Preston writes, 'the United Nations had given [Franco] a winning hand to play, allowing him to persuade the Spanish people that he was their heroic leader in yet another foreign attempt to destroy Spain'.[8] Why did this tactic work so successfully? The persuasive power of the Francoist propaganda machine was great, particularly in the absence of alternative, uncontrolled sources of inform- ation with which to contrast official messages and put them into perspective. In a country of massive illiteracy, the emotional impact of visual images and the spoken word could give them tremendous manipulative potential. Franco was fully aware of this. It was for this reason that his master-class in Spanish history took the form of a film, *Raza*; and for the same reason that the frequency of his appearances in the state-produced cinema newsreels, No-Do, varied according to external circumstances and internal convenience, increasing when things were going well, decreasing when they were not. Even so, the propaganda which set out to promote the aggrandizement of the figure of Franco, almost to the point of beatification, could not have succeeded without fertile ground in which to plant its seeds. It was possible to present Franco as a bulwark against foreign malice because, in the course of its history, Spain *had* been invaded or its fortunes adversely affected by foreigners on many occasions. It was easy, therefore, to touch the sensitive nerve of nationalism.

Franco never took major steps when in doubt. When he was unsure of his ground, or of the outcome of an action, he waited. When he felt fully in command of the situation, he acted decisively. So it was when, in the spring of 1947, he announced that he would shortly present to the Cortes the draft of a law which would regulate the question of who would succeed him as Head of State and, equally important, when this event would take place. Significantly, the text of the Law of Succession was made public on 31 March, the eve of 'Victory Day', the anniversary of the end of the Civil War. Spain was still deeply divided by the war and the choice of its commemorative dates (such as 'Victory Day', or 18 July) for the announcement of important political decisions was a tactic frequently used by Franco, reminding people that it was the outcome of the war that had given him the power to alter the country's course as he thought fit. For Franco himself and his partisans, the deliberate coincidence of military and political milestones was a way of reaffirming their conviction of their *right* to control their country and its inhabitants. To the regime's opponents, it was a signal that they had the *power* to do so. For both, the message was unequivocal: the legitimacy of the Franco regime derived from superior military force. The means of ensuring the imposition of law and order is necessary, but not sufficient, as a basis for the exercise of power in a democracy; whereas, in a dictatorship such as Franco's, it was not only necessary, but also sufficient.

It was this approach that Spaniards were reminded of on 31 March 1947, as they listened to Franco's reedy voice on the radio, telling them that the time had come to 'confront the ultimate definition of [their] State, inseparably linked to the statute of succession in its highest echelons'.[9] In spite of the collapse of King Alphonso XIII's monarchy in 1931, the millions of Spaniards whose sympathies were Republican and the horrors of the Civil War engendered by the inability of a group of soldiers to accept those two realities, General Franco had decided that the 'ultimate definition' of the Spanish state over which he presided would thenceforth be 'kingdom'. After his speech came a reading of the text of the proposed law. Although it enshrined the idea that Spain would one day be ruled by a prince of the blood, the key concept was 'one day', for no date was specified for this event. What *was* specified was that Franco would be Head of State for as long as he lived, and that he would designate his own successor, as king or regent. In addition, Franco would appoint the members of a Council of the Realm, to which his successor would eventually be responsible, and would also designate a Council of Regency, which would take his place until a successor was chosen, in the event that the *Caudillo* died without naming one. In effect, Franco had extended his all-encompassing grip on the present to ensure control over the future as well.

Don Juan de Borbón reacted with a statement published on 7 April, in which he rejected Franco's proposals outright. A week later, he gave an interview in the same vein to the *Observer*, which was reproduced by the BBC and by the *New York Times*. The Falangists were also displeased, partly because they were opposed to the principle of monarchy, and partly because, in stating specifically that the ideological basis of the regime would be provided by an amalgam of political forces, the Law of Succession choked off their hopes of making Spain exclusively a Falangist state. Their criticism, however, was half-hearted. Former Minister Arrese presented to the Cortes some 'Notes on the Law of Succession', but they were simply by way of personal observations, not rejection of the Law. As a Falangist critic commented years later, the Falange's attitude was 'reticent and vacillating'.[10] The discontent of the monarchists and Falangists was as nothing by comparison with the rage felt by the regime's left-wing opponents. For them, this new manifestation of Franco's megalomania was coupled with the distress and humiliation of physical and political repression, degrading social, economic and working conditions, and disappointment with the policy of the western democracies. On 1 May 1947 – traditionally Labour Day for the socialist, communist and anarchist movements – the industrialized provinces of Vizcaya and Guipúzcoa (in the north of Spain) were the scene of the first widespread strike since the end of the Civil War. In spite of the difficulties of organizing and sustaining such an action in conditions of clandestinity, it continued for almost a week – an unprecedented event in the Franco regime.

The *Generalísimo* was unruffled by these indications that large sectors of the population disagreed with the way he had planned their future, for they posed no real threat to his power. Don Juan was in exile and his supporters in Spain did not have the military or political support necessary to effect a successful coup. The Falangists derived what power they had from their positions as the instruments of Francoism; they had no organizational capacity outside the framework of the regime and no international support at all. As for the anti-Francoist labour movement, it was severely restricted by its illegal and, consequently, clandestine nature, and weakened by the internal wranglings of the exiled Leftist political parties to which it was linked. In any case, the repressive methods employed by the Armed Police, the Civil Guard and the legal system itself were more than a match for unarmed industrial workers. Moreover, strike action could be counterproductive. As well as enabling the regime to identify and arrest leaders, it might be interpreted by some western governments as a sign of the communist subversion claimed by Franco, to which they were particularly sensitive in the light of their worsening relations with the Soviet Union. In terms of domestic politics, there was no one to challenge Franco's decisions, however arbitrary they might be.

Franco was therefore in defiant mood in mid-1947. The very survival of his regime 'proved' that Spain did not need the western democracies, from whose European Recovery Programme (better known as the Marshall Plan) Spain was excluded when it was launched in June. Spain had friends elsewhere: on 8 June 1947 the wife of the Argentinian dictator, Eva Perón, began an official visit to Spain, during which she was displayed as a symbol of Argentinian solidarity to crowds of Spaniards anxious for a glimpse of 'Evita'. Carmen Polo threw steely sidelong glances as her husband (dressed always in military uniform) proudly escorted the glamorous Señora de Perón on her visit. In fact, the *Generalísimo*'s unprecedented attentions to the visitor were no more, but also no less, than a lavish propaganda exercise designed as a show of political strength to conceal or shore up the underlying economic weakness and isolation of the regime.

In self-confident mood, Franco pressed ahead with his plans for the Law of Succession. The day before Eva Perón was due to arrive, on 7 June 1947, Franco read the draft to a packed Cortes. Many of the members were there in Party uniform, despite the political unfashionability of such trappings. As Franco read the introductory Preamble, followed by the text of the Law itself, they listened intently, dutifully, interrupting only to applaud. There were no questions or interjections from the floor of the Chamber, as is customary in the British House of Commons, and as had been common debating practice during the Second Republic. But, then, the Francoist idea of parliament precluded discussion and dissent, in the same way that these two concepts were excluded from every area of social and political life under Francoism. At the end of Franco's presentation, the draft was unanimously accepted by the members and Franco left the Chamber to the accompaniment of a standing ovation. The whole performance had been little more than a formality, to give an appearance of government by consensus. The outcome was, however, a foregone conclusion; at no point did there exist the slightest possibility that the Law would not be approved.

Under the terms of the 1939 Law of the Administration of the State, Franco could have promulgated the Law of Succession without previously presenting it to the Cortes. His purpose in doing so was to create the illusion that major political decisions were not taken by one man, but in a collegiate way, by the representatives of the people. The attempt to disguise the fact that the decision itself was not made in or by the Cortes, was taken a step further with the announcement that the Law of Succession would be submitted to popular consideration in a national referendum on 6 July 1947. Throughout the intervening month, the Spanish public was subject to a relentless campaign of propaganda urging them to vote in favour of the Law. Any other kind of propaganda – in favour of abstention, or rejection – was illegal, and an ordinance was even passed detailing the sanctions to be applied to those who did not vote on 7 July. Not surprisingly, with their jobs and their rations at stake, 14,145,163 people placed their cross in the 'Yes' box on the ballot papers, against 1,074,500 who voted against or returned spoiled ballot papers.[11]

The Law of Succession came into force on 18 July in 1947, a deliberate 'celebration' of the beginning of the Civil War. The regime used the fact that it had been 'approved' in a referendum to prove two apparently contradictory notions, both of which served, nevertheless, to legitimate Franco's rule. First, that the referendum demonstrated that Spain was a democracy; and, second, that the result showed that the electorate wanted Franco, the champion of anti-democracy. On the one hand, the referendum was acclaimed as 'a magnificent act without equal in the . . . history of the most worthily-titled democracies', because it had offered the people the opportunity to limit the power of 'the National Government and its eminent leadership'.[12] On the other, 'the whole of Spain ratifie[d] with its vote . . . the powers of Franco'.[13]

Why, it might still be asked, did Franco go to so much trouble to give the impression that his regime had a basis other than sheer force, when that selfsame exercise made it clear that he did not need to? Why hold a referendum, when no one could challenge the imposition of his will? Partly in order to show the world (and, perhaps, reassure himself) that 'his destiny and that of Spain [were] consubstantial and that God [had] placed him in the position which he [occupied] for great things'.[14] Partly because, in spite of his professed indifference to the outside world, it nevertheless rankled with Franco that his regime was excluded from all the most important international circles, and he knew that it would continue to be blackballed for as long as it could be accused of denying the Spanish people free choice. The solution, therefore, was to make it look as though they did have a choice, but to ensure that they chose Franco. The 1947 referendum (and the law it had considered) were a further step in the strategy adopted in 1945 to improve the appearance of the regime without altering its underlying principles.

The ploy was at least partially successful, but more by luck than by tactical acumen. In the second half of 1947 international attitudes towards Franco began to alter but this was less in response to the 'changes' he had introduced than because Spain's strategic value was enhanced by the deterioration of east–west relations. Thus, when in November 1947 a resolution was put to the United Nations General Assembly (UNGA) Committee for Political and Security Questions, calling for a reaffirmation of the December 1946 resolution, it failed to secure the two-thirds majority required for adoption. Most significantly, the United States voted against the resolution. In January 1948 the US State Department began to consider posting an Ambassador to Madrid and supplies of petroleum and military and paramilitary *matériel* began to be sent through the Standard Oil Company. In March only President Truman's veto prevented the inclusion of Spain in the list of recipients of Marshall Plan aid, after it had been approved by Congress. That same year, France reopened the border and concluded a trading agreement with its southern neighbour. Britain, too, signed a commercial agreement with Spain in May 1948.

Although these unequivocal signs of changing western attitudes were tempered by continuing British and French opposition to the re-establishment of full diplomatic and political relations, they were sufficient to give an enormous boost to Franco's confidence in himself and the rightness of his own actions. Yet there was one cloud on the horizon: Don Juan. It was not that he posed any real threat (although he was discussing collaboration with moderate socialist exiles). What bothered Franco was that Don Juan was beyond his control. Don Juan did not recognize Franco as having any authority over him and openly challenged the *Generalísimo*'s public and self-image of omnipotence. However, in January 1948 Don Juan had been advised by

American representatives to mend his fences with Franco, and in August he accepted an invitation to meet Franco on board the latter's yacht, the *Azor*. Franco's main objective was to propose that Don Juan's son, Don Juan Carlos (then ten years old) be educated in Spain. Don Juan refused, but later acquiesced when, in October, Franco presented him with a *fait accompli* by leaking news that Juan Carlos was to come to Spain to continue his schooling. The young prince arrived in November.

That same month, Spain was invited to join the International Statistical Commission, which was a UN body. It was a small but clear sign that the western democracies wished to extend an olive branch to Franco, made clearer by the fact that Britain and the United States had voted in favour. By then, the Cold War was well under way and it was strategically expedient for the western powers to ensure the permanence of a stable anti-communist regime on Europe's southern flank. It was indicative of Franco's childishly egocentric view of politics that he now chose to ignore Allied overtures. In 1946, they had rejected his regime; now, when it could be of use to them, he was going to make sure that any cooperation was given on his terms and in his good time. Thus, although Franco's own Minister of Industry and Commerce told him in early 1949 that, without more foreign aid, the Spanish economy could survive for six months at most, the *Caudillo* insisted that Spain had no need of the international community. In the same way that, in 1941, he had been convinced that Hitler was in his debt for services rendered in the struggle against communism, Franco now believed the western powers owed it to him to recognize that he had been right all along. That being the case, it was not appropriate to seek admission to the United Nations or to NATO (the latter created in 1949); it should be offered to him as of right. When, in May 1949, a UN resolution recommending the re-establishment of full diplomatic relations with Spain fell only four votes short of achieving the requisite two-thirds majority, Franco interpreted this as vindicating his stance. And when, at the beginning of 1950, US Secretary of State Acheson conceded that the United States would now vote in favour of the return of UN members' Ambassadors to Spain, Franco knew that the thaw had begun.

However, there was still a long way to go for Spain to be fully integrated into the world concert of nations; indeed, this was not possible while Franco lived. But Spain would never again be as politically and economically isolated as it had been between 1945 and 1950. This in itself was to be a major factor in Franco's permanence in power in the years to come. Having survived the domestic and international challenges of the 1940s, Franco ended his first decade of post-Civil War power firmly established at what he liked to call the helm of the ship of state. His mood of self-satisfaction was far from justified in terms of social and economic realities, but even these were to be turned into personal triumphs for Franco in the course of the next two decades. It was ironic indeed (although, of course, no one mentioned it) that, having risen to power by lambasting the liberal democracies as 'anti-Spain', Franco's permanence from the 1950s onwards owed a great deal to the political and economic capital invested in Spain by those same nations.

. . .

NOTES

1. P. Preston, *Franco*, London: Harper Collins 1993, ch. 18.
2. Cf. R. Garriga, *Franco-Serrano Suñer. Un drama político*, Barcelona: Editorial Planeta 1986, p. 115.
3. Churchill was speaking two weeks before the Allied landings in Normandy on 6 June 1944 (D Day). Although the balance of the war had shifted considerably against the Axis since Jordana's warning about how Spain would interpret an Allied landing in North Africa (see above, p. 133), the Allies still viewed continued Spanish neutrality as vital to their success.
4. Quoted in J. Sinova (ed.), *Historia del franquismo*, (2 vols), Madrid: Diario 16 1985, Vol I, p. 93.
5. P. Preston, *Franco*, ch. 21.
6. Quoted in P. Preston, *Franco*, ch. 21.
7. Ibid., ch. 21.
8. Ibid., ch. 21.
9. *Arriba*, 1 April 1947. L. Suárez Fernández, *Françisco Franco y Su Tiempo*, Madrid: Ediciones Azor 1984, vol. IV, pp. 163–4; F. Franco, *Franco ha dicho, 1er apéndice*, Madrid: Ediciones Voz 1949, p. 242 dates Franco's radio broadcast as 30 March 1947.

10. J.M. Martínez Val, *¿Por qué no fué posible la Falange?*, Barcelona: Dopesa 1975, p.95.
11. *Arriba*, 27 July 1947. Cf. Preston, in *Historia 16*, No. XXIV, December 1982, who gives a total of 3,033,649 negative votes, spoiled ballots and abstentions.
12. *Arriba*, 10 June 1947.
13. *Arriba*, 8 July 1947.
14. Kindelán to Don Juan about the result of the referendum, quoted in P. Preston, *Franco*, ch. 22.

Chapter 7

THE 'SENTRY OF THE WEST' (1950–60)

Franco seemed to be riding on the crest of the wave as he entered the second decade of his rule – his 'magistracy' as he called it in his own grandiloquent language. At home, he had quelled the murmurings of those who wanted a clear sign of what the regime's institutional future was to be, without committing himself to a date for the return of a monarch to the leadership of the state, and without specifying who his successor would be. Abroad, gestures such as the dilution of the pre-1945 Falangist predominance and the 1947 referendum had achieved a certain relaxation in the hard line adopted by the members of the United Nations. Looking back over the first decade of his regime, in a radio broadcast made to mark the tenth anniversary of the end of the Civil War, Franco crowed,

> What other Regime would have resisted the very serious situations which the Nation has had to confront in these thirteen [*sic*] years? Thanks to [the regime] we were victorious in our war, we escaped another, we resisted the most serious international conspiracy ever recorded and we have overcome with minimum destruction the economic difficulties of two wars, the unending neglect to which our predecessors subjected our economy, and a terrible drought which has put the production and the resilience of our Fatherland to the test in this period.[1]

In fact, the material foundations of Franco's regime were far from secure. By the end of the 1940s, Spain was on the verge of a major economic crisis, because the country's infrastructure was incapable of sustaining the programme of self-sufficiency adopted for political reasons in 1939. At the end of the Civil War, and during the Second World War, it was relatively easy to persuade people that shortages of food, clothing, fuel and manufactured goods were due, first, to the destruction wrought by the 'reds' and, subsequently, to the difficulties resulting from international conflict. When the situation scarcely improved after 1945, Franco resorted to his theory of the international 'judeo-masonic–communist' conspiracy by way of explanation.

Franco's refusal to recognize that autarchy was economically and politically untenable was due partly to his belief that liberal democracy could not bring economic well-being, and partly to his lack of understanding of the complexities of economic policy-formulation. For both reasons, he resisted attempts to reinsert Spain fully into the international capitalist system until forced to do so by the prospect of a return to wartime rationing. His inability to grasp the intricacies of modern economics was due in large measure to limits of intellect and lack of appropriate training (although, as we have noted in Chapter 5, this did not prevent him from drafting, in 1939, his 'National Programme for Resurgence'). His ignorance was compounded by the fact that, in theory and in practice, the subject was becoming objectively more complicated. Indeed, the same was true of every sphere of human activity, including politics. In the course of the 1950s, the first signs appeared that the tactics used by Franco since 1936 to stay in power – repression, appeals for unity, apocalyptic visions of Republican 'chaos', and himself as arbiter among fractious regime forces – were less effective than they had previously been.

True to his dislike of sudden change (or, indeed, of any change which implied modernization) Franco altered the direction of his economic and foreign policies only cautiously. It was not until the second half of the 1950s that autarchy was definitively superseded by a firm commitment to international capitalism. Nevertheless, change was imminent from the start of the decade, powered by the twin motors of Spanish economic need and the military interest of the United States. There was no question of generalized armed conflict at this stage, but the rivalry between the two 'superpowers' meant that the struggle for domination did not cease. In June 1950 communist North Korea invaded South Korea. This war, the continuing conflict in Vietnam and successive wars in Africa, the Middle East and Central and South America were the flashpoints of the constant process of east–west confrontation which characterized international politics as the second half of the twentieth century opened.

It was in the context of this struggle for control that the western world, with the United States at its head, decided to readmit Francoist Spain to its circle. From a military point of view, the strategic importance of the Iberian Peninsula was evident simply from looking at a map. Situated between the Mediterranean and the Atlantic, and midway between the African and European continents, it was at the centre of a crucial communications crossroads. During the Second World War, in order to maintain Allied access to the Mediterranean, it had been enough to ensure Spain's neutrality. But the Soviet Union in the 1950s was an even more formidable adversary than Hitler's Germany had been. It was therefore thought necessary to take steps not only to secure the defence of the Iberian Peninsula, but also to give it the ability to assume an offensive role if necessary. From an ideological point of view, the anti-democratic nature of the Spanish regime became less significant once communism had replaced fascism as the perceived principal threat to world peace. There was no need to convince the Spanish regime of the alleged danger of communist take-over: the Spanish Nationalists had fought a war on precisely that platform between 1936 and 1939. Consequently, although Franco's offer of sending troops to fight in Korea, as part of a new 'crusade' against communism, was not taken up, there were lobbies in the United States and in Britain which were in favour of re-establishing full relations with Spain. At the same time, Portugal advocated the admission of Spain to NATO – a possibility to which Franco responded, in characteristically hispanocentric fashion, by deeming that the return of Gibraltar to Spanish sovereignty should be the quid pro quo of Spanish membership of NATO.[2] As he had done with the Axis in 1940 and the Allies in 1945, Franco considered that the foreign powers were in his debt and, therefore, that he, not they, should lay down the terms of Spanish cooperation.

His position seemed fully vindicated when, on 4 November 1950, the UN General Assembly voted by thirty-eight to ten (with twelve abstentions) effectively to withdraw the condemnation issued in 1946 by authorizing members to reinstate their Ambassadors to Madrid. Franco interpreted this move, not as a gesture of diplomatic expediency, but as a demonstration of western approval. Considering the moment propitious to pursue the Spanish claim to Gibraltar, he and Carrero Blanco mounted a press and radio campaign for the return of the Rock. At the end of 1950, the co-author of a book advancing Spanish claims to various overseas territories, including Gibraltar, Fernando María Castiella, was appointed as Spanish Ambassador to London. This, however, proved to be too provocative a move: Castiella was refused *agrément* and was therefore unable to take up the London posting. In February 1951, a huge rally in support of Spanish sovereignty over Gibraltar was staged in Barcelona, and Franco declared 4 August 'Gibraltar Day'.[3]

The United States showed no sign of wishing to intervene in Spain's quarrel with Britain over Gibraltar, but was not deterred from seeking closer relations with Spain. In November 1950 fact-finding missions from the Finance Committees of the US Senate and Congress travelled to Spain and a loan of $62.5 million was subsequently authorized. Then, on 27 December, the appointment was announced of Stanton Griffis as US ambassador to Madrid. For Franco, this was perfect timing for his end-of-year speech. In a highly self-congratulatory address, he pointed to 'the solemn international rectification of the United Nations agreement' and affirmed that 'the world, disabused of its false delusions, turns its eyes to our Fatherland, in the conviction that, above all, right accompanied Spain'. Nonetheless, he condemned that same deluded world for its previous exclusion of Spain from the European Recovery Programme, thereby exacerbating the effects of a long period of exceptionally low rainfall. 'If we have been unable to give Spain greater well-being', he said, 'let it be very clear that this has been due to foreign incomprehension.' Yet, against all odds, he continued, 'we have managed to take a gigantic step forward', and proceeded to enumerate the regime's achievements in grandiose – and extremely vague – terms. 'What Spanish regime', he enquired rhetorically, 'at any time, has been more productive in carrying out its tasks and has created for the Nation, in any respect, wealth comparable to that created up to now?'[4] Not everyone agreed with Franco's triumphant assessment. The spring of 1951 saw a boycott of public transport and a general strike in Barcelona, and a strike in the mining, ship-building and steel sectors of the Basque Country. If the concern Franco had expressed for the living and working conditions of the Asturian miners in 1917 had been sincere, it was long forgotten by 1951. Viewing the protests against low wages and high prices as the work of foreign communist agitators, he ordered heavy police repression.

Despite this indication that Franco had not changed the political principles on which his regime had been established in 1939, the US military establishment pressed ahead with its plans, on the one hand to secure bases in Spain and, on the other, to help Spain become militarily capable of joining NATO. In July 1951 the US Chief of Naval Operations, Admiral Sherman, began what would be protracted negotiations for the concession of air and naval facilities on the Spanish mainland. Franco responded as he had done with Hitler, presenting a shopping list and saying that the provision of the items on it (which ranged from aircraft to foodstuffs) was a prerequisite for Spanish cooperation. Unlike Hitler, however, the Americans were anxious for Franco's consent and found him a reasonable interlocutor. Admiral Sherman promised that Congress would be asked to approve a line of credit for Spain and, that summer, had economic and military delegations sent to the Peninsula to study the details of what Franco required. As had happened with the return of the Ambassadors, Franco had seemingly got what he wanted without altering his position. Certainly, this was the way he needed to present it for domestic consumption, for this new alliance and the concession of territory for military use by a foreign power scarcely seemed consistent with the many hours and column inches he had devoted to demonizing the western democracies and to denouncing the British 'occupation' of Gibraltar.

A new cabinet, announced on 19 July 1951, indicated that modifications to domestic policies could be expected to parallel the shift already apparent in external affairs. The economy was clearly at the centre of the *Caudillo*'s attention, and the accent was more on the practical qualifications of appointees than on ideological affiliations. It was the beginning of a move away from the belief that 'faith is more important than competence'.[5] For the first time since the Civil War, Industry and Commerce were not lumped together, but each given a separate ministry. The new Minister for Industry was José Planell Riera, then Vice-President of the state holding company, the National Institute for Industry. Manuel Arburúa, appointed as Minister for Commerce, had, until then, been Under-Secretary at the combined Ministry for Commerce and Industry and was, by profession, an economist specializing in financial and monetary policy. Agriculture, too, felt the wind of change, with an agronomist, Rafael Cavestany, taking the ministerial place of the Falangist Carlos Reín. Curiously, the man appointed head of the Treasury, Francisco Gómez de Llano, came from a different mould, being a lawyer and one-time civil servant under the dictatorship of General Primo de Rivera. This was perhaps a conservative precaution on Franco's part, and a reminder that, when it came to the nation's purse-strings, there would not yet be any hint of relaxation or liberalism.

Ever mindful of the utility of involving all the regime's political 'families' in the business of government, Franco distributed amongst them the remaining posts in his 1951 cabinet. In this way, he pre-empted possible rebellions on grounds of exclusion and fuelled the common interest of his diverse partisans in keeping the regime alive and himself in power. Yet, without altering the basic components of the mix, it was possible to detect a shift in the nuances. Old-style Falangists occupied the ministries associated with social and political control (Interior, Army, Labour and the Party Secretariat), but portfolios connected with the external image of the regime and the assurance of its future (such as Justice, Foreign Affairs, Education and Public Works) were assigned to men guided less by rigid ideological concepts than by their awareness that the world had changed since 1945 and that Spain needed to adapt if it was to be counted among the leading nations in the post-war world.

What was to prove the most far-reaching of the changes introduced in the July 1951 cabinet was the elevation to ministerial rank of Admiral Carrero Blanco's position as director of the office of the head of government; and the one which best exemplified the combination of new and old, change and ossification, was the creation of a Ministry of Information and Tourism. Had they been in vogue in 1951, the words *perestroika* and *glasnost* might have been used by observers. The substitution of the term 'information' for the old 'press and propaganda', and its promotion to ministerial level seemed to indicate a more wide-ranging approach to questions of what the general public might know and think of the regime; while the allocation of official attention to tourism suggested that, by contrast with the days of autarchy and isolationism, foreigners were henceforth to be encouraged to come to Spain. At the same time, however, the man appointed as Minister, Gabriel Arias Salgado, was a rigid Catholic and well known for the fanatical campaigns against sin and temptation in literature, cinema and theatre that he had master-minded from the Department of Popular Education in the 1940s. One of his more absurd measures had been to oblige chorus girls to appear on stage in knickerbockers which reached to their knees. The choice of this unyielding, deeply religious man for this particular post was a sharp reminder that, when it came to how Spaniards viewed their own country and the outside world, and to how outsiders would see Spain, their opinions would still be shaped from above according to the scale of values which had informed the Franco regime from the start.

The simultaneous process of relaxing autarchy and *rapprochement* with the western democracies moved very slowly in the first half of the 1950s. A more adventurous statesman, or one less determined to hang on to power, might have acted more quickly or taken more radical steps to achieve the same goal. Franco, however, did not fit that mould. He had not acted on impulse since his time as a young captain in Morocco, anxious to make his mark in an institution which deliberately massified people and sub-jugated their individuality. By 1936 he had consolidated his professional reputation; by 1939 he had established his political hegemony; and by 1949 he had survived ten years of internal and external difficulties. Moreover, Franco disliked change. It is not surprising, therefore, that not only did he consider that he alone would set the pace, but also that the pace he chose to set was that of a dilatory gastropod.

Franco's instinctive preference for slowness was strength-ened by signs that movement towards abandoning the well-worn paths of hispanocentric tradition would meet with fierce opposition from certain quarters. In February 1952 an attempt was made to burn down an Evangelical church in Seville, and Cardinal Segura published a virulently anti-Protestant pastoral letter, in which he effectively accused Franco of betraying the sacred identity of Spain as a Catholic nation. It was a delicate moment for Franco, who had so closely linked the legitimacy of his power to his presentation of himself as the defender of the Catholic faith. His immediate response was to stonewall. Later, he used the opening of the Cortes, on 17 May 1952, and the International Eucharistic Congress, held in Barcelona in June, to indicate that nothing essential had changed. The quasi-religious ceremonial which surrounded Franco's attendance at both events served both to sacralize power and to secularize religion, making the two indivisible in the person of Francisco Franco.[6] In purely pragmatic terms, such identification with Catholicism was a way of currying favour with the Vatican and with the influential Catholic lobby in the United States. For, by mid-1952, Franco had decided that Spain's international standing and his own personal prestige would be enhanced by concluding a bilateral agreement with the United States and a concordat with the Vatican. He secured both in 1953.

After months of negotiation, the agreement with the United States was signed on 26 September 1953. Known as the *Pacts of Madrid*, the two-part treaty was essentially military in character, but also contained economic and cultural provisions. Spain was to allow the United States to construct three Airforce bases (at Zaragoza, Torrejón de Ardoz, outside Madrid, and Morón de la Frontera, in

Andalusia) and a naval base (at Rota, near Cadiz). In exchange, the United States would pay a certain sum annually in the form of development-aid grants and would provide the Spanish Armed Forces with *matériel*. In addition, the two countries signed an agreement of mutual defence. The significance of this event was threefold. First, it meant that the Franco regime had the approval and protection of the most powerful nation in the world. Secondly, the Spanish economy was to receive a much-needed shot in the arm (in the first instance, some 200 million dollars-worth of military and technological assistance). Thirdly, the willingness of the United States to become militarily and economically involved in Spain gave North American and European financiers and businessmen the reassurance they needed to invest private capital there. The fact that Spain was not a democracy had warranted a UN condemnation in 1946. Now, less than ten years later, a blind eye was turned to this 'circumstance', for it was offset by the market potential of Spain, which offered plentiful labour at cheap prices and some thirty million consumers-in-the-making. Moreover, strikes were illegal, wages were controlled by the state and people were anxious to improve their standard of living after so many years of rationing and privation.[7] To the owners of foreign capital, the Franco regime no longer seemed a political embarrassment, but the guarantor of the political and social stability which would enhance their chances of making profits in Spain.

The international campaign against communism had a natural ally in the Catholic Church. Negotiations for a concordat had been going on between Spain and the Vatican for about the same length of time as those between Spain and the United States. When Franco made his cabinet changes in July 1951, his first choice for Minister of Education had been the Falangist turned Christian Democrat, Fernando María Castiella. However, he had refused the appointment. Surprisingly, Franco did not make an example of him as he had done in previous such instances of 'insubordination', but appointed him as Ambassador to the Holy See. As such, his principal task was to secure the concordat, which was signed at the end of August 1953. In practical terms, the concordat was not so important as the Hispano-US agreement. However, as a sign of international approval, Franco probably viewed it as more significant, for it was more of a personal triumph, bolstering his image as God's emissary. To the man who had declared himself 'responsible before God', but not before his fellow citizens, the conclusion of an agreement with God's earthly representative had an elevated significance. From the standpoint of more worldly considerations, the signing of the concordat soothed the irritation of those Catholics who did not like the trend towards closer relations with what they saw as Protestant – that is, heretic – America (although they must also have recognized that the Catholic political and economic lobby in the United States was large, rich and influential).

Franco's propagandists spared no efforts to demonstrate that the international community had at last recognized the rightness of his principles, or to extol what they called the enormous political skill of the man who had foreseen the Cold War years before it became reality. One of Franco's most fervent supporters, Luis Galinsoga, editor of the Barcelona daily, *La Vanguardia*, lauded the *Generalísimo* as the 'sentry of the west' and the 'guardian of the European spiritual fortress' – a description which undoubtedly fitted perfectly Franco's own image of himself and his role in Spanish and world politics.[8] The enthusiasm of official propaganda derived partly from the triumphalism inherent in a regime which had come into being by dint of a military victory, and partly from the need to conceal, or divert attention away from domestic problems. As we noted earlier, one of the reasons why Franco ultimately revised his former anti-western attitudes was that the crisis of economic autarchy left him little choice. The Spanish economy desperately needed external aid and, in order to get it, economic policy-makers had to accept the prescriptions of their benefactors as to how the economy should be organized. In the first place, the Pentagon had partial control over how the funds granted under the terms of the Pacts of Madrid were to be spent. Secondly, private investors had their own ideas about where they wanted to place their capital, which did not always or necessarily coincide with those of the Spanish regime. Consequently, while the method chosen to resolve the economic crisis brought political as well as economic benefits, it also involved the risk of setting up other political and economic tensions which might ultimately defeat the object of the exercise: the consolidation and continuation of the Franco regime.

It is difficult to decide whether the 'loosening [of] the unity under siege of the period 1945–53'[9] which followed the concordat and the Pacts of Madrid was a deliberate continuation by Franco of the controlled internal jockeying he had presided over since 1936, or a sign that he was being gradually overtaken by the speed of events. The traditional political 'families' still vied with each other in pursuance of their particular objectives; but the old clans of Catholics, monarchists and Falangists were now joined by a new breed of apolitical technocrat and a new kind of Falangist. This is not to say that they were anti-Francoist. On the contrary, their objective was not to overthrow the Franco regime but to adapt it to meet the demands of what promised to be a more international future. This idea was expressed by an article published in one of the newspapers of the official students' union, the Sindicato Español Universitario (SEU) in 1952:

> The Spanish regime born of the rising of 18 July 1936 has been consolidated, enjoys an indisputable prestige and has achieved, for the first time in centuries, an independent political line for the Spanish people . . . The figure of Francisco Franco and his political talent, like his military talent before, have made possible a situation in which we may look to the future with optimism. Precisely for that reason, it is urgently necessary to consolidate the present and make definitively sure of the future.[10]

Nevertheless, the people who voiced such sentiments were 'less bewitched by the magic of the *Caudillo*' than the previous generation of regime supporters.[11] They had no direct experience of the Second Republic or the Civil War and so were less fearful of the consequences of change. Indeed, having grown up with the privations of autarchy, they could see the potential benefits of inclusion in the international capitalist system.

In the monarchist camp, too, new ideas were being developed. In September 1953 a group of Don Juan's more liberal partisans, of whom the most prominent was the intellectual and journalist, Rafael Calvo Serer, began to propound the idea of a 'social monarchy' as an alternative to Franco, and themselves as a 'third force', in opposition both to the Falange and the Catholic conservatives. The liberal ideas of this group, and the fact that several of its members were known or alleged to belong to the secretive Catholic brotherhood, Opus Dei, made them anathema to the 'old shirt' Falangists and the Catholic integrists.

From the second half of the 1960s, the aims of these new sectors and the tensions between them and the Francoist old guard would contribute to the build-up of pressure for democracy which characterized the last decade of Franco's life. At the beginning of the 1950s, they were merely emergent and posed no threat to Franco, who was concerned to defuse two more immediate potential sources of internal unrest. The first was the ultra-nationalist core of his political support, which might react badly to the suggestion that the Fatherland was being 'sold' to foreigners – and liberal democratic foreigners at that. The second was the large and influential agrarian component in the regime's social, economic and political fabric, which was liable to feel unjustly treated if the regime abandoned it in favour of the programme of liberalization and industrialization recommended by the representatives of foreign capital. The opposition to change of these two sectors, whose views, moreover, reflected Franco's own social and political sympathies, strengthened his instinctive disinclination to make substantive policy modifications.

To soothe the nationalists, Franco resorted yet again to the rituals of Falangism to remind everyone what were the constants of his power. He authorized the organization of the first (and, tellingly, only) National Congress of FET y de las JONS in Madrid, on 29 October 1953, the twentieth anniversary of the foundation of Falange. This gesture also served to indicate that he was still in charge, for the event was held in the face of opposition from other sectors of the regime, who considered it 'madness to give this sensation of revitalization of the Falange'.[12]

To retain the support of the landowners, the regime continued throughout the 1950s to channel state funds into the agricultural sector and to support it with protectionist policies which merely sustained inefficiency and low productivity. Landowners' profits were protected by keeping rural wages down and by paying artificial, guaranteed prices for crops. Little was done to resolve the age-old problem of land-distribution. The large, powerful estate owners in Castile and Andalusia continued to exercise the social and economic power they had enjoyed for centuries, based on their monopoly holding of the principal economic resources. An attempt was made to improve the situation of those, especially in the Northern provinces, who were afflicted by the extreme smallness and dispersion of their holdings, but the administrative and social problems involved in applying the Law of Land Concentration proved insurmountable in many cases, particularly given the lack of political will to tackle them. In his message to the nation of 31 December 1950, Franco admitted that 'the rhythm of resettlement is still a long way below our ambitions', but immediately excused this by saying that a sector so vital as agriculture would be damaged by 'erroneous or precipitate reform'. The overall result of proceeding with such respect for the status quo in the countryside was the decline of agricultural production, the progressive deterioration of the social conditions of small farmers and farm labourers, and the gradual depopulation of the rural areas. The massive exodus of the rural populace to towns in Spain or abroad, which began in earnest towards the end of the 1950s, bore witness to the priority given, in the Francoist scale of values, to preserving the patrimony of the strong, rather than to caring for the welfare of the weak.

Part of Franco's concern, in assuring himself of the backing of his staunchest allies, stemmed from the resurgence in support for Don Juan visible in the 1950s. In October 1954 the coming-out of Don Juan's eldest daughter, the Infanta Pilar, occasioned a massive wave of congratulatory messages to the royal family, from hundreds of Spaniards of all social conditions. Alarmed by this sign of the strength of popular monarchist feeling, Franco's political adviser, Carrero Blanco, assured the *Caudillo* that it was all the work of Freemasons – an explanation Franco readily accepted. Nonetheless, in order to accommodate the monarchist lobby, when the first local government elections since the Civil War were held, in Madrid, in November 1954, Franco allowed a group of monarchists to stand as candidates alongside the official list. The election was to choose one-third of the members of the city council. The impression of democratization thus given was, in fact, dispelled by the restrictive nature of the suffrage, which was limited to heads of households and married women. This was a telling comment on Francoism's concept of 'normality' and, particularly, on its view of the intellectual and political capacity of women: men who were not the head of the household in which they lived and all unmarried women were disenfranchized, even if they had reached the age of majority. This hit the potential female electorate particularly hard, since the Civil War had frustrated the possibility of marriage for many women.

As was to be expected, the official candidates won. Franco and his henchmen had undoubtedly allowed the monarchists to stand in the hope that they would be discredited by defeat. In fact, their campaign and the probably well-founded suspicion that the result had been rigged had the opposite effect. In order to damp down monarchist hopes that it might now be possible to pressure him into resigning, Franco wrote to Don Juan on 2 December 1954, telling him that power would not be transferred in Franco's lifetime and that his successor would be bound by the guiding principles of the regime set up in 1939. Four weeks later, the two men met on the country estate of the Conde de la Ruiseñada, Don Juan's representative in Spain. Don Juan asserted confidently that he had the firm support of numerous followers. Franco repeated the message of his 2 December letter when he said that he did not 'see any advantage in change' and that if he were ever to delegate the leadership of the government, it would only be when he was no longer able to carry out the functions of that position as well as those of head of state. From this it was clear that he would never renounce the latter post. It was also a hint that, while he wanted to retain ultimate control for as long as he lived, he foresaw a time when it might be possible to relinquish his personal hold on the administration of the system without it collapsing. This was not an admission of dispensability. Rather, it was an expression of supreme confidence in the immutability of his creation. Not only did he see no advantage in change, he believed he could prevent it indefinitely. He thus revealed that he was out of touch with contemporary reality and that the complex dynamics of civilian society were more than ever beyond the grasp of his mechanistic, military mind.

Spain *was* changing, however, in spite of Franco's reluctance to recognize the fact, for it was slowly being drawn back into the international mainstream. By the second half of the 1950s, thanks to foreign loans, the economy was showing signs of recovery, and Spain had been admitted as a member of the United Nations, in December 1955. Regular television broadcasting began in 1956 and was soon to prove an invaluable addition to the arsenal of the regime's propaganda channels. In 1956, only 600 sets received the images produced by the state broadcasting company, Spanish Radio-Television (Radio Televisión Española, RTVE), but, by 1958, that figure had leapt to 40,000.[13] In 1956, too, a Spaniard, albeit an exiled Republican Spaniard, Juan Ramón Jiménez, won the Nobel prize for literature and Spain was the protagonist of another, undoubtedly more popular, cultural event: on 13 June 1956 the Real Madrid football team won the first European Cup championship.

Yet the picture presented by RTVE, the state-controlled press, and the official cinema newsreels was artificially rosy, for it was highly selective. What the media did not show was the concern of Spanish economists and financiers over rising inflation and a mounting balance of payments deficit; the widening gap between conditions of life and work in town and country; emigration on a rapidly growing scale; or the conflict latent in Spanish universities between a desire for greater intellectual freedom and the constraints of an antiquated, paternalistic education system. It was in the nature of the Franco regime, as it is to a greater or lesser degree in that of all authoritarian systems, not to provide the public with full information, for problems can be 'resolved' more rapidly if those in power have a free hand simply to suppress them. 'The custom of disguising reality so that it appeared to be perfect' had long been the tactic of the Franco regime.[14] It was relatively easy to do in the first years of the regime, with a war- and hunger-cowed populace, a subsistence-level economy, and a country cut off from the outside world. However, it became more difficult to achieve when those conditions no longer prevailed, as a result of the resumption of contact with North America and the rest of Western Europe.

As a time of transition from autarchy and isolation to developmentalist capitalism and international *rapprochement*, the 1950s in Spain were a time of ambiguity and uncertainty, in which the first signs of a limited degree of liberalism became visible at the same time as the use of the customary repression made it clear that nothing fundamental had changed. This was thrown into sharp relief by a crisis which blew up in February 1956, as a result of a clash between rival groups of students in a central Madrid street. Timid winds of change had been trying to blow in Spanish universities since 1951, when a relatively progressive Minister of Education, Joaquin Ruiz-Giménez, had initiated an attempt to revitalize and open up the torpid and reactionary Spanish education system. In this, he had the support of many educationists, intellectuals and students, including the Rector of Madrid's Central University, Pedro Laín Entralgo, that of the University of Salamanca, Antonio Tovar, and the Falangists in the SEU who wanted to adapt Francoism to the new era. However, they inevitably aroused the hostility of conservative Catholics and Falangist reactionaries, who saw in the liberalizing ideas of Ruiz-Giménez a threat to their respective preserves in the education system. Matters were made worse by the fact that Ruiz-Giménez was himself a practising Catholic and had, on appointment, sworn allegiance to the principles of the Francoist Movement, while Laín and Tovar were both erstwhile Falangists. The defenders of the 'true' faith therefore felt that they must strengthen their guard against the 'enemy within'. Three initiatives in particular 'confirmed' their fears: a seminar series held in 1954 and entitled 'Encounters between Poetry and the University', which were ostensibly purely cultural but always became highly politicized; a projected 'Congress of Young University Writers', planned for November 1955 by pro-democratic students and progressive Falangists, but banned by the Ministry of the Interior; and the idea of a 'National Congress of Students', in preparation for which a manifesto calling for the abolition of the SEU monopoly of student representation was circulated in universities throughout Spain in early 1956. Although the aims of these events were far from revolutionary, they gave the supporters of Francoist orthodoxy particular pause. For many of the students who took part in them did not have the working-class background traditionally associated with militant anti-Francoism, but came from prosperous, middle-class families which had benefited socially and economically from Francoism. Predictably, Franco believed that these were essentially good, but impressionable, young people who had been led astray by the agents of 'anti-Spain'.

On 9 February 1956 a large group of Falangist students had gathered in a street in the university quarter of Madrid to commemorate the anniversary of the death, in 1934, of one of the party's first martyrs, the student Matias Montero. On the way back from this ritual, they came upon a crowd of anti-Falangist students. In the ensuing mêlée, one of the Falangists, Miguel Alvarez, was wounded in the head by a bullet. His comrades immediately claimed that he had been the victim of Leftist aggression and demanded retribution. In fact, as an unpublished police report subsequently stated, the near-fatal shot had been fired by one of Alvarez's own comrades.[15] That finding could not be disclosed, for its publication would have revealed the regime's double dishonesty, in suppressing the truth and in using the incident to justify repressive measures against the liberalizers in the university and to rally the faithful around Franco. Falangist hard-liners made a stockpile of weapons at the headquarters of an extremist group, the Guardia de Franco, and drew up a hit-list of individuals to be attacked should the wounded Falangist die. The Falangist daily, *Arriba*, titled its 10 February edition 'They've killed Matias Montero again', even although Alvarez was still alive. On 11 February the monarchist *ABC* weighed in with a leader entitled 'Patriotic alert', in which it claimed solidarity with 'the Falangist faith' and issued dire warnings against the 'hidden hand' which lay behind the 9 February disturbance, by which was meant socialism and communism. An official newspaper, *El Español*, produced by

171

the Ministry of Information and Tourism, kept feelings running high by publishing on 24 February, an article entitled 'The conspiracy has names', in which a number of named students were attacked as 'communist intriguers', and the 'Congress of Young University Writers' as Leftist agitprop organized with the connivance of some of the regime's own officials (a thinly veiled reference to Ruiz-Giménez, Laín Entralgo and the reformist group within the SEU). *ABC* contributed to keeping the issue going by reproducing the *El Español* article in its edition of 4 March – almost a month after the Alvarez shooting had happened.

The press campaign and the Falangist demands for retribution were perfectly consonant with Franco's own view of the 9 February events. Describing the liberal-minded students as 'rowdies and trouble-makers', he treated their concerns not as a social, political or even intellectual matter of significance, but as a short-term problem of public order. The Central University was temporarily closed; the two clauses of the 'Spaniards' Charter' which recognized freedom of movement and limited time of detention were suspended; and the leaders of the student movement in favour of democracy in the universities were rounded up and arrested. On 14 February Ruiz-Giménez was dismissed, along with Laín Entralgo and the Technical Secretary General for Education, Manuel Fraga Iribarne, the Minister Secretary General of FET y de las JONS, Fernández Cuesta, and his Vice-Secretary, Tomás Romojaro. Fernández Cuesta was replaced by veteran Francoist, José Luis Arrese, and Ruiz-Giménez by José Rubio Mina. Both were unreformed Falangists. In a report presented to the Political Committee of FET y de las JONS on 1 April, the dissident Falangist, Dionisio Ridruejo, stated his belief that the whole affair had been a fabrication, as an excuse for a crack-down in academic and intellectual circles.

By turning to the Falangist component of the regime forces in this way, Franco was resorting to an old tactic. In view of the violent intentions of the Guardia de Franco, the military governor of Madrid, General Rodrigo Martínez, had placed the organization's premises under surveillance and had declared that he would mobilize troops if the

Falangist extremists attempted to take the law into their own hands. In addition, he and Generals Muñoz Grandes and Martínez Campos asked Franco what he proposed to do to control the Falange. Franco, however, was not a man to give way to this kind of pressure. In maintaining the Falangist content of his cabinet, he was intent upon showing the military that he was still in control and would not be pushed by them. In the event, the February 1956 crisis was the last time that Franco was able to apply old methods to new situations. He was very soon to be forced to face the fact that things had moved on since 1939.

On reappointment as Minister Secretary-General of the official party, Arrese was commissioned by Franco to produce a series of legislative drafts whose purpose was twofold. First, they were to give the regime the appearance of being based not on sheer superiority of armed force, but on objective political and juridical principles. Second, they were to turn the regime into a permanent institution, capable of withstanding the vagaries of circumstantial change and of surviving Franco's own eventual demise. Arrese got together a study-group of hard-line Falangists, whose mission was to draft four documents: a new version of the Party Statutes, which had last been revised seventeen years earlier, in August 1939; a law of the Fundamental Principles of the State, which was to encapsulate the basic tenets of Francoism; a law of the Movement, which was to give legal form to the distinction between 'the Party', FET y de las JONS, as a clearly delimited group of political activists, and 'the Movement', which encompassed all those who actively or passively subscribed to the values which inspired Francoism; and an Organizational Law of the Government, which was to lay down ground-rules for the legislative and executive powers of the government. Arrese made the package public when, on 4 March, he addressed a gathering of Falangists in Valladolid. This was a carefully calculated move, designed to underline the Falangist character of the project of which Arrese had been given exclusive charge, for Valladolid was the cradle of militant Falangism and 4 March was the anniversary of the fusion, in 1934, of Falange Española and the JONS. As so often, the Franco regime was using a date of significance only to itself to suggest that Spain had no history outside that which was officially approved.

Like Franco, Arrese was trying to hold back the march of history. It might be possible physically to suppress the signs of its advance in the universities, but there were other indicators which could not so readily be ignored or concealed. Two days before Arrese's Valladolid speech, France announced that it was to grant independence to its protectorate in Morocco. Franco had allowed anti-French nationalism to flourish in Spanish Morocco in the first half of the 1950s, naïvely and carelessly confident that pressure for independence would not be a problem in the Spanish protectorate. He was wrong. The French decision sparked serious disturbances in Spanish Morocco and, on 15 March, Spain found itself obliged to concede that it, too, would relinquish control over its protectorate. The agreement was signed on 7 April 1956.

Considering Franco's lifelong and obsessive involvement with Morocco and his equally characteristic reluctance to relinquish territorial gains, the speed with which independence was granted to Spanish Morocco was extraordinary. It was all the more remarkable given Franco's condemnation, years earlier, of the loss of the last remnants of the Spanish empire, as he saw it, without a fight, and his disapproval of General Primo de Rivera's decision to withdraw from Morocco in the 1920s. And, just as the conquest of Morocco had been undertaken at the turn of the century to counteract the divisive effects of 'the Disaster' by giving Spaniards a new, common enterprise with which to identify, one might have expected that in 1956 Franco would resort to a military campaign to save Morocco to unite the regime forces around himself and divert attention away from domestic problems. Looking back, we can now say that Franco's response to the Moroccan crisis gave a clear indication that 1956 marked a turning point in his political and personal life. From that year onwards, he became progressively more absent from the conduct of daily political affairs, relying as much on the inertia of the system he had created as on his ministers to keep the country running, while he devoted increasing amounts of time to hunting, shooting and fishing.[16] One of Franco's most sympathetic biographers, Suárez Fernández, maintains that the *Caudillo*'s penchant for such country pursuits reflected his 'typical custom of reflection in the solitude of nature before taking decisions'.[17] Given that Franco was not alone on these occasions and that he was busy destroying nature, rather than reflecting upon it, it seems more likely that advancing age and the duration of his mandate had reduced his appetite for playing an active role in Spain's political life.

This did not, however, mean that he was ready to relinquish his all-powerful position. Hard on the heels of the Moroccan crisis came a wave of strikes in Asturias, Navarre and the Basque Country, in protest against economic hardship. Even Franco, whose automatic reaction to labour unrest was usually to dismiss it as the work of communist agitators, was obliged by the arguments of the Minister of Labour to authorize a 23 per cent general wage increase. The depth of the crisis can be gauged from the fact that the minister (José Antonio Girón) was a hard-line Falangist not given to either reformist 'weakness' or left-wing sympathies. Soon afterwards, a group of monarchists began plotting to force Franco to step down, in order to thwart Arrese's plan to 'structure the regime' in the Falangist mould. Franco responded to these signs of internal opposition with what, effectively, was a show of force. Between 27 April and 1 May, he toured Andalusia, to the ecstatic, Falangist-organized acclaim of thousands of spectators. In his speeches to the multitudes, Franco's enthusiasm for the Falange put monarchists and military on notice that any attempt to push him into early retirement would have to contend with the mass opposition of his 'popular support'. In fact, of course, the 'masses' as seen in Andalusia were no more than paid extras in a grandiose propaganda operation. If Arrese chose Andalusia to stage it, it was because he could be sure that, in the rural south, the official party would not encounter the embarrassment of striking miners or protesting students.

There was, however, a potential pitfall for Franco in such ostentatious manifestations of admiration for the Falange, which was that, in siding so clearly with one of the regime's political 'families', he risked losing his position as arbiter between them all, and provoking the others into joining forces against him. Franco himself may have realized this,

175

for his erstwhile enthusiasm for Arrese and his project began to wane in the second half of 1956, as opposition to it became more widespread and vocal among the non-Falangist sectors of the regime. Perhaps in a deliberate attempt to reassert his authority by disconcerting all the interested parties, or simply following his instinct to play for time, Franco resorted to his old tactic of duplicity. On 17 July, at Arrese's suggestion, he addressed the National Council of FET y de las JONS. This seemed like a Falangist revival, for it was the first session that had been held since 1945 and Franco asserted that it was 'necessary that the National Council should recover the role which corresponds to it in the political tasks, because it is hierarchically the highest body in the Movement, whose duty it is to ensure the purity of the organization and the continuity of the doctrine'.[18] But many of those present, including the Vice-Secretary of FET, Diego Salas Pombo, detected behind the smokescreen of verbiage a lack of genuine commitment to Arrese's plan for a Falange-dominated future. In a private conversation with Salas Pombo after the National Council speech, Franco admitted that he thought the Falangist ideology outmoded.[19] The part of the project referring to the Party statutes was subsequently dropped.

Arrese and Salas Pombo made desperate efforts to convince military and Church leaders that the proposed laws were not a disguised attempt to make Spain a totalitarian state. In addition to opposition from these two quarters, however, they were faced by a barrage of criticism from Luis Carrero Blanco, from the Traditionalist Minister of Justice, Antonio Iturmendi, and even from some fellow-members of Falange. In contrast to Arrese's proposals, which left the form of the state and the succession issue very vague, Carrero's idea was for an authoritarian monarchy based on 'the principles which inform the National Movement', of which the 'fundamental elements' would be 'the Crown, the Council of the Realm, the National Council of the Movement, the Cortes and the government'.[20] When, in December, three of the four cardinals denounced Arrese's proposals to Franco, he decided that the project must be withdrawn. Typically, he did not break the news to Arrese himself, but instructed

Carrero to do it. Faced with opposition from his own forces, Franco was not guided by ideological principles nor personal loyalty, but purely and simply by whatever would keep him in power. Never before had he capitulated. That he was prepared to do so to retain his position was, in itself, a sign of changing times.

By the beginning of 1957 Franco found himself on the horns of a dilemma: both change and immobilism implied a high degree of risk for his continuation in power. The basic problem was that the switch from autarchy to internationalism had not been fully effected: a free-market economy could not exist as long as its component parts – especially investment, supply of raw materials, and the purchasing power of the domestic market – were still closely controlled by the state. The result was that the economy was in the grip of a crisis which could only be resolved by adopting measures to free it from the constraints of autarchy. The difficulty this offered Franco was that, to his authoritarian mentality, loosening control was synonymous with losing it. His response was to renew his ministerial team.

The composition of the new cabinet announced in February 1957 constituted Franco's attempt to resolve the dilemma he faced by being both immobile and innovative at the same time! Half-a-dozen old retainers acted as anchor-men in the positions they had had in the previous cabinet. In addition, whilst Falangists Arrese and Girón de Velasco were ousted respectively from the Party Secretariat and the Ministry of Labour, they were replaced by two men who were also Falangists but who, by contrast, were known to be more moderate and flexible in their views than their predecessors. In case anyone should be tempted to see this as a sign of weakness, the ultra-authoritarian Blas Pérez González was replaced as Minister of the Interior by the even more hardline Camilo Alonso Vega, former head of the Civil Guard and one of Franco's oldest and closest friends from their days as soldiers in Africa. The removal of Alberto Martín Artajo from the Ministry of Foreign Affairs, and his replacement by Fernando María Castiella, represented a change of incumbent, but not of political approach nor ideological commitment.

The same could not be said, however, for the men

appointed to the economic ministries. The portfolios for Industry, Agriculture, Public Works, Commerce and Finance were entrusted to people whose loyalty to the regime was, of course, unimpeachable, but whose political utility lay in their possession of technical skills, not in their allegiance to any particular ideological current, nor in having good connections with the traditional oligarchy of large, wealthy landowners. Their inclusion was a clear sign that what had been the order of the regime's stated priorities since the end of the Civil War must now be reversed. In the 1940s the official press had stated that economic goals would be subordinate to political objectives. The policies of autarchy represented the regime's attempt to implement that declaration of intent. By the end of the 1950s, however, the failure of autarchy as an economic programme had made it necessary to seek other options, and these implied at least the modification of the existing political framework. In effect, the political objective of Francoism – self-perpetuation – was now dependent upon the achievement of the economic aim of remaining solvent.

This promised to be a difficult task; hence the need for professional economists in the cabinet. In the industrial areas of Spain, the investment of foreign capital, technology and managerial skills had stimulated immediate improvement, but not definitive recovery. Growth was spectacular in the second half of the 1950s, both in absolute terms and by comparison with the levels of the preceding decade. Spanish industry and finance seemed to have taken a new lease of life, and the official propaganda machine lost no opportunity to attribute this trend to the sagacity of the *Caudillo*. Whereas his public appearances had been sporadic up to 1955, and largely prompted by political events, the second half of the decade saw a notable increase in his activities as the opener of factories, electricity generating stations, reservoirs and housing schemes. Yet it was not the case in Spain that 'if construction is going well, everything is going well'. Despite the improving state of industry, the economy as a whole was lop-sided, unbalanced by the deteriorating situation of the agricultural sector. The overall effect of coupling the Spanish wagon to the international economic train was to destabilize the former, for its antiquated methods and structures could not readily assimilate and apply efficiently the benefits of the latter.

The imbalances and strains occasioned by the change of economic policy were not limited to the strictly economic areas, but also spilled over into the social and political spheres. In the first place, the working classes naturally wanted to participate in the economic benefits they were helping to produce in the industrial and service sectors. Secondly, it was in the interests of factory owners and investors that they should participate, for it was of little use to produce increasing quantities of goods if the mass of the population could not afford to buy them. Wage rises were therefore granted not only as a response to disruptive strikes, but also to enable demand to absorb supply. This had the effect of attracting people from the rural areas into the cities, in search of work and a better standard of living; which, in turn, placed unbearable strains on urban social and economic infrastructures. Overcrowding, insanitary conditions and inadequate services (particularly medical, educational and cultural), together with the accompanying problems of health risks and rising crime rates, began to make their appearance in Spanish cities in the 1950s, just as they had already appeared in large connurbations elsewhere in the world.

In the spring of 1957 spiralling inflation stimulated a fresh wave of strikes in Asturias. Franco could not believe that the miners wanted more than he had already given them and, as always, viewed their discontent as political subversion. In a sense, he was right, for despite the Civil War, the ensuing repression and the stranglehold of the official trade unions, Leftist ideals had not been totally exterminated in the Spanish working classes. The contrast between increased industrial output and deteriorating social and economic conditions sharpened their political consciousness and strengthened support for the clandestine labour movement, especially among the younger workers, who had not experienced the Civil War and did not have the 'peace at any price' outlook of some of their parents' generation.

In the context of changing national and international social and economic conditions, the maintenance of an inflexible, narrow political framework became increasingly untenable. From the Presidency of the Government, Carrero Blanco worked to preserve the Catholic and conservative essence of the regime and, at the same time, to adapt its structures and administrative procedures. In the same way that Franco had been heavily dependent on Serrano Suñer's political acumen when dealing with unfamiliar problems in the period 1937–42, he was now increasingly reliant on Carrero. Thus, three days after the February 1957 cabinet changes, a law was passed which, by giving Carrero's department the power to 'initiate, draft and programme legislation', effectively transferred the onus of policy-making to the Presidency. In addition, inter-ministerial committees were to be set up to settle administrative questions which, until then, had been discussed at ministerial level. Finally, an Economic Coordination and Planning Office was created within the orbit of the Presidency, specifically to address the problems facing the economy.

These changes effectively distanced Franco both from policy-making and the administration of the regime. Nevertheless, legislation still required his sanction, and he continued to preside over cabinet meetings. He could and did play a decisive role. In February 1959, despite Spain's increasing dependence on outside inputs and its deepening economic difficulties, Franco refused to countenance the provision of a Stabilization Plan by the International Monetary Fund (IMF). It was only when the Finance Minister, Navarro Rubio, confronted Franco personally, impressed on him the absolute and urgent necessity of devaluing the peseta, and asked him how he would feel if ration cards had to be reintroduced, that Franco reluctantly gave in. The IMF plan was adopted and the peseta devalued in early March 1959.

That Navarro Rubio should stand up to Franco in this way was indicative of how power relations within the regime had changed since the Civil War. Twenty years earlier, those who had dared to dissent from Franco's view, or who had merely questioned it, had been dismissed, exiled, imprisoned, demoralized or professionally ruined. In 1959 Navarro Rubio had not only *not* immediately fallen under suspicion of disloyalty, but had actually made Franco back down. In the same way that repression was less effective than twenty years earlier as an instrument of socio-political control against the anti-Francoist opposition, the spectres of the Republic and the Civil War were less useful as a means of holding the regime forces together. This did not mean, however, that Franco was prepared to relinquish them. On 1 April 1959 he presided over a lavish ceremony the purpose of which was the inauguration of an extraordinary church, built, in Franco's own words, 'in memory of my victory over communism, which was trying to dominate Spain'.[21]

That reconciliation was not Franco's guiding principle was clear from the decree he had issued on 1 April 1939 (the same day he had signed the final war bulletin), ordering that a monument be built 'to perpetuate the memory of those who fell in the Crusade of Liberation' and to honour 'those who gave their lives for God and the Fatherland'.[22] What this meant in ordinary language was that only those who subscribed to Francoist ideals would be remembered and honoured. This would include 'the Catholic fallen from both sides', but not non-Catholic Republicans, who, in Francoism's terms were worthy of no memorial. On transferring his official residence from Burgos to Madrid, in October, Franco 'toured the Sierra de Guadarrama, looking for a place he had already seen during the war' in which he planned to locate his war memorial. On 21 October he found the valley of Cuelgamuros.[23] Henceforth, it was to be known as 'el Valle de los Caídos' – the Valley of the Fallen. It seems rather more than fortuitous that Franco should have chosen this spot, for it was only 10 kilometres from the imposing palace, monastery and royal pantheon of El Escorial, built by Philip II in the sixteenth century. Franco's project stopped short of a royal palace or royal tombs, but it attempted to emulate El Escorial in virtually everything else, including its monastery, its panoramic vista towards Madrid, across the plain at the foot of the Sierra de Guadarrama, the bellic nature of its origin[24] and the massive scale of its construction.

Work began on 1 April 1940. It took nineteen years to complete what was not only a remarkable feat of engineering but also an outstanding example of Francisco

Franco's single-minded pursuit of self-aggrandizement and immortality. In order to excavate the site itself, a new road had been built and a viaduct constructed to carry it across the valley before it climbed through the wooded hillside to the rocky crag chosen for the location of the church which formed the heart of the project. At the top of the road, two flights of ten steps each (symbolizing 'the ten Commandments, or the ascent to moral perfection inspired by faith')[25] led to 30,600 square metres of paved esplanade, in the shape of a cross, which, in turn, led to an arched doorway, flanked by an arched colonnade. Above it towered a 150-metre high concrete and granite cross, the arms of which 'were wide enough inside for two average-sized motor cars to pass each other'.[26] At ground-level, a huge bronze door, decorated with panels depicting in relief the fifteen mysteries of the rosary and other biblical scenes, opened on to the interior of the church. This had been constructed underground, by tunnelling into the rock. It was designed to impress and overawe by its sheer size: 262 metres long and 41 metres high at its highest point, over the transept. Six side chapels were each dedicated to the Virgin Mary in relation to the Civil War: Our Lady of Africa; the Immaculate Conception, patroness of the Army; Our Lady of Carmen, patroness of the Navy; Our Lady of Loretto, patroness of the Air Force; Our Lady of the Pillar, patroness of Zaragoza and declared Captain-General of the Army during the war; and Our Lady of Mercy, patroness of Prisoners. The last of these was ironic, not to say cynical, for much of the manpower used in the building of the Valle de los Caídos had been provided by political prisoners, who were allowed to redeem part of their sentences in what was, effectively, a labour camp. Conditions were extremely arduous and the work exhausting but at least, as one former prisoner testified years later, unlike conventional prisons all over Spain, there was neither the obligation to sing the Falangist hymn, nor the nightly selection (*saca*) of prisoners to be shot next day.[27]

Franco personally monitored progress on the project from its inception, frequently appearing on site without prior warning, and often accompanied by doña Carmen. In 1956, with the interior of the church nearing completion, the architect, Diego Méndez, constructed a lead-lined tomb under the floor in the transept, behind the high altar.[28] This was, in fact, for Franco, although its existence did not become public knowledge until almost thirty years later. A second tomb, situated directly opposite that destined for Franco, in front of the high altar, was not kept secret, for it was very soon to receive its occupant. On 30 March 1959 the remains of José Antonio Primo de Rivera were transported from the basilica of El Escorial, where they had been buried in 1939, for reinterment in the Church of the Holy Cross of the Valley of the Fallen. The following day, Franco's 'private pyramid' [29] was formally inaugurated. The choice of 'Victory Day' for the occasion was the *Caudillo*'s way of restating his belief in the legitimacy of his regime and of reminding its members of their shared responsibility in its creation and their common interest in its continuation.

By 1959, some of the regime forces were beginning to organize politically outside the limits of FET y de las JONS. Liberal supporters of Don Juan had formed Unión Española and two former CEDA members, Manuel Gimenez Fernandez and José María Gil Robles, were the instigators, respectively, of Izquierda Democrática Cristiana and Democracia Social Cristiana. Although these groups were very small and certainly not revolutionary in character, the return of the words 'Left' and 'democracy' to the political vocabulary of people not proscribed by the regime undoubtedly gave Franco pause. In his end-of-year speech for 1959, he condemned what he called 'inorganic' (i.e. liberal) democracy. He continued, too, to denounce strikes and clandestine labour and political activity as evidence of an international 'judeo-masonic–communist' conspiracy to destroy Spain. He did not seem to appreciate the contradiction between his virulent denunciations of parliamentary democracy and the increasingly close economic ties being woven between Spain and the western democracies; nor between his belief that economic nationalism was best and the fact that unless Spain liberalized its economic policies, it would remain isolated from the growth then beginning to be enjoyed by the rest of Europe. When the US President, Eisenhower, visited Madrid on 21 December 1959, Franco persisted in interpreting it as a sign of recognition of his rightness, not as an indication that times were changing and he would have to move with them or be left behind.

To a large extent, the cabinet reshuffle of 1957 marked the point at which the Franco regime adopted the style which was to become its hallmark in the 1960s and 1970s. From then until Franco's death in 1975, it was no longer simply the victory in the Civil War that was invoked as the basis for Franco's right to rule, but his role as the provider of material wealth and prosperity. As the leader of the Nationalist armies, he had been hailed in 1939 as the restorer of peace and order to a country allegedly on the verge of ruin thanks to Republican bad faith and malpractice. By the end of the 1950s that argument was becoming less effective as time blurred the collective memory of the Republic and an increasingly large sector of the population had no direct experience of either the Republic or the Civil War. If people were no longer so easily frightened into docility, new ways would have to be found to make them ductile. The answer was to present Franco as the guarantor of the peace and stability which enabled Spain to flourish economically and individuals to enjoy an improved standard of living. It was still implied that, without him, there was a danger that the political disorder of the past might return, but the emphasis would, henceforth, be much more on what people stood to lose in material terms if the system which provided those benefits were substantially changed.

It was an unsubtle and false logic, but one which was effective when presented without alternatives to a populace which had endured great hardship for a prolonged period. The creation of a capitalist, consumer society and the rapid expansion of the urban middle classes which characterized Spain in the 1960s took place without making any fundamental modification to the political premises on which the regime was posited. The tensions generated by this contradiction deepened and broadened with the passage of time. Franco's mere presence prevented radical change, but his role as guarantor and arbiter became increasingly irrelevant as different strands of regime and anti-regime opinion converged in agreement on the need for the return of democracy.

. . .

NOTES

1. F. Franco *Franco ha dicho (1er apéndice)*, Madrid: Ediciones Voz 1949, p. 184.
2. P. Preston *Franco*, London: Harper Collins 1993, ch. 23.
3. This was because 4 August was the date in 1704 on which a British Admiral, Rooke, captured the Rock of Gibraltar from the Spanish garrison defending it, during the Spanish War of Succession.
4. F. Franco *Discursos y Mensajes del Jefe del Estado, 1951–1954*, Madrid: Dirección General de Información, Publicaciones Españolas 1955, pp. 7–20.
5. The phrase was used by Franco to refer to his choice of Castiella as Ambassador to London; P. Preston, *Franco*, ch. 23.
6. Cf. E. Gentile, 'Fascism as Political Religion' in *Journal of Contemporary History*, vol. 25, Nos 2–3, May–June 1990, pp. 229–51.
7. Ration cards were finally done away with in 1953, fourteen years after the end of the Civil War that had made them necessary.
8. *La Vanguardía Española*, 1 October 1953; 'Sentry of the West' was the title of a biography of Franco written by Galinsoga and Franco's cousin and aide de camp, Francisco Franco Salgado-Araujo, *Centinela de Occidente: semblanza biográfica de Francisco Franco*, Barcelona: AHR 1956.
9. P. Preston, *Franco*, ch. 23.
10. M. Arroita-Jauregui, '18 de julio: punto de partida', in *Alcalá*, No.13, 25 July 1952.
11. P. Preston, *Franco*, ch. 23.
12. R. Fernández Cuesta, interview with the author, Madrid, 15 July 1977.
13. J. Sinova (ed.) *Historia del Franquismo*, (2 vols) Madrid: Diario 16 1985, vol I, p. 335.
14. L. Ramírez, *Franco*, Paris: Ruedo Ibérico 1976, p. 307.
15. L. Suárez Fernández, *Francisco Franco y Su Tiempo*, Madrid: Ediciones Azor 1984, vol. V, p. 255.
16. On Franco's 'sporting' activities in this period, see P. Preston, *Franco*, ch. 23.
17. L Suárez Fernández, *FFST*, vol. V, p. 256.
18. F. Franco, *Discursos y Mensajes del Jefe del Estado, 1955–1959*, Madrid: Dirección General de Información, Publicaciones Españolas 1960, p. 216.
19. Interview with the author, Madrid, 21 November 1977.
20. L. López Rodó, *La larga marcha hacia la monarquía*, Barcelona: Noguer 1977, p. 127.

21. R. de la Cierva, *Franco*, Barcelona: Planeta 1986, p. 428.
22. *ABC*, Madrid, 20 November 1975.
23. L. Suárez Fernández, *Franco. La historia y sus documentos*, Madrid: Ediciones Urbión vol. 4, p. 55.
24. The palace and monastery of El Escorial were built to celebrate a Spanish victory over French forces at Saint Quentin (Picardy), in 1557.
25. *Santa Cruz del Valle de los Caídos*, Madrid: Editorial Patrimonio Nacional, 1983, p. 12.
26. Ibid., p. 13.
27. Gregorio Peces-Barba del Brío in J. Sinova (ed), *Historia del franquismo*, (2 vols) Madrid: Diario 16 1985, vol. I, p. 25.
28. *ABC*, Madrid, 20 November 1975.
29. Gregorio Peces-Barba, loc. cit., p. 24.

Chapter 8

THE TWILIGHT OF THE GOD
(1960–75)

On balance, and in purely economic terms, the effects of the 1959 Stabilization Plan were positive and a crisis was avoided. Certainly, this was achieved at the expense of a massive rise in unemployment (34.7 per cent between 1959 and 1960)[1] and a fall in production and domestic demand; but, in seeking a response to the ensuing social and labour unrest, Franco was not constrained by any constitutional limitations to his powers, and the combined forces of the police, the official trade union system and the Francoist press were fully deployed to hound, punish and discredit those who dared to protest. The Plan itself was sufficient only to provide a stop-gap solution to the problems of the Spanish economy, but its application coincided with a period of economic growth in the rest of Europe, in the wake of post-war, 'Marshall Plan' reconstruction. Consequently, recession in Spain was offset, at the start of the 1960s, by an influx of capital from foreign investors looking for new areas into which to expand, and of revenues from North European tourists seeking the hitherto unaffordable pleasures of Mediterranean beach holidays. To take advantage of this situation, the Stabilization Plan was followed by a five-year Development Plan, announced at the end of 1960. Economic growth became the leitmotiv of the 1960s, as foreign investment capital flowed in, industrial exports rose, and earnings from foreign visitors became one of the mainstays of the Spanish economy. Franco was unhappy that this was taking place under the auspices of the World Bank, since he was convinced that the leader of the Bank's delegation in

Spain, Sir Hugh Ellis Rees, was a Freemason and, therefore, part of 'anti-Spain'.[2] He was sufficiently pragmatic to realize, however, that without such external assistance, the Spanish economy would collapse and, foreseeably, his regime with it.

In 1961 Franco's propagandists launched a campaign to celebrate 'Twenty-five Years of the National Movement'. The title itself was indicative of the ambiguity of a regime undergoing transition. That there should be a celebration at all indicated that the regime's fundamental *raison d'être* was still the fact that Franco and his forces had defeated the Second Republic. Yet the absence of an explicit reference to 18 July 1936, the day of the military rising, and the implicitly all-encompassing overtones of 'National Movement' suggested a desire to play down the overtly divisive aspects of the anniversary. There had to be a commemoration, for certain domestic audiences; but it had to seem inoffensive, for the gallery of foreign interests now present in Spain – many of them from countries which had not supported the rebel cause in 1936. Perhaps, too, the orchestrators of the campaign were aware that, for a growing proportion of the population, the words '18 de julio' struck no heroic chords. The distance between that date and the life-experience of an ever-increasing number of Spaniards would only become greater in the future. Even the organizers of the 'celebrations' seem to have been less than wildly enthusiastic about them, as though they, too, realized that the time had come to look for new points of reference from which to justify the continued existence of a regime founded in national and international circumstances very different from those of 1961.

Franco, however, was as triumphalist as ever when he addressed the assembled members of the Cortes on 3 June 1961. 'The grandeur of the Crusade', he said, 'lies in having achieved the active and mutual participation of all good Spaniards . . . in the most glorious epic of our History.' Naturally, by 'good Spaniards' he meant only those who had not supported the Republic. He went on: 'Never was there in the History of Spain a State more legitimate, more popular and more representative than that which we began to forge a quarter of a century ago.'[3]

Again, the fact that the Francoist state was the result of a military coup and a war was conveniently ignored.

That this was an exercise undertaken to bolster the figure of Francisco Franco was highlighted by the fact that the climax of the commemorative events was reached on 1 October, the anniversary of his appointment as Head of State. As in 1936, the ritual was acted out in Burgos. Franco's speeches were full of laudatory references to himself: 'at the very critical moment at which Spain was falling apart, I received into my hands the bloodless body of the Fatherland in order to save it and create a State', he proclaimed from the balcony of the Town Hall, going on to say that 'Under our Régime . . . the nation is reborn in every respect and, now that the principal political lines have been laid down, progress can be seen in every sphere: spiritual, cultural, sanitary, agricultural, naval and industrial.'[4]

Despite Franco's constant references back to the Civil War, reality had moved on since then. The regime's propagandists were fully conscious of this, even if the *Caudillo* himself appeared not to be. The change which occurred in Franco's public image, as it was presented in official cinematographic newsreels in the 1960s, illustrates rather well both the contemporary change in the regime's style and official awareness of how useful the media could be in achieving mass transmission and acceptance of ideas. Between 1943 (the year in which the newsreel company was created) and 1960, the number of times per year that Franco featured in major reports tended to be erratic, never exceeding five and, in one year – 1945 – making no appearances at all. It was no coincidence that this was the year in which the Second World War ended in defeat for Franco's erstwhile Axis allies. From then until 1955, while Spain remained ostracized from western political and economic circles, Franco kept a relatively low public profile – a tactic which enhanced the semi-regal, semi-divine image he held of himself, and which made less immediate the association in the popular mind between Franco and the penury in which many of the people who saw the films lived. By contrast, from 1960, during five consecutive years, Franco's appearances on cinematographic screens rose steadily, as Spain became accepted in Europe and North

America as a trusted member of the anti-communist world, a lucrative investment market and a cheap, sunny place to spend holidays. With standards of living improving for most people, Franco could allow himself to be seen more often by his 'subjects'. When he toured Catalonia, in April 1960, and Andalusia, in April 1961, he drove through the streets in an open car or, more rarely, went on foot. This was some distance from the immediate post-war years, when his public appearances were virtually limited to appearing on official balconies to receive the ovation of the crowd below. In the 1960s Franco literally came down to street level, although he did not go so far as to allow the masses to press forward to shake his hand, in the manner of democratic heads of state.

There were other changes, too, in the way in which Franco was presented to the public in the 1960s. Until then, he had appeared as the restorer of peace, unity and national dignity after the supposed chaos of the Second Republic and the vicissitudes of the Second World War. The 1960s saw a subtle shift of emphasis, in line with the changes then occurring in society at large. Now, it was the image of Franco the provider of wealth and prosperity which shone from cinema and television screens. By the end of the decade, Franco had become increasingly marginal to the mechanics of day-to-day government and it was Franco the family man who predominated. In retrospect, we might be tempted to surmise that, in attempting to promote a more open, popular image of himself, Franco was influenced by the style of the new occupant of the White House, John F. Kennedy, elected to the US Presidency in November 1960. Certainly, the modernizing ideas and the relative youth of the technocrats who had recently entered the Spanish cabinet were closer to the transatlantic model than any of their predecessors had been. In fact, Franco was deeply suspicious of Kennedy. In this, as in so many things, he was influenced by Carrero Blanco who, in February 1961, produced a report on the new American President in which he recommended that Spain take a hard line in the forthcoming negotiations to renew the agreement granting the use of facilities on Spanish territory to the US Armed Forces. Franco remained more akin to his autocratic Portuguese neighbour, Antonio Oliveira Salazar. Indeed, a photographic portrait of Salazar occupied a prominent place near the *Generalísimo*'s desk in his study at the Pardo Palace (alongside another of Pope Pius XII). Although the regime appeared to be becoming less restrictive in its attitudes, and although the economic indicators suggested that Spain was well on the way to being a modern, consumer society in the western tradition, its political system was still deeply authoritarian, repressive and undemocratic.

Between them, the benefits of economic prosperity and the threat of repression were sufficient to assure the short-term stability of the regime. But Franco was nearly seventy years old and beginning to show signs of physical decline. Although it was not admitted officially for some years to come, he was in fact suffering from Parkinson's disease, a paralytic illness caused by the progressive degeneration of nerve cells at the base of the brain. Consequently, there was increasing concern among his followers about the future and, in particular, about the regime's ability to survive without the man who had made it so heavily dependent on his own unifying role. Some provision for the post-Franco era had been made with the 1947 Law of Succession and the 1958 Fundamental Principles, but the necessary development of these had not yet been completed. The worry was that Franco might die without having named his successor and without having laid down legally enforceable rules which would guarantee the continuation of the political status quo.

In June 1961 Franco announced his intention of passing a law which would specify how the state should be structured, how the legislative, executive and administrative apparatus should be organized, staffed and run, how the Head of State should be chosen and what his powers would be. The importance of this proposed Organic Law of the State was that it made legally binding what, until then, had been general guidelines. Certainly, such documents as the Spaniards' Charter, the Workers' Charter, or the Fundamental Principles of the State had the status of laws. The precepts enshrined in such texts, however, referred to the existing *content* of the state, whereas the proposed Organic Law of the State was about its *form* and was intended to take care of its as yet uncertain future. In characteristically dilatory fashion, Franco allowed another five years to pass before presenting the law to the Cortes for approval.

Two non-political events in the second half of 1961 focused further attention on the question of what would happen beyond Franco's lifetime. In September Don Juan de Borbón informed Franco that Prince Juan Carlos was engaged to Princess Sofia, eldest daughter of King Paul and Queen Frederika of Greece. The legitimate Spanish dynasty thus acquired a prospect of continuity which underlined the need to make provision for the future. Then, on Christmas Eve, Franco had a hunting accident. Few details were made public about what had happened, but it appears that his shotgun had exploded while he was using it, seriously injuring his left hand. He was not in danger of dying from the injury, but the incident brought home the *Caudillo*'s mortality to his followers and, by extension, the urgency of completing the arrangements for the institutionalization of the regime. Franco himself, clinging as tenaciously as ever to power, did not consider even a temporary withdrawal for convalescence. Although the injury caused him considerable pain, he broadcast his end-of-year message as usual.

Franco's failure to set in train the elaboration of the Organic Law of the State in 1961 reflected partly his inveterate tendency to act slowly and partly the concern of the regime's economists and their international advisers to secure the economic future as a prerequisite for political institutionalization. The first step was the creation, in January 1962, of a special department within the Office for Economic Coordination and Planning (Oficina de Coordinación y Planificación Económica, OCPE), entitled the Commissariat for the Development Plan (Comisaría del Plan de Desarrollo). At the suggestion of Carrero Blanco, the Commissariat was headed by the Director of the OCPE, Laureano López Rodó, who thus became a kind of commander-in-chief of the regime's economic forces. As the title of the new department indicated, 'development' had replaced mere survival as the regime's prime economic objective. Accumulation, profit and growth were now to be the key concepts, rather than simply balancing the books and breaking even. A second innovation was that these goals were to be achieved by 'planning'. In itself, this was not so new. Under Francoism, the state had always tried to control what was produced, how much was imported, how credit was assigned and so on. The difference between 1940s and 1960s planning was that, whereas in the early years of Francoism the state set the economic goals and controlled the means to achieve them on the basis of its assessment of what would be required, now the state would simply indicate how it thought resources should be deployed to satisfy the requirements of supply and demand, as determined by the operation of a free market.

Franco played no direct role in the elaboration of the new approach, but he remained indispensible to those who *were* in charge of the intricacies of economic planning, because he exercised supreme authority. No legislation could be passed without his approval. It was the task of ministers, therefore, to persuade him to sanction the changes necessary to stimulate the economy. It was not easy. In the first place, he was not, by nature, an innovator. On the contrary, he was deeply suspicious of change and clung to what was familiar and traditional. Secondly, the kind of liberalization envisaged for the economy by the Spanish technocrats and their international advisers also implied a relaxation of controls in other areas in order to create a thriving domestic market, attract more foreign investment and enhance Spain's chances of being admitted to the European Economic Community (EEC), to which application was made in February 1962 for associate status. All this was a lot to ask of a man for whom liberalism, the exercise of individual, personal freedoms, and European cultural and political influences were all anathema. Predictably, Franco was opposed to Spanish membership of the EEC, because he believed it to be 'a fief of freemasons, liberals and Christian Democrats'.[5] Thirdly, anti-Francoist protest had been increasing in frequency and intensity since the second half of the 1950s. This was partly as a result of increased awareness of the benefits of democracy, brought by greater contact with Europe and the United States after 1950, and partly because ideas and ideals can rarely be eliminated by repression. Franco, however, believed that only the first of these two factors was involved, and ordered ever harsher police measures against the strikes and demonstrations which increasingly characterized the 1960s. It was hardly surprising, therefore, that the EEC would not countenance political discussions with Spain, agreeing only to negotiate a preferential trade arrangement.

The year 1962 illustrated the contradictory nature of Spain under Franco at that time. On the one hand, Foreign Minister Castiella approached the EEC with a view to negotiating Spanish entry; the 'Opus Dei technocrats' spearheaded efforts to rationalize and liberalize the economy; and voices in support of greater equality and freedom began to be heard from social sectors – the middle classes and the Catholic Church – which had hitherto largely ignored the injustice and repression of which they were rarely the victims. On the other, Franco harked back to the Civil War in speeches which reassured the faithful that, while he lived, the values of '18 July' would be upheld; and a great furore was caused by the attendance of a large contingent of Spanish democrats at a congress on Spain organized in Munich by the European Movement.

Several strikes took place in the spring of 1962, particularly in the industrial areas of the Basque Country, in protest against the wage-freeze and unemployment resulting from the Stabilization Plan. Such action would not normally have worried the Francoist authorities unduly, except that, this time, it was actively supported by two Catholic labour organizations and a number of priests. The Catholic Workers' Youth Movement (Juventud Obrera Católica, JOC) and the Catholic Action Workers' Brotherhood (Hermandad Obrera de Acción Católica, HOAC) had two major advantages over the more overtly political labour organizations: first, they were not clandestine and so were able openly to hold meetings, distribute propaganda and maintain publications; secondly, they were not left-wing and therefore offered a means of expression and organized action to a sizeable proportion of the working classes which, though anti-Francoist, was not socialist, anarchist or communist. These two organizations and their partisans in the Church hierarchy progressively became a source of increasing irritation and perplexity to Franco, for he was accustomed to believing that the Church was on his side and dissent was the work of a communist–masonic–Jewish conspiracy. This rigid, Manichaean scheme of things could not admit, still less accept, that practising Catholics and priests could support, and even take part in, acts of protest.

Against this back-drop, on 27 May 1962, one of the Civil War veterans' organizations – the 'Brotherhood of Provisional Sergeants'[6] – held a rally in parkland to the west of Madrid to commemorate the twenty-fifth anniversary of the creation of their wartime corps. On the Garabitas ridge in the Casa de Campo, the ex-combatants evoked the days when, from that same spot, the Nationalists had besieged the capital during the war. General Franco's presence at the rally gave a clear indication of the importance he attached to what it stood for, since he rarely attended military gatherings other than the annual Victory Parade, and had never before participated in an event like this. The basic theme of his speech to the assembled veterans was the familiar argument that the Civil War and his regime were justified as the continuing struggle to defeat the enemies not only of Spain but of western civilization:

> The orchestration of our enemies is led by the Russia of the soviets, which spends hundreds of millions on broadcasting propaganda, on buying and recruiting agents, and on financing the machinations of its 'fellow travellers'. We are the keystone of western political resistance; we are the country in which, through your efforts, communism has been defeated for the first time; and, in this respect, we are the firmest bastion in the whole of the West.[7]

The social protest of the preceding months, he affirmed, reflected no more than the growing pains of progress; 'a natural consequence of our growth and vitality'. 'The excesses of the occasional separatist Basque cleric', he continued, 'or the clericalist [sic] errors of some other excitable priest . . . represent nothing in the great spiritual resurgence of our Fatherland', even though 'external propaganda' and foreigners might 'attempt to take advantage of labour unrest in the North' and use such excesses 'against our regime'. Finally, he made clear that, although he was nearly seventy years old, he had no intention of retiring. In response to those who 'engaged in clumsy speculation about [his] age', he said that he felt young and that, in any case, his work would be guaranteed for all time 'by the will of the vast majority of Spaniards . . . and by the faithful and insuperable guardianship of our Armies'.[8]

When he made his Garabitas speech, Franco may well have been aware of the impending Fourth Congress of the European Movement, which took place in Munich ten days later, between 5 and 8 June. Its theme was contemporary Spain, as a gesture of solidarity with those who were trying to bring democracy back to that country. A number of Spaniards had been invited to attend, representing virtually the whole spectrum of anti-Francoist opposition, including socialists, liberal monarchists, dissident Falangists, Basques, Catalans and progressive Catholics (but – ironically, given Franco's obsession – excluding communists). Franco and the regime reactionaries were outraged. The term they used to refer to the gathering, 'the Munich machination', was intended to deride and reject what they saw as yet another example of foreign-inspired hostility to 'true' Spain (and instantly entered anti-Francoist folklore as the epitome of regime absurdity).

On 8–9 June, the cabinet sat in all-night session to decide what action to take. The Congress was, of course, denounced; the Spaniards' Charter was suspended; and the Spaniards who had been in Munich were arrested on their return and their passports confiscated. When Franco made a speech in Valencia, on 16 June, his words were as fervently and openly condemnatory of outsiders as they had been on 27 May, but now he also included an explicit attack on 'the natural enmity of political parties', 'communist infiltration in Europe' and the free foreign press, most of which, he alleged, had been bought off with 'Soviet gold'. Rejecting 'that liberal world which is still fashionable in Europe', he lauded the creation in Spain of 'an efficient set of political ideas which, in accordance with the dictates of the Christian faith, takes up all the basic and efficient elements of past political theories'. 'The fact is', he said, 'that we must resign ourselves for a few years to being misunderstood . . . . If we hold fast, the barking out there from communism and its associates will matter little to us; what matters is what goes on here at home.'[9]

Not since 1937, when he had moved swiftly and decisively to end Falangist and Carlist squabbles, had Franco reacted with such speed and virulence to a manifestation of opposition to himself. For, in 1962, as in 1937, he was alarmed by the prospect of an alliance of political forces against him. However, whereas it had been relatively easy in 1937 to justify the suppression of dissidence in the name of the need for wartime unity, in 1962 no such exonerating circumstance was present. In 1962, moreover, the Francoist backlash was directed not only against some of Francoism's erstwhile followers, but also against the democratic Europe to whose 'Common Market' Spain wished to gain entry. Franco's reaction to the Munich conference must have made it clear to those politicians, entrepreneurs, financiers, etc. who wanted to be in the European mainstream that Spain's main problem was not labour unrest nor alleged communist subversion, but Franco. It seems possible, therefore, that Franco's gradual disappearance from day-to-day government in the course of the 1960s was due not only to his advancing age and infirmity, but to a deliberate attempt by pro-Europeanists such as López Rodó, Navarro Rubio and Ullastres to marginalize him, because he was becoming not just an obstacle but a veritable liability. Be that as it may, when the cabinet was modified on 10 July 1962, the most significant change was the creation of the position of Vice-President of the Government, occupied by Franco's old friend and comrade-in-arms, General Muñoz Grandes. His appointment distanced Franco from the day-to-day mechanics of government and indicated recognition of the fact that it was becoming increasingly likely that someone would soon have to deputize for Franco as head of government.

At the Garabitas gathering in May, Franco had reiterated his belief that the Civil War was not yet over: 'I have often said that our war did not end with our victory, nor with the internal unity of all Spaniards, for covert attacks have continued from outside Spain over the last twenty-five years.' That this was not just empty rhetoric was brutally demonstrated by the arrest, torture, trial and execution of a communist activist, Julián Grimau, in April 1963. Franco remained impervious to the international outcry provoked by the case, and to pleas for clemency from political and religious leaders world-wide. In so doing, he did irreparable damage to Spain's political image and confirmed the view of the EEC member-states that Spanish entry could not even be considered. Franco had evidently learned nothing from the heavy international criticism attracted by his reaction to the Munich congress. The creation, in May 1963, of the Courts of Public Order (Tribunales de Orden Público, TOP) may, at first sight, have seemed to be a liberalizing measure, in so far as, thenceforth, political offences were no longer to come under military jurisdiction. In fact, however, the TOP were the direct heirs of the wartime and post-war military courts and, as such, zealously continued their task of persecuting all forms of left-wing dissidence.

Franco's decision to take the unusual step of appearing at the veterans' rally in 1962, the menacing tone of the speech he made there and the increase in repressive measures throughout 1963 betrayed a lack of confidence in the reliability of the material prosperity promised by the economic planners as a guarantee of social and political stability. Franco's scepticism towards economic modernization seemed to be confirmed when, after a brief period of improved economic performance and stable domestic prices, inflation reappeared in 1964. Ironically, this trend coincided with the début of the First Development Plan, produced by López Rodó's Comissariat in November 1963, for the period 1964–67. As a result, the planners were obliged to incorporate unpopular *ad hoc* measures such as currency devaluation and wage freezing. This resolved the immediate problem, but had undesired side-effects on the planners' forecasts. These were based to an important degree on the assumption that increases in productivity could be achieved in return for wage rises which, in turn, would stimulate greater domestic consumption, and that these two factors together – production and consumption – would encourage national and foreign investors to put their capital into Spanish firms. In reality, development in Spain was erratic to the extent that it might be argued that it occurred despite, not thanks to, state efforts to promote it.

Nevertheless, when, in 1964, the regime celebrated 'Twenty-five Years of Franco's Peace', it did so with considerably more conviction than when, three years earlier, it had commemorated 'Twenty-five Years of National Movement'. The keynotes of the propaganda campaign organized by an *ad hoc* committee set up in the Ministry of Tourism were the economic progress made by Spain since 1939 and Spain's equality with the rest of Europe. The message transmitted by a flood of books, pamphlets, articles, speeches, exhibitions and so on was that these two achievements were entirely thanks to Francisco Franco, because he had brought peace; peace was the key to material well-being; and material well-being should be everyone's prime objective. The paradigmatic exponent of this logic was a documentary on the life of General Franco, made for the cinema by the director of Franco's own epic film, *Raza*,[10] José Luis Sáenz de Heredia. The title of the film, *Franco, ese hombre* (*Franco, the man*) was reminiscent of the biblical *ecce homo* and designed to propagate the image of Franco as a figure made of flesh and blood, but endowed with superhuman qualities and capabilities. Franco himself saw the film in the small theatre at the Pardo Palace where he regularly had private showings of commercial films. The director was present, anxiously awaiting his verdict. Franco said nothing throughout the ninety minutes that the film lasted. At the end, his only comment was a crushing 'Too many parades'. It is impossible to know whether he meant that the film was technically deficient or that it devoted too little attention to his own person. Either way, his remark was a fine example of the coldness characteristic of Franco the *real* man.

What Franco's mortifying comment almost certainly did *not* mean was that even he felt ill at ease with such unbridled exaltation of 'his' work, when there was so much evidence to counter official euphoria. Strikes were occurring all over the country with increasing frequency, as workers organized to protest against low pay, long hours, poor conditions and the prohibition of free trade union activity. More worrying to Franco were the signs of increasing disapproval emanating from the Catholic

Church in general and the Vatican in particular. In the speech he made at the opening of the Cortes on 8 July 1964, Franco laid emphasis on the Catholic inspiration of his regime and on the services he had rendered the Church since 1936, saving it from persecution at the hands of an atheistic Republic and protecting its interests thereafter. As with the Axis and, later, the western powers, Franco viewed as ingratitude Catholicism's rejection of his regime in the mid-1960s, due, so he believed, to its underestimation of the gravity of the communist threat. It may be that Franco's failure to understand the role of the Catholic Church as a liberalizing force in the light of the Second Vatican Council was due to his increasing isolation from the real world, together with his natural suspicion of change and the deeply conservative influence of his immediate entourage (in particular, his wife, Carrero Blanco, his doctor and his priest). It may also have been, however, that he understood only too well that the Church's inclination towards 'decoupling' itself from his regime undermined one of the latter's most basic principles: the consubstantiality of Catholicism and national identity. Consequently, when in September 1964 the Vatican Council approved a resolution asking states to renounce the privilege of nominating their bishops, Franco refused to comply. He thus revealed the self-interest which underlay his defence of Catholicism and alienated the Vatican still further.

If Franco's attitude did little to encourage the Catholic Church to maintain its once firm support for the Spanish regime, it did even less to soften the negative attitude of Spain's European neighbours. In his New Year speech of 30 December 1963 Franco condemned the West as offering only 'out-of-date political systems, centuries-old injustices inherent in the liberal capitalist system, inorganic democracy which divides and weakens them and freedom lessened by the realities of misery'.[11] Thus it was hardly surprising that in March 1964 the EEC again declined to contemplate anything other than a purely economic relationship with Spain. This merely confirmed Franco's belief that the western democracies were the enemies of Spain. In a speech made to the National Council on 9 April Franco reviewed the twenty-five years of his rule in tones of glowing self-congratulation and condemned the 'inorganic democracy' of the rest of Europe. Such diatribes dismayed those both inside and outside the regime who saw in *rapprochement* with Europe the way to loosen the ties which kept Spanish society trussed up like a captive chicken. In Franco's view, there was nothing amiss in condemning the political system espoused by the west whilst seeking to attract its economic assistance. Yet again, his notion that the west was in his debt distorted his view of international relations. In the late 1940s and early 1950s he had believed that the onset of the Cold War would vindicate his life-long struggle against communism and bring the Allied powers round to accepting Spanish membership of the western political and defence community. The return of the western ambassadors in 1951, the 1953 Hispano-US Agreements and admission to the United Nations in 1955 had seemed to prove him right. Ten years later, he was applying the same tactic to the EEC. In 1964, however, it was less demonstrably successful. In June negotiations were initiated for a Preferential Trade Agreement, but there was still no question of full membership as long as Spain continued to be governed by an undemocratic regime.

The second half of the decade saw the regime on a continual see-saw between gestures which appeared to concede greater freedom of movement in social, political and cultural matters, and knee-jerk repressive reaction to pressure for those appearances to become reality. Thus, for example, in 1965, the Basque and Catalan vernacular languages were allowed to be used in church services for the first time since the Civil War, but a Catalan priest, the abbot of Montserrat, was obliged to leave the country for his support of Catalan separatists, and a massive demonstration organized in the Basque Country to celebrate the region's National Day was broken up by police. The official students' union, the SEU, was dissolved, but those who participated in student assemblies which called for democracy were arrested, and lecturers and professors who supported the students were expelled from their universities. The Penal Code was reformed in 1965, but strikes were still considered a criminal offence if they were motivated by anything other than purely economic claims. A new Press Law was passed in 1966, to replace one which had been in force since the time of the Civil War and whose overt censorship was at variance with the regime's attempts to give Spain the appearance of an open, liberal society in the eyes of western observers. In fact, the new law was more severe than the previous one for, instead of clear, if draconian, censorship being exercised prior to publication, it was now left to editors to decide whether or not to publish and, therefore, to run the risk of having material confiscated after publication, and of suffering the serious financial loss that this might entail. The effect was to make authors, editors, film-makers, etc. more cautious than before, with self-censorship replacing the official variety.

While the Franco regime paid lip-service to change and took minimal steps to make it look as though it might ultimately evolve into a system compatible with other European states, Francoism was, in fact, digging in its heels and preparing to make itself eternal. In 1947 it had been decided that, eventually, Spain would again be ruled by a monarch; but Franco had deliberately left open the question of when and how this transition would take place. He had been urged many times to step down; there had been conspiracies and ultimatums to force him to hand over power. Each time he had resisted and had made clear that he had no intention of relinquishing his position as Head of State. In June 1961 he had announced his intention of passing a law which would prearrange the lines along which the post-Francoist monarchy would run. In this way, 'everything [would] be securely tied up', as he had said at Garabitas a year later. But that was as far as he went. Despite pressure from Carrero Blanco, López Rodó and other ministers to turn his attention to the succession question; despite the potential hiatus brought sharply into focus by his hunting accident in 1964; and despite his advancing age and infirmity, Franco doggedly refused either to name his successor or to complete the provisions for the institutionalization of the regime. Indeed, when in April 1965 ministers Fraga and Castiella pressed him at a cabinet meeting to discuss the future, Franco became very angry, asking them if they thought he was some kind of circus clown. At the end of the day, however, he did nothing. The question of Spain's political future remained in a state of suspended animation for as long as Franco chose, since he alone could appoint a successor.

Why was he so reluctant to take steps to institute the 'stability and continuity' which he himself had recommended in numerous speeches and interviews since the beginning of the decade? In the first place, he disliked and distrusted change. Secondly, he enjoyed power and did not want to relinquish it. Thirdly, he was both stubborn and inflexible; he would not be pushed or persuaded to go in any direction against his will. Fourthly, he suspected that, if Prince Juan Carlos were to become king, he would allow the restoration of the political pluralism which was anathema to Franco. Finally, his belief in his own special providence made him reluctant to contemplate the notion that he was dispensable; that life would, in fact, carry on without him. Consequently, it was not until the end of 1966 that he finally presented the long-awaited Organic Law of the State to the Cortes.

As ever, a date close to one of Francoism's ritual milestones had been chosen for the occasion: 22 November, two days after the thirtieth anniversary of the execution of José Antonio Primo de Rivera. Sitting on a raised daís before the semi-circle of representatives, Franco read in a droning monotone the speech which explained the content of and reasons for the new law. The Civil War was still the fundamental reference point, for it was this, according to Franco, that was the source of the 'political order of unity, authority, justice and progress' which was to be preserved indefinitely. In other words, the future was to be consciously conditioned by the past and manipulated in such a way as to sustain an interpretation of the past which deliberately excluded certain options whilst legitimating others. That there were to be 'flexible institutions capable of adapting to inevitable change' in fact meant nothing, for the aim was not to promote internal change, but simply to adapt to changing external circumstances in such a way as to preserve intact the values which had always been the pillars of Francoism. These were still to provide the basic criteria for political action. And in case there should be any doubt as to the temporal extent Franco intended these provisions to have, he made it clear that the Organic Law of the State laid down 'not only . . . the guarantees and formal procedures of the first succession, but also of subsequent successions, once the normal order has been established'. That is to say, he assumed the right and the power to determine what happened not only during his lifetime, but also in years to come, when he would no longer be physically present. It was Franco's way of attempting to achieve immortality.

Not content with simply putting the law on the statute book, Franco decided that it should be submitted to public approval in a national referendum. As everyone was perfectly aware, this was no more than an empty gesture, since the conditions for a free poll did not exist and, in any case, Franco's unilateral legislative powers precluded the need for anything other than his signature. Besides, the Franco regime was based on military principles of authority and obedience, not on the idea that the opinions of ordinary citizens must be taken into account in the legislative process. The real purpose of the referendum was to give the impression that Spaniards *did* have a say in the political development of their country and, perhaps more important, that they supported Franco unequivocally, both as their present leader and as the creator of a system which would outlast him. The referendum was, thus, not about the Organic Law of the State, but a plebiscite for Franco's personal rule. The propaganda campaign leading up to polling day (14 December 1966) accordingly emphasized that the electorate was being asked to vote for Franco. Propaganda encouraging people to vote 'No', or to abstain, was prohibited. The published results gave a participation rate of 88 per cent and a vote in favour of the law of over 95 per cent. Both these figures are highly questionable. When municipal elections were held only a month earlier, the abstention rate had been 85 per cent, so it seems highly unlikely that it should have sunk as low as 12 per cent in the referendum, even bearing in mind that many who did not vote in local government elections may have considered a national referendum too important to miss. Even if the turnout *had* been 88 per cent (indeed, especially if it had been), it is difficult to believe that 95 per cent of those who voted did so in favour of Franco, for the extent and intensity of anti-Francoist protest registered throughout the 1960s was likely to be reflected in the number of people voting 'No' or returning blank ballot papers. The regime's supporters, however, naturally upheld the results as genuine and claimed them as a massive vote of confidence in the *Caudillo*. The Organic Law of the State duly came into effect on 10 January 1967.

Four days before the referendum, on 10 December 1966, Carrero Blanco had stated in a televized speech, 'the Organic Law of the State ends all speculation about the future of the regime'. This was not quite accurate, for Franco had not yet named his successor, but it was true in the sense that the law mapped out the form of the state that Franco's heir would take over. It was complemented, in June, by a trio of further laws which, between them, guaranteed the officially Catholic nature of the Spanish state, confirmed the political and trade union monopoly of the Movement, and defined suffrage more precisely (and more narrowly) with respect to the vote corresponding to heads of families. Franco undoubtedly did not intend any irony when he said, in his end-of-year message on 30 December 1968, 'immobilism is not viable in our time'. What he meant was not that radical changes should or would be introduced, but that the regime would be adapted in ways which would allow the fundamental power relations to remain the same, whoever was Head of State.

With the institutional framework in place which would ensure the continuity of his system of 'inorganic democracy', Franco withdrew almost completely into his leisure pursuits and his family circle. All that remained to be done was to establish formally the line of succession. It had long been generally assumed that the son of the rightful Pretender to the throne, Prince Juan Carlos, was being groomed for the position. On 15 January 1969, Franco informed the Prince that he would be officially designated as the *Generalísimo*'s political heir before the end of the year, but still gave no more detailed indication of the timing. Franco's agonizingly crab-like manner of proceeding greatly worried those of his cabinet ministers who were anxious for the monarchy to be restored. At a time when internal unrest was gathering pace again (particularly on university campuses and in urban, working-class areas) and Spain faced difficult negotiations with the United States, over the renewal of the military bases agreement, and with Britain, over Gibraltar, they hoped that the resolution of the succession question would put an end to speculation and contribute a much-needed note of political and institutional stability.

Throughout the spring of 1969, Franco was pressed to name his successor by Carrero Blanco (who had taken over from Muñoz Grandes as Vice-President of the Government in September 1967) and by his old friend and fellow-soldier, Alonso Vega. This time, Franco did not fly off the handle as he had done when similarly pressed four years earlier. On 21 July he informed the cabinet and the Council of the Realm that Prince Juan Carlos would, indeed, succeed him. On the following day, thirty years after the end of the Civil War, but characteristically close to the anniversary of its beginning, Don Juan Carlos was officially designated 'Prince of Spain'.[12] The absence of any indication as to when Juan Carlos would take over from Franco confirmed the latter's intention not to relinquish power until forced to do so by incapacity or death. Given his age and the irreversible nature of his illness, it seemed reasonable to suppose that it would not be long before that moment arrived. For the anti-Francoist opposition, it could not come soon enough, even though it was far from clear that the return of the monarchy would bring democracy in its wake. On the contrary, it seemed highly likely that, between them, the die-hard Francoists and the Movement reformers would ensure that Spain continued to be governed by a regime which proscribed and excluded certain political options. As the 1960s drew to a close, it appeared that Franco had, indeed, made sure that everything was 'securely tied down' for the future. In fact, the last five years of his life were to show how futile had been his efforts indefinitely and totally to control the course of Spanish history.

August was usually a political millpond in Spain, with the Cortes in summer recess, the Administration reduced to a skeleton staff, and patricians and plebeians alike seeking relief from the heat away from the cities. In 1969, however, the customary summer tranquillity was broken by news of the discovery of a major scandal in the business world, in which senior government officials and even cabinet ministers were rumoured to be involved. A manufacturer of machinery for the textile industry, Matesa, was alleged to have obtained some ten billion pesetas in export credits under false pretences, with the connivance of people in the Administration.[13] However, it was not the immorality of the scandal nor the magnitude of the deceit that gave the political classes pause, but the wider economic and political implications of the affair. In the first place it revealed the glaring contradiction between the developmentalist ethos inspiring economic policy and the restrictive official framework within which business had to operate. For Matesa claimed that it had invented export orders as the only way to obtain money to tide the company over until it was paid by its export customers. Secondly, the political aspect of the matter was that the owner of Matesa, Juan Vilá Reyes, was said to be a member of Opus Dei and to maintain excellent relations with the group known as the 'Opus technocrats' in the ministries of Finance and Commerce. The Falangists in the regime seized on the affair as a long-awaited opportunity to retaliate against what they considered their political displacement by the men of Opus Dei, by reasserting themselves as the guiding force of the regime. They were to be disappointed. Franco remained relatively unperturbed by the scandal itself, but was irritated by the Falangist campaign to discredit the technocrats. Once more, opposing factions within the regime were squabbling amongst themselves, as they had done in Salamanca in 1937, over the clash at Begoña in 1942, and in the wake of the shooting of the student Miguel Alvarez in 1956. For what was, in fact, to be the last time, Franco exercised his authority as supreme arbiter, although, in truth, the whip he cracked had been put in his hand by his Deputy Prime Minister, Carrero Blanco.

There had been speculation about a cabinet reshuffle for some time. 'New Government before Successor is named?' had been the headline of *Mundo* on 19 July.[14] Dilatory as ever, Franco had preferred not to act, despite Carrero Blanco's advice that action was necessary to counter a growing sense of confrontation between those who favoured further, albeit limited, changes to the regime, and those who thought that the reform process had already gone quite far enough. The Matesa affair brought this latent conflict to crisis point, making its resolution urgent.

On 29 October the composition of the new cabinet was made public. The two Opus Dei ministers implicated in the Matesa scandal, Juan José Espinosa San Martín (Finance) and Faustino García Moncó (Commerce), were dropped, as were the Falangist moderates Solís and Fraga, whom Franco regarded as having allowed the Party's reactionary wing to try to exploit Matesa to their own advantage. In that thirteen of its eighteen members were new, the 29 October cabinet constituted a real shake-up; but it did not herald any sweeping change of political direction. At most, it confirmed the ascendancy of the Catholic technocrats over the Falangists, for two-thirds of the new cabinet could be identified either with Opus Dei or the slightly more conservative National Catholic Association of Propagandists (Asociación Católica Nacional de Propagandistas, ACNP). It was the most homogenous cabinet in the history of the regime. Its composition betrayed the influence of Carrero Blanco who, increasingly, was the real power behind the throne at the Pardo Palace.

While Franco became more wasted by Parkinson's disease and, in consequence, less able to govern, Carrero worked to square the circle of preparing a continuist future for a society in which pressure for radical change was building up on all sides. Franco persisted in invoking the Civil War and the achievements of his regime in his – now far less frequent – public appearances, and in claiming that he could only relinquish his position when God relieved him of the onerous duties he had, throughout his lifetime, sacrificed himself to carry out. The truth was, however, that by the beginning of the 1970s, his regime was held together by no more than its legal corset and the personal loyalty of a relatively small group of die-hard reactionaries. Franco's words were empty rhetoric for the majority of Spaniards. Worse, they were a provocation to those who fervently desired an end to dictatorship.

A strong sense of frustration undoubtedly contributed to the escalation of anti-Francoist protest in this period. The basic problem was that the restricted mould into which Franco and his followers had forced Spain for so many years was no longer capable of containing the resurgence of the country's inherent social, political and cultural diversity. Franco no longer exercised real power, except in his capacity to prevent change, but he refused to step down. And while contemporaries such as Salazar, de Gaulle and Alonso Vega died of old age,[15] Franco clung doggedly to life. The feeling of desperation among anti-Francoists was sharpened by the almost certain knowledge that, even if Franco were to die or retire, Carrero Blanco would be there to ensure that, as the *Caudillo* himself was given to saying, after Franco would come 'the institutions'. Carrero's appointment, on 8 June 1973, as Head of Government, constituted another turn of the screw. It turned out to be one turn too many. On 20 December 1973 Admiral Carrero Blanco was assassinated in Madrid as he returned to his house by car after hearing mass at a nearby church. A tunnel had been secretly excavated under a central street, then filled with a huge explosive charge which was detonated as Carrero's vehicle drove over it.

The attack was the work of the militant Basque nationalist organization, Euskadi Ta Askatasuna (Basque Homeland and Liberty), more commonly referred to by its acronym, ETA. Repression against Basque nationalism had been particularly virulent throughout the Franco regime, and never more so than in the 1970s, when frustration on the part of the Basques and fear on that of the regime became locked together in an intensifying spiral of hatred and violence. Indeed, the decade had opened with a show trial in Burgos, at which the prosecution asked for a total of nine death penalties and a total of 752 years in prison for sixteen members of ETA accused of terrorist activities. Franco ultimately commuted the death penalties, not because he genuinely felt inclined to mercy, but because Spain had, at last, concluded a preferential agreement with the EEC in June and had received considerable economic assistance for much-needed infrastructural projects from the World Bank and the government of the Federal Republic of Germany. With economic difficulties again on the horizon, the Franco regime could not afford to alienate the western democracies. Moreover, at that time, ETA commanded and could mobilize considerable sympathy among anti-Francoists throughout Spain. For this reason, while many were shocked by the enormity of the crime perpetrated against Carrero Blanco in 1973, they also considered it a positive step in the direction of opening the way to a non-continuist post-Franco era.

Franco was devastated. He had known Carrero since the 1930s when, as General Commander of the Balearic Isles, he had asked the then young naval captain for a plan to improve the maritime defences of the islands. The two men had many things in common: a naval vocation; belonging to a generation marked by the collapse of the Spanish empire; participation in the Moroccan wars; an aversion to liberalism, communism and Freemasonry; and an unquestioning, unhesitating belief in the rightness of the values on which Francoism rested. In 1940 Franco made him First Secretary to the Presidency of the Government, to which Carrero subsequently added the responsibilities of Vice President of the Cortes and National Councillor of FET y de las JONS. Since he was also a convinced monarchist and maintained good relations with the Catholic Church, he had a finger in many political pies and was uniquely placed to report to Franco on what was going on within the regime. Yet, despite the potential his position afforded him for political self-advancement, Carrero never so much as appeared to want to overshadow or compete with Franco. For over thirty-five years, he had served Franco with utter fidelity, a paragon of loyalty and discretion.

As ETA had anticipated, the assassination of Carrero Blanco dealt a severe blow both to Franco and to Francoism. Gonzalo Fernández de la Mora, the ultra-conservative Minister for Public Works, commented accurately, 'No harder blow could have been struck at the future prospects of the [Francoist] state.'[16] However, although the regime was rocked back on its heels, it did not fall. This was in no small measure due to the calm efficiency with which the Vice-President of the Government, Torcuato Fernández Miranda, took over the leadership. His rejection of the extreme Right's demands for retribution earned him the respect of the general public. However, in the view of the regime's most reactionary sector, including Franco's most intimate circle, he was too weak to prevent what they feared was going to be a repetition of the assault on the Russian Winter Palace. This, together with his known liberalizing preferences, was the reason for the exclusion of Fernández Miranda from the list of possible successors to Carrero Blanco. Franco was anxious and indecisive, as could only be expected in a man of eighty, suffering from a serious nervous disease and the effects of a severe emotional shock. When he most needed Carrero Blanco to tell him what to do and whom to choose, Carrero was not there. On 28 December Franco informed the Council of the Realm that he wanted Carlos Arias Navarro to be the next Head of Government. This seemed an astonishing choice, for Arias Navarro was Minister of the Interior and, therefore, ultimately responsible for the protection of government ministers. Notwithstanding his failure to protect Carrero, a number of factors favoured Arias's candidacy as the Admiral's successor. In the first place, he could be expected to adopt an authoritarian approach to government in general and to anti-Francoist opposition in particular: he had earned himself an enduring reputation as a hard-line Nationalist during the Civil War, when, as state prosecutor of Malaga in 1937, he had overseen rearguard repression so brutal that the Italian government had protested to Franco. It was his unbending attitude towards Francoism's 'enemies of Spain' that, secondly, had gained him the esteem and patronage of another regime hard-liner, Franco's intimate crony Camilo Alonso Vega. Thirdly, Arias, like Carrero, had no political aspirations other than total loyalty to Franco. Last, but by no means least, Arias was much liked by Franco's wife, doña Carmen. In appointing Arias, Franco seemed to have reverted to the criterion which in 1950 had led him to choose Fernando María Castiella as prospective ambassador to London, when he had explained his choice by saying, 'Faith is more important than competence.'[17]

When the composition of the first Arias government became known on 3 January 1974, the inclusion of men considered relatively liberal in outlook seemed at first sight a hopeful sign. In fact, the mix of progressives and reactionaries represented a return to the old Francoist tactic of containing internal tensions by giving all the regime's political 'families' a place in government. But the past success of that tactic had been due in large measure to two factors which were no longer present: Franco's role as supreme arbiter among his followers, and their common fear of the consequences of his absence. Now, Franco was little more than a figure-head, whose absence was only feared by Falangist extremists who knew that, if political pluralism were to return, the active life-expectancy of their groups would be very short. From the standpoint of social and political stability, the Arias government was a failure, for the period during which he was Prime Minister – December 1973 to June 1976 – saw a tremendous escalation of strikes; demonstrations in favour of democracy; open criticism of the regime from Church, regionalist, business, artistic, intellectual and press spheres; political violence; and state repression. At the same time, however, it was an impossible task to reconcile the demands for reform which underlay these protests with pressure from Franco to purge the cabinet of liberals; sabre-rattling in certain sectors of the Armed Forces; and the overtly threatening attitude adopted by hard-line supporters of Franco. In addition, Arias had to cope with the unsettling example of the April 1974 revolution in Portugal and a situation of deepening economic crisis. As he himself and many others must have suspected, Arias was, in practice, overseeing the death throes of the regime.

Those suspicions were suddenly intensified in the summer of 1974, when on 9 July Franco had to be admitted to hospital, suffering from phlebitis in his right leg. Despite the seriousness of his condition, Prince Juan Carlos did not temporarily assume the position of Head of State, partly because Franco's family argued against the transfer at this stage and partly because Don Juan Carlos himself did not want to be 'a temporary understudy with no clear role'.[18] On 18 July, however, Franco suffered a relapse, apparently brought on by watching a television programme about his own life. On the following day, Prince Juan Carlos took over as Head of State, in accordance with the provisions of the 1967 Organic Law of the State. It was not to be for long. On 2 September Franco informed Arias Navarro that he would resume the functions temporarily transferred to Prince Juan Carlos, which he did on 9 September, despite still undergoing an intensive programme of physiotherapy to help him recover his mobility and overcome frequent bouts of depression. As if to confirm that he was back in control, on 4 October, the feast day of Saint Francis, he remained standing while greeting over 400 people who wished to pay him their respects.[19] Then, on 24 October, he instructed Arias to dismiss the Minister of Information and Tourism, Pío Cabanillas, on the grounds that the press was becoming too outspoken. There followed an unprecedented flurry of resignations in solidarity, from the Finance Minister and a number of top civil servants.

The state of constant tension and agitation which characterized the first half of the 1970s in Spain reached a climax in the summer of 1975. On 27 September two convicted members of ETA and three of another extreme Left-wing organization, FRAP (Frente Revolucionario Antifascista y Popular) were executed, in accordance with a draconian anti-terrorist law passed a month earlier. The executions were carried out in spite of a massive national and international campaign of protest and revulsion, which included pleas for clemency from the United Nations and the Vatican. On 1 October Franco was acclaimed by thousands of cheering supporters when he appeared on the balcony of the Royal Palace in the centre of Madrid, to celebrate the thirty-ninth anniversary of his appointment as Head of State. The pathetic, drooping figure who laboriously raised his arms in greeting to the crowd below was a far cry from the stout, energetic Franco who had revelled in the adulation of other crowds, in Burgos and Salamanca, in 1936. The determination physically to eradicate all vestige of Left-wing thought, however, had not changed at all.

That was, in fact, the last time that Franco ever appeared in public. On 15 October he suffered a heart attack. Three more followed between 20 and 24 October. On 30 October, in view of the respiratory and intestinal complications which had set in, he ordered that Prince Juan Carlos take over as Head of State. This time, the transfer was to prove permanent. Franco was admitted on 5 November to a Madrid hospital, where he twice underwent major intestinal surgery in an attempt to stop massive internal haemorrhaging. For two weeks the whole of Spain held its breath as the announcement of Franco's death was awaited at any moment. Meanwhile, he was kept alive, but not conscious, by a horrendous array of tubes, bottles, drugs and machines. He died in the early hours of the morning of 20 November. It was the thirty-ninth anniversary of the death of the founder of Falange Española, José Antonio Primo de Rivera. To the last, Franco kept his tryst with the rituals of his regime.

. . .

NOTES

1. S. Lieberman, *The Contemporary Spanish Economy. A Historical Perspective*, London: Allen and Unwin 1982, p. 206.
2. P. Preston, *Franco*, London: Harper Collins 1993, ch. 25.
3. F. Franco, *Mensajes y Discursos del Jefe del Estado, 1960–1963*, Madrid: Dirección General de Información, Publicaciónes Españolas 1964, p. 209.
4. Ibid., pp. 292, 300.
5. P. Preston, *Franco*, ch. 26.
6. The 'Provisional Sergeants' (*alfereces provisionales*) corps was created in the spring of 1937 as a means of providing temporary NCO status to volunteers in the Nationalist Army. A great many wartime *alfereces provisionales* subsequently entered the Franco regime's sprawling civilian bureaucracy.
7. F. Franco, *Discursos y mensajes del Jefe del Estado, 1960–1963*, pp. 391–2.
8. Ibid., pp. 392–7.
9. Ibid., pp. 399–404.
10. See above, pp. 127–8.
11. J. Sinova (ed.), *Historia del franquismo*, (2 vols) Madrid: Diario 16 1985, vol. II, p. 591.
12. The heir to the Spanish throne traditionally used the title 'Prince of Asturias'. The creation of the title 'Prince of Spain' was designed to underscore Franco's contention that he was not restoring the old monarchy but installing a new one.
13. For a more detailed discussion of the Matesa affair, see E. Alvarez Puga, *Matesa. Más allá del escándalo*, Barcelona: Dopesa 1974, passim and E. de Blaye, *Franco and the Politics of Spain*, Harmondsworth: Penguin 1976, pp. 260–4, 387.
14. Equipo Mundo, *Los 90 ministros de Franco*, Barcelona: Dopesa 1970, p. 420.
15. Salazar and de Gaulle died, respectively, on 27 July 1970 and 9 November 1970. Alonso Vega died on 1 July 1971.
16. J.P. Fusi, *Franco. A Biography*, London: Unwin Hyman 1987, p. 148.
17. See above, p. 158.
18. J.P. Fusi, *Franco. A Biography*, p. 157.
19. Ibid., p. 160.

Chapter 9

THE BEGINNING OF THE POST-FRANCO ERA

At six o'clock on the morning of 20 November 1975, the Minister for Information and Tourism, León Herrera Esteban, announced on Spanish National Radio that, according to the bulletin issued by Franco's Civil and Military Households at 5.25 a.m., His Excellency the *Generalísimo* had died 'from a cardiac arrest, culminating a process of toxic shock caused by peritonitis'.[1] At the same time, the Minister informed listeners that 'in accordance with Article 7 of the Law of Succession, the powers of the Head of State have been assumed, in the name of His Royal Highness the Prince of Spain, by the Council of Regency'. Finally, Herrera gave out 'an important notice': the Prime Minister, Carlos Arias Navarro, would address the nation on radio and television later that morning.

At ten o'clock, an emotional, but controlled, Arias Navarro spoke for exactly seven minutes. He began by pronouncing the words that were already the headlines of all that day's newspapers: 'Franco ha muerto' ('Franco has died'). He then read 'Franco's last message', which the *Caudillo* had written at his El Pardo residence on 18 October, and later given to his daughter, Carmen, for typing and safe-keeping.[2] In it, Franco asked forgiveness of all, as 'with all [his] heart [he] forgave all those who declared themselves [his] enemies'. 'I hope and believe', he continued, 'that I had no enemies other than those of Spain, which I love until the last moment and which I promised to serve until my last breath, which I know to be at hand.' After thanking those who had collaborated with him, he asked his fellow countrymen and women to

215

'surround the future King of Spain, Don Juan Carlos de Borbón, with the same affection and loyalty' as they had shown Franco, and not to forget 'that the enemies of Spain and of Christian civilization are on the alert'. The message ended with Francoism's ritual cries, 'Arriba España! Viva España!' ('Up with Spain! Long live Spain!')[3]

During his short broadcast, the Prime Minister said he knew that, in many homes, his words would be 'blurred by the murmur of weeping and prayer'. In fact, many people did not hear or see Arias's historic broadcast in their own home for, by then, the streets of towns and cities up and down the country were thronged with people. The newspaper kiosks could barely keep pace with the demand for the numerous editions published by all the national dailies, while transistor radios and television sets in bars and cafés came into their own. The prevailing sensation that morning was of disbelief. For some, this meant grief and dismay at the realization that the man who for four decades had presided over Spain's destiny was no longer there to protect and guarantee the survival of such values as national unity, anti-communism and Catholicism. For others, it meant incredulity that now, at last, the dictator would not be able to stand in the way of a return to democratic, pluralist forms of government, society and culture.

Soon, a sense of expectation took over which, like the initial reaction, meant different things to different people. The regime's supporters hoped that the answer to the question, 'What now?' would be 'the institutions', as Franco and Carrero Blanco had promised. By contrast, those who, at the time of Carrero's death, had sensed that change was suddenly a real possibility, were equally hopeful that Francoism would not survive its creator. For all of them, the key question was whether or not the Prince of Spain, designated Franco's political heir in 1969, would carry on where Franco had left off, as he had been groomed to do since childhood. The mouthpiece of the ultra-right-wing National Confederation of Combatants, *El Alcazar*, affirmed that 'the laws passed in 1947, 1967 and 1969' provided the 'mechanism necessary to fill the void which has occurred in the country's principal Magistracy'. 'In this way', it continued, the simple application of the law guarantees the continuity of the institutions and the certainty that the words, so often pronounced, 'Everything is securely tied down' reflect reality and constitute the last and finest service rendered by the man who ruled over the fortunes of the Fatherland for nearly forty years. At the same time, the political wisdom and intelligence of the Prince, demonstrated throughout his life and especially on the two occasions on which he assumed temporarily the Headship of the State, allow us to feel not only sadness at the death of Francisco Franco, but also confidence in the performance of his successor.[4]

For years, Don Juan Carlos had stood at Franco's elbow on important occasions such as the annual Victory Parade, but he had never voiced his opinions publicly. His reluctance to assume only temporary leadership of the state in July 1974 had suggested to Franco's inner circle that he was a man of decisive and independent character but, for the mass of the population and most outside observers, he was an unknown quantity. In accordance with the 1947 Law of Succession, the three-member Council of Regency met as soon as news of Franco's death had been made public, and called a plenary session of the Cortes and the Council of the Realm for Saturday, 22 November. Thirty days official mourning were also declared. All academic activities were suspended until 27 November. Cinemas and theatres were closed and sporting events postponed until the afternoon of 23 November. Radio stations broadcast nothing but appropriately solemn music, interspersed with news bulletins, and the Mayor of Madrid, Miguel Angel García Lomas, issued a municipal edict inviting his fellow citizens to pay their last respects to Franco at the funeral chapel to be opened next day in the Royal Palace and to attend the mass and military parade to be held on the day of Franco's burial, Sunday, 23 November.

Saturday, 22 November dawned bright and intensely cold. An air of expectant silence hung over Madrid, for the new king was to be installed at noon and the day had been declared 'non-working for all purposes'. Before the assembled members of the Cortes, Don Juan Carlos de Borbón swore 'to keep and cause to be kept the Fundamental Laws of the Kingdom and to remain loyal to the Principles which inform the National Movement'. He was then proclaimed King of Spain, 'to reign with the name of Juan Carlos the First'.[5] He then made his inaugural speech, from which it was clear that he intended to establish from the outset that his assumption of power stemmed, not from his designation by Franco, but from his position as rightful heir to the Spanish throne. The new king devoted one respectful, though hardly effusive, paragraph to the recently deceased *Caudillo*, but the main theme of the speech was the future and the need for pluralism and change. His words surely strengthened the misgivings of those who feared Juan Carlos I might not follow meekly in Franco's footsteps.

The first public engagement of the newly installed monarch was Franco's state funeral on 23 November. For two days, thousands of people had queued day and night for up to fourteen hours, to file past Franco's embalmed body as it lay in state, dressed in the gala uniform of Captain-General, in the Royal Palace.[6] Many raised their right arm in fascist salute as they stood before the coffin. Some knelt briefly in prayer. An eighty-year-old man fell dead as he reached the bier, overcome by the emotional stress of the occasion and the physical strain of standing outside in the bitter cold for several hours.[7] All over Spain, special masses were said for the eternal rest of the *Caudillo* and balconies were draped with the Spanish flag and black ribbons, as a sign of mourning. A large platform, a bier and an altar had been erected in front of the main entrance to the Palace, from which mass was to be celebrated in the presence of the coffin, the king and queen and the Franco family. Flags and tapestries adorned the balconies of the Palace. A unit of Franco's personal guard stood to attention before the platform and thousands of people filled the Plaza de Oriente, in front of the Palace where, in the past, they had so often gathered to cheer the *Caudillo*. Franco would have revelled in the pomp and solemnity of the occasion.

After the mass, celebrated by the Archbishop of Toledo and Primate of All Spain, Monseñor Marcelo González Martín, guardsmen of 'His Excellency's Own Regiment' carried the coffin to the open military vehicle which was to serve as a hearse. A military parade and a rendering of the national anthem then preceded the departure of the funeral cortège, which began, as dictated by a decree of 1963, with a twenty-one gun salute. Five vehicles carrying wreaths and flowers led the way, followed by twenty one Civil Guard motorcyclists and four cars containing the heads of Franco's Civil and Military Households and a number of high-ranking churchmen. They were followed by the military vehicle carrying the coffin and an open car in which stood King Juan Carlos. These two vehicles were flanked by two lines of mounted lancers, with flowing cloaks and shining helmets. An unmounted horse, supposedly Franco's, accompanied them. Then came an interminable motorcade conveying the Franco family, the President of the Cortes, the Royal Family, and innumerable ministers, diplomats, top civil servants, military men, Movement officials and local government representatives. At 1 p.m. the first vehicle reached the entrance to the 'Valley of the Fallen', in the Guadarrama mountains, where, on 'Victory Day' 1959, Franco had inaugurated the huge underground church built as his monument and his mausoleum.[8]

On the esplanade in front of the entrance to the basilica were gathered some 80,000 fervent Francoists. They had come from all over Spain in convoys of coaches and cars, and represented the hard core of Franco's erstwhile support: the Federation of Combatants, the Blue Division Brotherhood, the Provisional Sergeants' organization, the Carlist Requeté, the Youth Front, the Women's Section, the 'José Antonio' Training School, and many more, all with their flags and emblems, all desolate at the passing of their lifelong patron. They broke into their ritual chant of 'Franco! Franco! Franco!' when the military 'hearse' reached the esplanade, but a voice over the loudspeaker system demanded silence as members of the Franco family carried the coffin up the steps and over to the entrance to the church. Eight uniformed members of Franco's personal guard then bore the coffin down the nave to the bier which had been set up in front of the high altar. King Juan Carlos, dressed in military uniform, sat behind and to the left of the altar; to his right, the government and, behind them, serried rows of regime officials. On the other side of the altar, sat the Archbishop of Madrid, Monseñor Vicente Enrique y Tarancón; to his left, the diplomatic corps and the representatives of nearly one hundred foreign countries, including the Chilean dictator General Augusto Pinochet and his wife, and the wife of the President of the Philippine Islands, Mrs Imelda Marcos.[9]

After a brief burial service, taken by the abbot of the Valley of the Fallen, Monseñor Luis María de Lojendio, the dark mahogany coffin was carried to the place behind the altar where, twenty years earlier and at Franco's behest, a cavity six feet long and four feet deep had been built beneath the marble floor. As the coffin was lowered slowly into the lead-lined tomb, and a 1,500-kilogramme, polished granite slab bearing the inscription 'Francisco Franco' was moved into place to close it, the more acute and dispassionate of the assembled mourners and observers may have reflected on the life and times of the man now being laid to rest with such lavish ceremony.

Francisco Franco Bahamonde was born towards the end of a long period of economic, social and political crisis which culminated in the loss of Spain's last overseas colonies in 1898. The 'Disaster' caused the Spanish upper and middle classes to initiate a collective soul-searching, in the hope that the regeneration of national pride and confidence would enable Spain to recover what they considered the country's 'rightful' place among the world's great nations. The military campaigns undertaken from 1906 onwards to protect and further Spain's interests in Morocco were viewed by the political élite as an enterprise which would at once involve all sectors of society and provide an opportunity for Spain to reassert her lost international prestige. In addition, the Moroccan war was seen by Spain's politicians as a way of placating the military for the humiliation and frustration of the 1898 débâcle.

Francisco Franco was a product of this particular configuration of historical circumstances. Without it, he might well have remained an anonymous soldier; if, indeed, he had become a soldier at all. This is not to say that his life and career were entirely determined by events external to himself. But, from an early age, the choices he made with regard to his personal destiny were intimately bound up with the course of his country's history. It may well be that it was his parents rather than he who decided that he should enter the Toledo Military Academy in 1907, but he does not appear to have opposed this decision or to have considered any alternative. Once at the Academy, the values instilled in him during his conservative, middle-class, Catholic upbringing began to take more explicit shape as the anti-liberal, anti-democratic socio-political opinions widely held in contemporary Spanish military circles. By the time Franco graduated as a Second Lieutenant, in 1910, he saw himself as a member of an élite body which alone was capable of saving Spain from the ruin and ignominy into which she was supposedly being led by the self-seeking incompetence of politicians.

As we saw in Chapter 2, Franco's career as a soldier in North Africa was crucial to his personal and professional development, to his view of himself as a man with a mission and, equally important, to other people's perception of him as a charismatic figure. In Africa were laid the foundations of his future power and of a long period of Spanish history. It was for this reason that Franco used to say, 'I am inexplicable to myself without Africa.' His role during the revolutionary crisis of 1934, during which he deployed Moroccan troops to devastating effect, constituted the next milestone along the road to power, in that it enhanced his self-confidence and, above all, confirmed the belief of Spanish conservatives that here was a man who would neither question nor stint the use of violence to crush 'the enemies of Spain', whether these were Rif tribesmen or Spaniards with left-wing views.

Then came the anti-Republican conspiracy and the military rising of 18 July 1936. Franco's initial reluctance to join the rebels was due to two facts which may have been related in his mind: first, he was not the leader of the conspiracy and, second, he was not convinced that it would succeed. 'When I rise, it will be to win', he is reported to have said in 1932, for he knew that failure would mean the end of his career and, possibly, of his life. Consequently, once he had thrown in his lot with the insurgents, he was bound to do his utmost to ensure they did not fail. Did this also imply, in his view, taking over the leadership of the rising? There is no testimony to the effect that such was his intention when, on 13 July, he sent word to the 'Director' of the conspiracy, General Mola, that he was with the rebellion. Yet, from the instant he landed in Tetuán on

19 July, he did not behave like just another cog in the rebel machine, but with the confidence and authority of someone in charge.

Paradoxically, his position was enhanced by the initial failure of the coup. With Madrid, Barcelona, Valencia, Bilbao and the Hispano-French border in government hands, and a large part of the Armed Forces loyal to the Republic, the fate of the rebellion depended on whether or not the Spanish Army's best troops, the Army of Africa, could be transported across the Straits of Gibraltar to the Peninsula. The achievement of this important immediate objective, thanks to Franco's determination and his appeals to Hitler and Mussolini, made him seem indispensable to the attainment of the rising's ultimate aim, namely the overthrow of the Republic. The conquest of Extremadura, the swift and devastating advance on Madrid from the west, and the relief of Toledo, all under General Franco's overall command, further increased his stock, placing him in a position of unanswerable superiority when, in September 1936, the military complexity of the conflict demanded that a single commander-in-chief be appointed in the rebel camp.

Franco also achieved supreme political power in, and largely thanks to, the exceptional circumstances of the Civil War. It was a position he was unlikely to have reached otherwise. With the possible exception of February 1936, he had never attempted to carry on the long tradition of military intervention in politics by leading a *pronunciamiento*, as General Primo de Rivera had done in 1923, and he had been reluctant up to the last moment to participate in the July 1936 coup. Certainly he had views on political issues and was acquainted with several politicians, but he appeared not to harbour strong ambitions to pursue a career in politics nor, still less, to found or lead a political party. It was this apparent detachment from particular creeds which clinched his appointment as political supremo in 1936. It also helped him to retain power for thirty-nine years thereafter, for it enabled him to act as uncommitted arbiter among the rival factions supporting him. Within the narrow confines of his anti-democratic system, Franco allowed his own partisans certain room for manoeuvre. Although all Left-wing and liberal thought was repressed, Alphonsine and Carlist monarchists, Falangists and Catholic conservatives retained their pre-war ideological affiliations and aspirations, as the political 'families' of Francoism. Franco did not identify with any one of them in particular nor did he actively promote a new, unitary identity for the party which formally bound them together from 1937 onwards, Falange Española Tradicionalista y de las JONS, even though he was its National Chief. On the contrary, it suited him that its components should maintain different and even divergent aims to some extent, for this lessened the risk of their joining forces to oust him and provided the justification for his own permanence as guarantor of internal peace and stability. Rarely can anyone have been so successful at holding on to power while appearing to have nothing to do with politics.

This was one side of the coin. The other was continuing repression of those who opposed (or were thought to oppose) Franco or his system. Both strands of policy very effectively curtailed any overt challenge to his authority until the day of his death. His handling of political matters, like his conduct of war, centred on the relentless pursuit of his own ends and the calculated grinding down of opposition, from whatever quarter. Yet Franco's ability to remain in power cannot be explained solely by reference to coercion of adversaries and manipulation of partisans. A number of other factors must also be taken into consideration. In the first place, although the Franco regime was loathed by many thousands of people inside and outside Spain, it also enjoyed the active support, or at least the acquiescence, of as many other people who sincerely believed that Franco had 'rescued' Spain from the 'chaos' of the Second Republic and the ultimate threat of communist subversion. Secondly, this popular view of Franco as guarantor of Right-wing stability on Europe's southern flank was in part accepted by governments in western democratic countries, whose inhibition during and after the Civil War was due partly to their fear of the advance of communism and partly to their reluctance to run the risk of becoming embroiled in further political, and possibly military, entanglements. After 1944 Franco had no reason to fear intervention from outside Spain.

Thirdly, because information was tightly controlled and

carefully disseminated, it was easy for Franco's propagandists to distort the truth in such a way as always to present Franco and his regime in a favourable light, inflating their successes and diminishing their failures or, as often happened, blaming difficulties on 'envious' foreign communists and Freemasons. Thus, the fact that Spain did not participate as a belligerent in the Second World War was attributed to consummate skill on Franco's part, which allegedly enabled him to resist Axis pressure to enter the war on the side of the Nazi–Fascist alliance. Food shortages and black marketeering, by contrast, were put down to external hostility and the machinations of 'bad' Spaniards.

Fourthly, although relations with the Vatican became increasingly strained in the final decade of Franco's life and certain sectors of the Spanish Church were closely involved in the movement, which gathered pace from the mid-1950s onwards, to make Spanish society more democratic it could not be denied that the Catholic Church had given its blessing to the Civil War as a 'crusade' in 1936, that Pope Pius XII had congratulated Franco in 1939 on achieving 'Spain's Catholic victory',[10] and that the Vatican had signed a concordat with the Franco regime in 1953. Franco could always count on a solid core of support at all levels of the Church hierarchy, in the Catholic press, and in the education system – traditionally the preserve of the Catholic Church – which would keep alive the memory of the 'crusade' and the image of Franco as the benefactor of Catholicism, the protector of Spain's identity as a Catholic nation, and the 'saviour' of Christian civilization.

Finally, in the early days of his regime and again in its (and his) later years, Franco relied on a small group of politically acute, personally honest and totally loyal men. This is not to say that he favoured them with his trust: he once commented to Don Juan de Borbón that he never placed complete confidence in anyone. It is to say that Franco's successive use, as assistants, counsellors and intermediaries, of his brother, Nicolás, Ramón Serrano Suñer, Agustín Muñoz Grandes, and Luis Carrero Blanco reveals him as an astute judge of character and a master of the art of exploiting other people to further his own ends. Nicolás Franco acted as his brother's rearguard political factotum at a time (the latter half of 1936) when the *Generalísimo* needed to concentrate all his energies on the military campaign against Madrid. Serrano Suñer played a more specific and executive role. While Franco pursued military victory in the Civil War, Serrano took on the task of laying the juridical and political foundations of the post-war regime. Franco deployed Serrano's political experience, professional acumen and ideological pre-ferences by appointing him first as Minister for the Interior and later, after the outbreak of war in Europe, as Minister for Foreign Affairs. In this way, Franco used him to consolidate the regime internally and externally until he felt sufficiently confident to dispense with him, in 1942. The appointment in 1962 of Agustín Muñoz Grandes as the first vice-president of a Francoist cabinet intimated Franco's recognition of the fact that, although he might claim to feel young, he was in fact ageing and tiring. Important though this development was, it was based solely on pragmatic considerations and did not mean that Franco was placing limitations on his own power, nor that he wished to modify the anti-democratic nature of his regime. On the contrary, the choice of Muñoz Grandes, a soldier with Falangist sympathies, indicated clearly that the fundamental values underpinning the regime had not changed.

Similarly, when Muñoz Grandes was replaced by Luis Carrero Blanco, in September 1967, it was not because Franco wanted to make his regime radically different, but partly because he was declining physically and mentally, and partly to ensure the political preservation of the regime. But whereas the choice of Muñoz Grandes had been redolent of the spirit of 18 July 1936, the designation of Carrero Blanco to succeed him reflected the conviction of Franco's political advisers (among whom was Carrero himself) that Francoism would only survive as a political system if it were modified in accordance with national and international economic and political circumstances very different from those which had accompanied its birth in 1936. Carrero was not hidebound by fidelity to particular ideological principles. He was imbued with the practical adaptability characteristic of the technocrats who, in the late 1950s and especially the 1960s, had decisively influenced the course of Spain's economic development. But Carrero was also a member of the Armed Forces, a loyal Francoist, a fervent Catholic, and a staunch monarchist. He thus embodied a combination of authoritarianism, conservatism and pragmatism ideally suited to the task of shoring up the regime in what were, foreseeably, Franco's final years, and of preparing its continuation even after the physical demise of its founder.

The impunity with which the Basque terrorist organization ETA assassinated Carrero Blanco in 1973 revealed that, despite its Praetorian pretensions, the Franco regime was not as strong as it appeared. Even so, it would have been difficult for observers in 1975, however acute, to have predicted the future and, in particular, the extraordinary speed and apparent ease of the transition to democracy which followed Franco's death. Paradoxically, the carefully calculated degree of flexibility employed by him to stay in power had ultimately made the regime untenable. For, although limited in scope, it was still sufficient to allow Spain to change socially, culturally and economically over the years. Indeed, from the 1960s onwards, the legitimation of Franco's permanence in power was that he not only continued to be the guardian of Christian civilization but he was also responsible for the transformation of Spain into a modern, industrialized society. By the 1970s, however, he was superfluous in his role as political ringmaster for, with the exception of a small band of recalcitrant '18 July' loyalists, all the regime forces were agreed on the need for political pluralism as a prerequisite for further economic and social development. The model originally used to impose national unity had become a threat to that unity, because it carried with it the seeds of its own destruction and had reached the limit of its capacity to assimilate their growth.

If after Franco's death in 1975 his regime crumbled with a speed that belied the forty years of its duration, it was because by then it was irrelevant to the society over which it presided. Within fourteen months of Franco's demise, a Law of Political Reform had been passed, which opened the way towards the legalization of political parties and the holding of a general election based on universal adult suffrage. The first democratic general election since

1936 was held in June 1977 with the participation of political organizations ranging right across the political spectrum, including the Communist Party of Spain and groups to its left. A new constitution, drawn up by a seven-man committee representing the major parties represented in parliament, was approved by popular referendum on 6 December 1978.[11]

Since then, with the exception of one notable incident, Spanish political life has followed a course similar to that of any other western democratic country. That incident took place on 23 February 1981, when a group of extreme Rightist Civil Guards and Army officers attempted a *coup d'état*, taking the entire Chamber of Deputies hostage in the Cortes, in the centre of Madrid. The decisive intervention of the king, who made a television broadcast in his capacity as Commander-in-Chief of the Armed Forces condemning the coup, was central to its failure. When it was all over and the perpetrators had been arrested, two sensations were prevalent: first, a sense of relief, mixed with repulsion and indignation; second, the dream-like quality of the eighteen hours that the crisis lasted. The coup seemed unreal because it belonged to a bygone era and was totally inappropriate to the Spain of the 1980s. Contrary to what Franco and his supporters had envisaged, he had not been succeeded by Francoist institutions, but by a constitutional monarch and a generation of political leaders born after the Civil War, who were intent upon breaking down the barriers Franco had erected between different groups of Spaniards and between Spain and the outside world. Unlike Franco, their guiding principle was not 'divide and rule', but the search for consensus and the peaceful coexistence of all Spanish citizens.

The year 1992 was Spain's *annus mirabilis*: year of the Universal Exposition in Seville, the Barcelona Olympic Games, the quincentenary of Columbus's landfall in the 'New World' and Madrid's turn as 'Cultural Capital of Europe'. It also saw the centenary of the birth of Francisco Franco. But those who visited Spain for the multitude of cultural and sporting events held that year, or because the accompanying flood of media reports on Spain had aroused their interest in the country, would have had to look very hard to find visible signs of the *Generalísimo* or his regime. The Spanish national flag no longer bears his emblem, but the crown and shield of the monarchy. The national anthem remains the same, because Franco had merely restored the pre-Republican Royal March, but the Movement anthem, *Cara al sol (Face to the sun)*, is no longer sung, except by the supporters of extreme Rightist groups, and the once nation-wide structures of the Movement bureaucracy have long since been dismantled. Curiously enough, there were never many statues of the *Caudillo* and none have been erected since his death. Streets and squares named after Franco and his wartime collaborators have reverted to their pre-war designations. Even the town of his birth, at one time called El Ferrol del Caudillo, is now simply El Ferrol again. The indigenous languages and cultural heritage of Spain's distinctive regions have returned with new vigour, particularly in Catalonia, the Basque Country and Franco's native Galicia, after four decades of proscription. Indeed, one of the most significant innovations of the 1978 constitution was the administrative and juridical reorganization of the entire state into seventeen self-governing communities, in order to secure the cohesion of the country's component regions by recognizing, rather than repressing, their inherent diversity.

Those who visited Spain in mid-November or early December 1992 might more easily have been aware of the late General Franco. On 22 November the Civil War veterans' organizations and a small number of extreme Rightist political groups made their annual tribute to mark the anniversary of his death with an open-air rally in the Plaza de Oriente. But attendances at such gatherings had been dwindling since the first, in 1976, when some 70,000 Francoist nostalgics had cheered the rantings of their leaders and chanted 'Franco! Franco! Franco!' as though he might still appear on the balcony of the Royal Palace. By 1992 barely 5,000 stalwarts rallied to the Francoist flag; the attempt of one extreme Rightist leader to address them was drowned by jeering from the supporters of a rival faction; and, for the first time, Franco's daughter stayed away. When the centenary of the *Generalísimo*'s birth was reached, on 4 December 1992, a mass for his eternal rest was celebrated at the parish church in El Pardo, but there were no rallies and no official commemoration. The national press published special supplements in which intellectuals, academics, politicians and others, of all shades of opinion, analysed the contribution made by Francisco Franco to the history of Spain, and a small flurry of books was added to the existing bibliography of secondary sources. But there was no popular celebration of the anniversary and those who hoped that this might be the occasion on which a collection of hitherto secret memoirs might appear were disappointed.

Towards the end of the twentieth century, with Spain fully integrated into the network of western political and economic institutions, and with democracy firmly established as the system of government, the possibility of a Francoist revival seems remote. As the results of successive elections have shown, the vast majority of today's Spaniards reject the repressive, authoritarian, anti-democratic values which held sway in their country for so many years. That this should be so is, perhaps, Franco's most important, if unintended, legacy.

. . .

NOTES

1. *ABC, El Alcazar,* Madrid, 20 November 1975. *Nuevo Diario,* 20 November 1975, gives 4.40 a.m. as the actual time of death.
2. J. Sinova (ed.), *Historia del franquismo,* (2 vols.) Madrid: Diario 16 1985, vol. I, p. 163.
3. *Informaciones,* Madrid, 20 November 1975. The Ministry of Education subsequently printed 2,300,000 copies each of Franco's last message and King Juan Carlos's inaugural speech for free public distribution; *Arriba,* 25 November 1975.
4. *El Alcazar,* 20 November 1975.
5. *Informaciones, Ya,* Madrid, 22 November 1975. The crown and sceptre lay on a footstool near Don Juan Carlos, but, following Spanish custom, there was no coronation as such.
6. *Arriba,* 25 November 1975, gives a figure of 300,000.
7. *Arriba,* 25 November 1975.
8. Ibid. and personal observation.
9. *Arriba, Informaciones,* 25 November 1975.
10. H. Thomas, *The Spanish Civil War,* Harmondsworth: Penguin 1965, p. 754.
11. The members of the Drafting Committee were Gabriel Cisneros, Miguel Herrero de Miñón and José Pedro Pérez-

Llorca (Unión de Centro Democrática); Gregorio Peces Barba (Partido Socialista Obrero Español); Jordi Solé Tura (Partido Comunista de España); Miquel Roca Junyent (Convergencia Democrática de Catalunya); and Manuel Fraga Iribarne (*Alianza Popular*); J. Sinova (ed.), *Historia de la Transición* (2 vols), Madrid: Diario 16 1984, vol. I, p. 534.

CHRONOLOGY

1892 Francisco Franco Bahamonde born at El Ferrol (Galicia), 4 December.

1898 Final collapse of the Spanish overseas empire, July.

1902 King Alphonso XIII ascends the Spanish throne, 17 May.

1907 Franco enters the Infantry Academy at Toledo, 29 August.

1910 Graduates as Second Lieutenant; posted to La Coruña (Galicia), 13 July.

1912 Arrives in Melilla (Spanish Morocco), 6 February.

1914–18
First World War; Spain remains neutral throughout.

1916 Franco seriously wounded at El Biutz (Spanish Morocco), 24 June.

1917 General strike throughout Spain. In Asturias, Franco takes part in military operations against striking coal miners, August.

1920 Franco returns to Morocco to take command of a unit of the recently created Spanish Foreign Legion, October.

1923 Appointed Chief of the Foreign Legion, May.

General Miguel Primo de Rivera stages a *pronunciamiento* in Barcelona and forms an anti-democratic government, 13 September.

Franco marries Carmen Polo Martínez Valdés in Oviedo (Asturias), 22 October.

1926 Promoted to Brigadier General – the youngest in Europe – and posted to Madrid, February.

Birth of Carmen Franco Polo, the first and only child of Francisco Franco and Carmen Polo, 14 September.

1927 Franco chosen as Director of a new General Military Academy, to be established at Zaragoza, March.

1930 General Primo de Rivera resigns; succeeded by General Dámaso Berenguer, 30 January.

Republican military rising at Jaca (Huesca); rapidly suppressed, 12 December.

1931 Second Republic proclaimed after collapse of monarchy and dictatorship, 14 April.

Decree closing Zaragoza Military Academy (and three others), 30 June.

1932 Franco posted to La Coruña (Galicia), February.

Attempted military coup (*la Sanjurjada*); Franco refuses to become involved, 10 August.

1933 Franco appointed General Commander, Balearic Isles, February.

José Antonio Primo de Rivera founds the fascist *Falange Española*, 29 October.

General election won by the right wing CEDA and Radical Party, 19 November.

1934 Franco promoted to full General – youngest in Europe, March.

Revolutionary strike action in Madrid, Catalonia and Asturias. Franco organizes repressive operations in Asturias and Catalonia, October.

1935 Franco appointed Chief of the Central General Staff, May.

1936 General election won by the left wing *Popular Front*, 16 February; Franco tries to make the Prime Minister hand over power to the Army, 17 February.

Franco posted to the Canary Isles, 21 February.

José Calvo Sotelo, leader of the right wing *Renovación Española*, assassinated in Madrid, 13 July.

Military rebellion begins in Spanish Morocco and mainland Spain. Franco arrives in Spanish Morocco, 17–19 July.

Rebels set up Committee for National Defence, 23 July; Franco made Chief of Armies of Morocco and Southern Spain, 24 July.

France, Britain, Belgium, Holland, the United States, Poland, Czechoslovakia, the Soviet Union, Germany, Italy and Portugal agree to a French proposal of non-intervention in Spain, August.

Franco sets up headquarters in Seville, 7 August.

Rebels take Badajoz, 13–14 August.

General Varela lifts the siege of the *alcazar* of Toledo, 28 September.

Franco designated *Generalísimo* of the rebel (self-styled 'Nationalist') Armed Forces and Head of Government of the Nationalist state, 28 September.

Nationalists begin all-out attack on Madrid, 7 October.

Republican government leaves Madrid for Valencia. First units of International Brigades arrive in Madrid, November.

Italy and Germany recognize Franco government, 18 November.

José Antonio Primo de Rivera executed in Alicante, 20 November.

1937 Battle of the Jarama Valley (Madrid), 6–23 February.

Battle of Guadalajara; the end of Nationalist efforts to take Madrid quickly, 8–22 March.

Franco signs Decree 255, creating the 'single' party, FET y de las JONS, 19 April.

Guernica (Vizcaya) destroyed by German and Italian aircraft, 26 April.

Battle of Brunete (Madrid), 6–25 July.

1938 Franco appoints his first cabinet, 30 January.

Battle of the River Ebro; Republican forces attempt to detain the Nationalist advance on Catalonia and Valencia, 25 July – 16 November.

1939 Nationalist General Yagüe occupies Barcelona, 26 January.

France and the UK recognize Franco government, 27 February.

Madrid surrenders, 27 March.

Franco issues the final war bulletin, 1 April.

Outbreak of war in Europe; Spain adopts position of neutrality, September.

1940 Spain changes stance to 'non-belligerence', 13 June.

Franco and Hitler meet at Hendaye, 23 October.

1941 Alphonso XIII dies in exile, having abdicated in favour of his son, Don Juan, 28 February.

Hitler invades Russia, June.

Spain modifies status to 'moral belligerence', July.

1942 Falangists and Carlists clash at Begoña (Vizcaya); serious political crisis ensues, 16 August.

Allied landings in French North Africa, 8 November.

1943 Hitler's forces defeated at Stalingrad, 1 February.

Allied landings in Sicily, 10 July.

Italy declares war on Germany. Spain returns to 'neutral' status, October.

1944 US suspends petroleum supplies to Spain, January.

Winston Churchill expresses Allied gratitude to Spain for not closing the Straits of Gibraltar, 24 May.

Allied landings in Normandy ('D Day'), 6 June.

1945 'VE Day'. Spain breaks off diplomatic relations with Germany, 8 May.

Creation of the United Nations Organization; Spain banned from membership, June.

1946 UN condemns the Franco regime, 9 February.
US, Britain and France issue a Tripartite Note condemning the Franco regime. Churchill makes his 'Iron Curtain' speech, March.
UN recommends withdrawal of members' ambassadors from Madrid; massive demonstration of support for Franco in Madrid, December.

1947 Law of Succession formally designating Spain a kingdom approved by referendum, 6 July.

1950 UN General Assembly authorizes reinstatement of members' ambassadors to Madrid, 4 November.

1953 Spain signs Concordat with the Vatican, 27 August.
Bilateral treaty signed with the USA ('Pacts of Madrid'), 26 September.

1955 Spain admitted to the UN, December.

1956 Falangist and liberal students clash in Madrid; cabinet crisis ensues, 9 February.
Spanish Morocco becomes independent, 7 April.

1957 Treaty of Rome, creating EEC, 25 March.

1958 Fundamental Principles of the Movement published, 17 May.

1959 Economic 'Stabilization Plan' published, 21 July.
US President Eisenhower visits Madrid, 21 December.

1960 5-year Development Plan announced, 12 December.

1962 Spain applies for associate status in the EEC; EEC agrees only to negotiate preferential trade agreement, February.
Prince Juan Carlos de Borbón marries Princess Sofía of Greece, 14 May.

General Agustín Muñoz Grandes appointed as first deputy Head of Government, 10 July.

1964 Regime celebrates '25 Years of Franco's peace'.

1966 The Organic Law of the State approved by referendum, 14 December.

1967 Admiral Luis Carrero Blanco replaces General Muñoz Grandes as deputy Prime Minister, September.

1969 Don Juan Carlos de Borbón designated 'Prince of Spain' and Franco's successor, 22 July.

1970 Preferential trade agreement concluded with EEC, 29 June.
16 members of ETA tried by military tribunal; six death sentences, ultimately commuted by Franco (the 'Burgos trials'), 3–28 December.

1973 Carrero Blanco appointed Head of Government, 8 June.
Carrero Blanco assassinated by ETA; succeeded as Prime Minister by Carlos Arias Navarro, December.

1974 Bloodless revolution in Portugal, 25 April.

1975 Franco suffers heart attack; Prince Juan Carlos takes over as Head of State, October.
Franco dies; Prince Juan Carlos proclaimed King, November.

BIBLIOGRAPHICAL ESSAY

The long and intense period of Spanish history examined in this book has generated an enormous literature, in many languages. On the Civil War alone, for example, more books are said to have been written than on the First and Second World Wars put together. The following bibliography constitutes no more than a small sample of what has been published and includes only titles available in English. Unless otherwise specified, the place of publication is London.

Three biographies of Franco appeared during his lifetime, all of which present him in a favourable light: Brian Crozier, *Franco, a Biographical History* (Eyre and Spottiswoode 1967); George Hills, *Franco. The Man and his Nation* (Robert Hale 1967); and J.W.D. Trythall, *Franco. A Biography* (Rupert Hart-Davis 1970). Juan Pablo Fusi's *Franco. A Biography* (Unwin Hyman 1987) devotes only eighteen pages to the period 1892–1936 and contains judgements with which some observers (including partisans of Franco) might disagree (for example that Franco was a brilliant military strategist) but, overall, offers a more objective assessment than any of its three predecessors. The standard work in any language is Paul Preston's *Franco* (Harper Collins 1993) which explains Francisco Franco and his historical context in terms of each other, charting the course of both with a wealth of fact, anecdote and original insight. Chapter 1, which approaches Franco from a psychoanalytical point of view, is particularly thought-provoking. The extensive use made by Preston of Franco's speeches and other Spanish, Portuguese, German and

Italian sources makes available for the first time to English-only readers much material not translated elsewhere.

The most illuminating short history of twentieth-century Spain is Raymond Carr's characteristically lucid *Modern Spain, 1875–1980* (Oxford: Oxford University Press 1980) which covers the period stretching from the first restoration of the Bourbon monarchy, in 1874, to its 'second coming', in the person of King Juan Carlos I, a century later. Carr's much longer *Spain, 1808–1975* (Oxford: Oxford University Press 1982), does not deal with the immediate post-Franco period, but this is amply compensated by the attention devoted to the nineteenth century. More than thirty years earlier, 1808 had been the starting point of Antonio Ramos Oliveira's extensive, well-informed and sensitive 'history of 130 years of civil war in Spain', *Politics, Economics and Men of Modern Spain, 1808–1946* (Victor Gollancz 1946). Gerald Brenan's classic work, *The Spanish Labyrinth* (Cambridge: Cambridge University Press 1943; reprinted 1991) also devotes attention to the nineteenth-century roots of the social and political upheavals of twentieth-century Spain, and is essential reading for an understanding of both. These 'classics' have recently been joined by Adrian Shubert's *A Social History of Modern Spain* (Unwin Hyman 1990), which looks at the interplay of social, economic, political and cultural factors in shaping nineteenth and twentieth century Spain.

The collapse of the monarchy of King Alphonso XIII and the gestation and birth of the Second Republic are the subject of Shlomo Ben-Ami, *The Origins of the Second Republic in Spain* (Oxford: Oxford University Press 1978). Gabriel Jackson's *The Spanish Republic and the Civil War* (Princeton, N.J.: Princeton University Press, 1967) is, perhaps, a little dated now, but it remains a useful overview of the Republic as well as a good general account of the war. Richard A.H. Robinson's *The Origins of Franco's Spain: the Right, the Republic and Revolution, 1931–1936* (Newton Abbot: David and Charles 1970) and Paul Preston's *The Coming of the Spanish Civil War: Reform Reaction and Revolution in the Second Republic 1931–1936* (Methuen 1983) analyse from contrasting perspectives the contribution made by Right and Left to the destruction of the Republic. The origins of the Civil War are also examined in a number of the contributions to Martin Blinkhorn (ed.), *Spain in Conflict* (Sage 1986) and Paul Preston (ed.), *Revolution and War in Spain, 1931–1939* (Methuen 1984).

As we noted at the beginning of this essay, the Spanish Civil War gave rise to a bewildering quantity of literature. Hugh Thomas's *The Spanish Civil War*, (Harmondsworth: Penguin 1965) was the first comprehensive history of the war in English. It has been revised and reprinted a number of times since its initial publication and remains an essential point of reference for any student of 20th century Spain. Sheelagh Ellwood's *The Spanish Civil War* (Oxford: Basil Blackwell 1991) is intended as a 'beginner's guide' to the complexities of the conflict, outlining the basic sequence of events and identifying the main social and political issues involved. Paul Preston's *The Spanish Civil War, 1936–39* (Weidenfeld and Nicolson 1986) offers a more detailed account, bringing out particularly well the interplay of national and international factors, while Raymond Carr's *The Civil War in Spain* (Weidenfeld and Nicolson 1986) presents what is probably the best interpretative summary written to date. Students of particular aspects of the war will find the respective bibliographical essays contained in these volumes helpful for picking their way through a myriad of works, too numerous to list here, of widely varying historical and literary quality. Two important additions to the bibliography of the Civil War, published since the four volumes cited above, are Helen Graham's incisive analysis of the political role of the Partido Socialista Obrero Español (PSOE), *Socialism and War: the Spanish Socialist Party in power and crisis, 1936–1939* (Cambridge: Cambridge University Press 1991) and Tom Buchanan's revealing study of how British socialists responded to the war, *The Spanish Civil War and the British Labour Movement* (Cambridge: Cambridge University Press 1991).

Max Gallo was probably the first to write a comprehensive assessment of the Franco regime, in his book *Spain Under Franco* (George Allen & Unwin 1973). It has since been superseded by Stanley G. Payne's *The Franco Régime, 1936–1975* (Stanford, Calif.: Stanford University Press 1987) yet it remains a useful and interesting chronicle of the thirty years between the end of the Civil War in 1939 and the designation of Prince Juan Carlos de Borbón as Franco's political heir in 1969. The essays contained in the collective volume edited by Paul Preston, *Spain in Crisis* (Hassocks: The Harvester Press 1976), trace the evolution of the regime through that of its component parts, up to and including the final crisis in the first half of the 1970s. Edouard de Blaye's *Franco and the Politics of Spain* (Harmondsworth: Penguin 1976) offers a general guide to Spanish politics at the time of Franco's death and includes a number of useful appendices giving e.g. the members of Franco's cabinets, and the names of Francoist and anti-Francoist political organizations.

The analysis of the Franco regime offered by these studies fills out the picture which emerges from a number of personal contemporary accounts. The first British Ambassador to Spain after the Civil War, Sir Maurice Peterson, included a chapter recounting his brief posting to Madrid in his memoirs, *Both Sides of the Curtain* (Constable 1950). His successor, Sir Samuel Hoare, played a crucial role in Allied efforts to prevent Franco from joining the Second World War on the side of the Axis; his book *Ambassador on Special Mission* (Collins 1946) provides a fascinating account of his part in those efforts and some incisive comments on Franco and his regime. Herbert Feis, *The Spanish Story* (New York: Norton 1948; reprinted 1966), paints a gloomy and altogether credible portrait of the Spain of the 'hungry forties', as does Thomas J. Hamilton's *Appeasement's Child. The Franco Regime in Spain* (Victor Gollancz 1943). Herbert Matthews's *The Yoke and the Arrows* (Heinemann 1958) assesses the Civil War and the subsequent development of the Franco regime, particularly with regard to its external relations, from the perspective of an American journalist who had lived and worked in Spain for over twenty years. Another American journalist, Benjamin Welles, is the author of *Spain. The Gentle Anarchy* (Pall Mall Press 1965), which looks at the regime's main institutional pillars (the Falange, the Church and the Army), at the relationship with the United States, the economy, the then future king, and the *Caudillo* himself. Regrettably, no comparable memoirs have yet been written for the final decade of the regime.

There are fewer monographs in English than in Spanish on particular aspects of Francoism, but, between them, the following titles cover the waterfront reasonably well. Stanley Payne's *Politics and the Military in Modern Spain* (Stanford, Calif.: Stanford University Press 1967), is probably still the standard work on the role of the Armed Forces (although it does not refer solely to the period of the Franco regime). However, Paul Preston's, *The Politics of Revenge. Fascism and the military in twentieth-century Spain* (Unwin Hyman 1990) constitutes a fascinating and original study of the role played by the military 'as instruments of right-wing dominance' between 1931 and 1981, with particular attention to the Franco regime. As the title indicates, Preston's book also looks at the part played by the anti-democratic Right in the creation and survival of the regime. The contribution made to the permanence of the regime by one sector of the Francoist Right, the Falange, is the subject of Sheelagh Ellwood's book, *Spanish Fascism in the Franco Era* (Macmillan 1987). Frances `Lannon's authoritative study, *Privilege, Persecution and Prophecy: the Catholic Church in Spain, 1875–1975* (Oxford: Oxford University Press 1987), traces the development of the Church as an institution and as a disseminator of ideas and values throughout the period covering Franco's lifetime. Sima Lieberman, *The Contemporary Spanish Economy* (Allen and Unwin 1982), and Joseph Harrison, *The Spanish Economy in the Twentieth Century* (Sage 1985), chart the transformation of Spain from a predominantly agricultural, to an industry- and service-based, economy. Two books guide the reader through the often labyrinthine complexities of Basque nationalism: Robert P. Clark's *The Basque Insurgents: ETA, 1952–1980* (Madison, Wisconsin: University of Wisconsin Press 1984) and John Sullivan's *ETA and Basque Nationalism. The Fight for Euskadi 1890–1986* (Routledge 1988). The most comprehensive study to date of the anti-Francoist opposition, Hartmut Heine's *La oposición política al franquismo* (Crítica 1983) is unfortunately not available in English. However, the history of one sector of that opposition, the Partido Socialista Obrero Español (PSOE), is exhaustively detailed in Richard Gillespie's *The Spanish Socialist Party: a History of Factionalism* (Oxford: Oxford University Press 1990), and students of Spanish communism should consult Guy Hermet, *The Communists in Spain* (Farnborough: Saxon House 1971) and Paul Preston, 'The PCE in the struggle for democracy in Spain' in Howard Machin (ed.) *National Communism in Western Europe* (Methuen 1983).

The formal rebirth of democracy with the general election of June 1977 provides both the starting and the finishing points for Raymond Carr and Juan Pablo Fusi, *Spain: Dictatorship to Democracy* (George Allen and Unwin 1979), in which the authors discuss the return of democracy as the result of both the social, economic and cultural evolution of Spain during those years and the internal dynamics of the Franco regime as a political system. David Gilmour's *The Transformation of Spain: from Franco to the constitutional monarchy* (Quartet 1985) has the advantage of having been written six years later, by which time democracy was well on the way to consolidation and it was possible both to know more about how the transition had occurred and to assess with greater certainty the relative significance of each of the factors involved. Paul Preston's *The Triumph of Democracy in Spain* (Methuen 1986) reconstructs what was an extraordinarily intense period of Spanish history with the meticulousness and wealth of factual detail which are the author's hallmarks. Finally, an entertaining and astute eyewitness account of the latter part of the regime and, above all, of post-Franco Spain, is provided by John Hooper's excellent study, *The Spaniards* (Harmondsworth: Penguin 1987).

. . . .
MAP

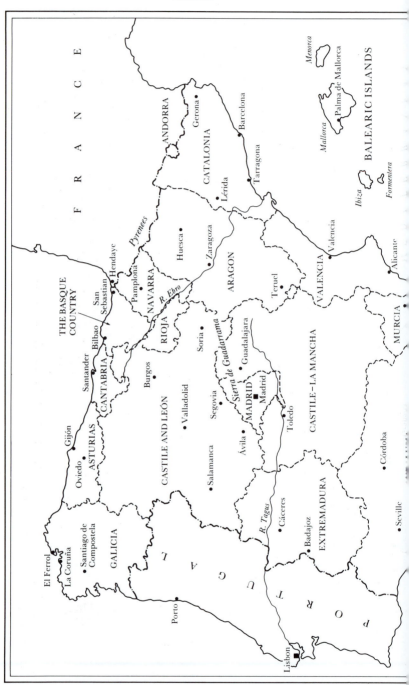

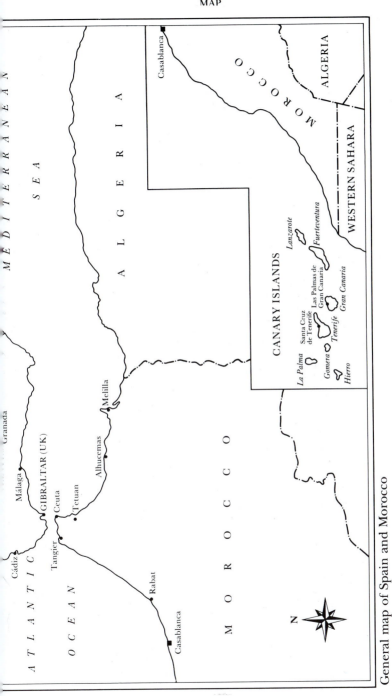

General map of Spain and Morocco

INDEX